T0365960

TOUCHSTONE

TRANSITION

*A Sentimental Story of
One Mind and One Era*

by WILL DURANT

A Touchstone Book
Published by Simon and Schuster

1 2 3 4 5 6 7 8 9 10

ISBN 978-0-671-24203-9

To a
Tender Mother
and a
Perfect Father

FOREWORD

DEAR READER:

Perhaps this is your story as well as John Lemaire's. It tries to show the effect, upon one growing mind, of the profound transformation which modern science and research have brought in the faith of the western world. In a lesser way it tries also to show the political experiments and disillusionment of our time, and to trace the evolution of a fairly typical rebel from Utopian aspiration through a cynical despondency to some measure of reconciliation and good cheer.

These changes have not been as impersonal as the abstract chronicle of history represents them; they have brought to sensitive individuals much suffering in mental transition and readjustment; they have broken up families and friendships; and they have unsettled the mind and morals of many generations by uprooting the customs and beliefs in which those generations grew. It is with this personal aspect of the Great Change that the story is concerned.

WILL DURANT

Sea Cliff, May, 1927.

CAUTION

This book was originally written and published as "A Sentimental Story of One Mind and One Era," in the form of a novel; consequently it added, to the actual experiences and memories of the author, some events and conversations not actually his own. This applies chiefly to Chapter III of Part II, "I Am Blown Up," and the conversation that concludes Chapter XI of Part II: "I Play Politics." Otherwise the account is basically autobiographical.

CONTENTS

PART ONE: THE GREAT CHANGE

PART TWO: THE NEW WORLD

CONTENTS

PART ONE

THE GREAT CHANGE

CHAPTER I

I LOSE MY INNOCENCE

My earliest memory pictures me held up high in the
hands of a rough but kindly Italian, and searching
for candy in the pockets of his coat, that hung upon
the wall. I was always a hearty eater, and perhaps
it is a little symbolical that this vivid operation of the
primal instinct is all that I see when I reach back
as far as I can into my childhood years. Apparently
this Italian lived with our family; at least I yet see
him, across these pitilessly moving years, coming in
at the close of the day, and hanging his coat and hat
upon his individual nail. Sometimes there were peanuts in the coat, sometimes candy, sometimes pop-
corn, sometimes nothing; and then my benefactor
would not lift me up as usual, but would soothe me
by bouncing me on his knee. He was a handsome
fellow, as almost every Italian is; and though his
coat shone with time and work, I loved him with
what my memory describes as a mute and ardent affection. It is strange that I remember him so clearly,
and yet have no vision at all of how my mother or
father, or any of my brothers or sisters, looked in
those early days. But some remembrance is his least
due; for I am sure that his gruff bestowal upon me of

3

part of his unused fund of paternal tenderness
taught me, almost in my swaddling clothes, the genial
kindliness that lies in the hearts of men.

We lived, it seems, in a little town called Readsboro, in Vermont. Already, in 1885, it was industrial.
I remember it as whitened with the dust of pumice
or cement mills, and inhabited by simple laborers who
had long since abandoned the effort to keep clean.
They worked hard, probably twelve hours a day; but
they were a jolly crew nevertheless, and had energy
enough after their toil for games and brawls that
made the place no paradise for philosophers. On Sat-
urdays and Sundays the square in front of our house
was animated with baseball; all the noise that makes
amateur sport so much more exhilarating than the
calm routine of professional games, filled the streets
and poured in at doors and windows and echoed to
the limits of the town. Sometimes the ball would follow the noise; once it crashed through a window and
fell almost at my feet. We were not greatly astonished; we could put in a pane of glass ourselves in
those days, and we knew that in these hilarious ceremonies America expressed one element of its spontaneous religion. The other element was in the factories.

Yet these blunt and hearty men, who fed the
machines in the mills, exchanged hospitalities in the
saloons, settled various national and sexual problems
in their street-corner conferences, and retired at last
to their homes, their sporting-sections, and their

pipes,—these men and their wives, though they constituted nearly all the population of the town, were hardly accorded the name American by the bent and wrinkled farmers who clung with timorous piety to the ancestral hinterland. To the sons of the Puritans these factory-workers were "Polocks," "Guineas," "Micks," "Sheenies," and "Canucks"; they belonged to strange and presumably inferior peoples who had chosen America as the cesspool for their waste. The farmers, encrusted in thirty years of dirt, looked with stern disapproval upon these workers dusted over with the pumice of the mills, heard with horror their score of dialects, and wondered what America was coming to. They saw their fields turned into factory yards, their streams poisoned with chemicals, their clear skies darkened with smoke, themselves unnoticed and displaced. Even they knew the tragedy of transition.

I think I can recall—or am I reading between the lines of my memory?—a fundamental difference between these farmers and the later immigrants who filled the town. The farmers looked tired and worried and unhappy; the factory workers looked strong and self-confident, and were always ready with smile and jest. The isolation of the farmers had made them unsocial; the deterioration of the soil had led to the exhaustion of their energy; the hardness of their lives had embittered them to all the world; and their religion was sterner and crueler than life itself. But those men who passed our house after the whistle blew, or filled the square on holidays, had a strange exuberance, a freshness of spirit as of people who had found renewed youth. In the midst of exploitation and hardship they remembered the stagnant misery of their native shores; and of an evening they would sit content on their steps, smoking the pipe of peace, trading stories with their neighbors, and listening with the calm of nicotine as their sturdy wives retailed to them the accumulated gossip of the day. Beyond these ruined farms they saw the promised land; and though they knew they had but seen its portals, they nursed the silent hope that their children would enter the kingdom.

They were a believing generation. They believed that in this endless expanse called America there was a road for every talent to rise to wealth and power. They frowned upon the employer who worked them ruthlessly; but they scorned with superior pride the young orator or the pallid student who suggested that they take over these factories and send members of their own class to rule the cities and the states. They found a secret zest in this gamble of the individualistic life; they were aware that most of them would lose; but as long as they did not know just who would win, they wished the game to go on. Its uncertainty was its lure.

And they believed in God. They never doubted that He was seated somewhere in that cloudy sky, surrounded with myriads of angels, and watching with paternal affection the fortunes of these queer crea-

tures whom He had placed upon the earth. For the
most part the men and women of those industrial New
England towns were Catholics; they listened with
gratitude to their priests' weekly assurance that they
had the one true faith; they even liked his denunciations of their occasional drunkenness and their devia-
tions from monogamy; they thrilled when he spoke
of Hell, but they always thought of it as the terminus
of other men, and felt intuitively that some day they
would see the blessed saints. They came away from
the confessional eased with avowal and reproof; they
almost saw Christ when they ate the Holy Wafer in
Communion; they were soothed with the recital of
the Rosary, uplifted with the sonorous chant of the
Vespers, and refreshed with the singing of the psalms.
They were reconciled to having the gates of matrimony close upon them forever, it was done with such
sacramental splendor; surely it was a fine thing to
marry a woman with a High Mass and a special
Communion. And then the priest came to their
homes, blessed their households, and asked the ages of
their children; he was a jolly old pastor, not too hard
on their sins, and always with a kind word for every
soul in his flock. Perhaps, if they worked hard, and
denied themselves, and saved, they could send a son
away to college and to the seminary, and have the
honor and blessing of a priest of their own family and
their own name to intercede for them with God. And
when they grew old and fell sick, and at last faced
the Great Enemy, what a comfort it would be to have

the old Curé by their bedside praying for them, anointing their hands and feet, and speaking of the heavenly hosts that waited to welcome them into everlasting happiness and peace. It was a believing generation.

My father was one of the workers in those mills. I am a little ashamed that I cannot recall how he looked in those early days; perhaps he went off to work while I still slept, and returned only when I slept again. He always worked hard; I do not remember ever to have seen him idle. What memories I have of him from that period belong to the Sundays, when friends came to the house and frolicked noisily. My father was quieter than most of the others; but he could tell a story and sing a song with the jolliest. We were French Canadians who had a tradition of drinking-songs and saucy stories that went back to the times of Rabelais. *"Ah la bouteille est bonne, bon garcon,"* and *"Br-r-r-r, Madame, il foit donc froid,"* still ring in my ears from the days when as a lad of five I listened with awe to those wild chants of love and wine. It took many a cup of forbidden drink to drown the memory of a week's insolence in the factory; and it was good that these simple joys were left as some atonement for endless months of toil.

I remember my mother even more vaguely than my father. I know—because she is yet beautiful in her white-haired seventies—that she was as pretty a wife

8

as any man had among the workers in that town. But
her face is so familiar now that every earlier image
has been covered over. She too worked hard, for
children came abundantly, unhindered; the Church
had prohibited any impediment to the increase and
multiplication of its fold. All the women of the town
who were able to bear children bore as many as they
could; every house was littered with them. It was a
method of procedure that cost the children something
in growth and education, and cost the mothers something in comfort and leisure. But it had its compensa-
tions: the children tamed and taught one another;
and the mothers were kept from boredom and adult-
ery. Such families could not be brought up on the
latest and most lenient principles; the tired mothers
found that spanking took less time than reasoning,
and penetrated sooner to the seat of memory. My
mother spared the rod, because she preferred to use
her hand. We loved her none the less, for we suspected that we deserved a little more than we received.

There were eleven of us; but only eight survived
the ordeals of infancy. Excepting small-pox, we
passed through the gamut of the diseases with which
children are graduated into youth: we wheezed with
the whooping-cough, and swelled with the mumps,
and scratched with the measles, and burned with the
fever of diphtheria. Perhaps Napoleon was right
when he told Antommarchi that at the Last Judgment physicians would have as much to answer for

as generals: it is as easy to make fun of medicine as it is to make fun of monogamy; neither comes naturally to us, and wit is our revenge. Nevertheless, through better medical knowledge, children now escape many of the disasters which came to us then with almost the inevitability of the tides. Probably those of us who survived enjoyed a strength and immunity not otherwise to be won; but perhaps, too, some of the finest souls among us returned in childhood into the darkness from which they had come at the cost of so much pain.

When I first felt the blinding light and deafening noises of the world, three boys and one girl were already on the scene. The oldest was Harry, who lived a jolly and carefree life, never hungry for gold or power, never awed by prohibitions (even when written into the Constitution), always ready to help a friend, always the life of every group that he joined, and in general the most open-hearted fellow of our tribe. Then there was Delia, whom I could never understand so well because she belonged to the strange sex; she married and went off when I was too young to do more than catch the faint corona of her romantic love-affair. Leo came next, pale and thin, and given to books; ill at ease in the hard industrial world in which he had to live, and always looking wistfully into that realm of the arts and sciences which he was never permitted to enter. After Leo another brother came, of whom I remember little, for he died in my earliest years. And then Fred, handsomest of them all, dark and proud and silent; perhaps more like his father than any of us—and I could yield him no finer compliment. I was a little jealous of his good looks, but I admired him humbly, and prayed that I might some day be as clever and handsome as he. After me came Ben, whose big head is still pictured in the memory I have of the time when I rocked his cradle, and who was to be, of all the family, my one unflinching friend in the days of my tragedy. And finally, two incomparably pretty young sisters, of whom, as still within the blushing age, I must say no more until they cross the current of my history.

The Reader will perceive that I have described our little family as almost perfect. He will understand that we all had our vices and absurdities, but he will not expect me to advertise them while we have still so many years (I hope) to live in this rude world. And he will smile at the way in which I shall make myself the center of this circle; it will be ridiculously unhistorical, for certainly each one of us placed the core of the world's affairs in his own heart, and only by literary license may I presume, henceforth, to focus the story upon myself. If these brothers and sisters had the "gift of gab" and were, like me, heavers of wind and hewers of words, what a different story they might tell!

We boys managed to live in a fairly moderate degree of warfare, considering that we were brothers. Many mad ventures we had together—many more, no doubt, than our memories have had room to hold. I recall one as particularly impressive to me, because it introduced me to sin, and gave me the new and awful experience of breaking one of the ten commandments.

We had all gone to play near the river that ran beside the town; attracted partly by our mother's standing prohibition against treading those slippery banks, and partly by the procession of logs that floated downstream from the forest to the mill. Leo and Fred, bare-legged, waded in with that timid audacity which blooms in us when we know that we are observed. Some of the logs drifted so near the bank that the boys caught them, and had great fun in rolling them about. At last the idea occurred to Fred and Leo to stand with one foot on one log and the other foot on another. So for a while they towered like brave Colossi, while I, too young for this achievement, pranced on the bank in admiring ecstasy.

Then one log took a mind to roll over, and Fred plunged up to his neck into the water. Leo was so disturbed by this turn of events that his own footing slipped and he joined Fred in his involuntary bath. I shouted with fright, but they commanded me to hold my peace. They found their way to the shore, shivered a while, and then conferred on the problem of keeping this log-rolling business from our mother. With youthful decision they made a fire, undressed, and tried to dry their clothes over the flames. However, as supper-time was at hand, and to be late would invite questioning, Leo and Fred got into their

12

clothes before the drying was quite complete, trusting that the journey home would finish the process. But suddenly it came to them that I might blurt out the whole story.

"Listen, Johnny," said Leo, "you won't tell on us, will you?"

"Oh, I won't tell on you," I said, like a man of four big years.

"If ma asks where we've been we'll say we were looking for berries."

"All right."

"And whatever we say, you say the same thing—understand?"

I tried to understand, though I was a little frightened at this multiple mendacity. I had lied before, but it had been natural, instinctive lying, not lying aforethought as now. My mother had told me how awful it was to lie, and how if I died just after a lie I would go to Hell and never see the face of Jesus. I trembled a little, but probably less than Fred and Leo, who feared no such distant and purely hypothetical punishment. Nevertheless we screwed our courage to the sticking point, and marched into the house as unanimous in falsehood as Lord Melbourne's Cabinet.

The questions were asked, and Fred and Leo lied like statesmen. My turn came, and I did my best, gulping down my theology and reciting my terrible untruths with an exaggerated positivity. I mourn to think that my unnatural insistence on what should have been offered as obvious and unworthy of em-

TRANSITION

phasis may have aroused the suspicions of my mother.
At all events, she spied the limp sag of Leo's shirt
and Freddie's trousers; she felt them and sniffed
them,—and the game was up. Then there was weeping
and gnashing of teeth, and the fire of discord was
not extinguished until we were all of us tossing in
troubled sleep.

My mother looked at me sadly the next day. I am
absurd enough to think that before Ben and the
younger girls grew up I was her favorite, and my im-
moralities hurt her more than those of the hardened
sinners who had been favorites before me. That dear
mother of ours was bound to make a saint of one of
us, and tried her best to inoculate me with every
virtue. To think that after all her love and all her
lessons and all her prayers I should stand up and lie
to her like a young Lucifer—this was hard to bear.
I am afraid there was some doubt about my sainthood
in the little mother's heart as she cared for her brood
that day.

CHAPTER II

I PUT ON PANTS AND BECOME A SAINT

HOWEVER, even a terrible thing like a lie can be forgotten, especially if other troubles succeed it. The time was coming soon when I was to make my début at school. I was not to be five till November; but the parochial school might accept me in September if I came in the proper moral and physical condition. The physical condition meant that my face and neck should be washed, my hair brushed back from my eyes, my shoes shined, and my legs clad in holeless stockings; while the rest of me was to be covered with pants, and a pretty blouse with a great stiff collar that fell over my shoulders, and a flowing tie that hung down on my breast. It was a tremendous experience to be so thoroughly accoutred; and I pleaded successfully with a fond mother to let me practice in the new equipment on the Sunday before school opened. I went to church with the pride of an alderman, said my prayers like a starched Aloysius, and came back throbbing with maturity and perfection.

Suddenly a group of boys, meeting me, burst out laughing, and called upon other boys to look at me; and when they too burst out laughing my new manhood melted into hot and helpless tears. I looked angrily about me to see the source of the laughter; but I saw nothing, and my anger grew. Then one lad pointed, and looking down I discovered that a button had come loose in the most strategic portion of my pantaloons, and a certain secret which decent lads conceal had been betrayed to the public eye. I covered up the error in mad haste, and ran home sobbing. It was no fun being a saint when one was built just like other boys.

That unseemly episode made a thinker of me. I brooded for hours, even in the midst of ball-games and walks, over the mysteries and melancholies of anatomy. Why were certain portions of me so much more sacred than others, requiring to be veiled in sanctuary from eyes that looked unhindered on my questionable nose? What were other people like? Were they all like me? What were these queer things called women? How were babies born?—I constructed for myself a marvelous system of physiology, which later life painfully brought nearer and nearer to what I now presume to be the truth. Curiosity burned like lava in me; and yet I dared not ask questions; it was sinful to be interested in such things. Perhaps, in school, when I learned to read, I might ferret out these holy secrets of human origin and female form.

And so I went to school,—with the button replaced, and a gold ring on my finger, and a heart a-flutter with the expectation of strange events. It was a Catholic school, taught by the Sisters of Charity. I was taken to the Sister Superior, and introduced as a candidate for education. However, the good Sister would not have me. She petted me and praised my blouse and approved of my trousers without suspicion of their shameful history; but she gently informed my sponsor that I was too young.

"Bring John back in February," she said, and turned away to other applicants—real, sensitive boys and girls who were watching the universe revolve about their focal selves even as you and I. And I came home defeated.

When I reached the house I found that the gold ring was gone from my finger. I quite understand that the Reader does not care about that ring; that he suspects it was only gold-plated, and not worth bothering about. But that missing ring meant tragedy for me; it brought to a suffocating climax the failures and indignities of two days which had promised to be heroic stepping-stones in my career. I swear I cared almost nothing for the ring; but my throat ached with the desire to repair at least one of the stupidities of my matriculation day. I can see myself now, over the hills and valleys of the intervening years, retracing every step that I had taken from the school, and searching every foot of the road and the path, with a heart beating and pounding as perhaps the rise and fall of nations would not make it beat again. And then when I could hardly walk any more I came home in utter humiliation, convinced that I would never amount to anything in this hostile world.

My mother was kind to me that day,—hardly scolding me, and understanding, with a word, just how my little cosmos had collapsed about me, leaving me poised in cold thin air, disconsolate.

A queer gap in my memory, and then I see myself kneeling on the floor of the classroom in the school, punished for some misdeed.

Apparently February had come, school had opened its arms to me, and perhaps, even, I had been there for a year or two; I cannot tell. But certainly I had done something villainous; for this business of kneeling was the penultimate penalty inflicted on the young criminals of that institution. It was no way to make piety palatable; but it awed us as few punishments would have done, and achieved a transient efficacy.

Now this habit my memory has (contrary to the most highly guaranteed psychology) of picking out the dark spots of my past, must not deceive the Reader. I would have him understand that I was a bright boy, led most of my classes, and in general astonished my teachers with a voracious intellectuality. If the things that I remember and record seem to stamp me as a dunce and a culprit, the Reader must take my word for it, in place of specific memories, that I was an unusually clever student, who always knew more than was good for him. Perhaps I was something of a trouble-maker, pretty nearly the worst-behaved boy at school in some of my younger years; I may decently concede that, for no-body is ashamed of misbehavior at school, except in his children. Schools are unnatural contrivances; and though we enjoyed reading and arithmetic, we hated to sit still for three hours in the morning, and then two in the afternoon, and then—for us bad boys—an hour after class. Unconsciously we longed for those ancient pedagogues who took their boys out for a walk, and taught them the nature of things not from blackboards and slates and books, but from the illuminating face of the world itself. Nothing learned from a book is of much use anyway.

Nevertheless, here I was in school. Now that I look back upon them, it seems that they must have been happy and exhilarating days. What adventures we had on the way back and forth, what lively quarrels and exciting games! I should like to record that I could "shoot marbles" with the best, and brought my marble-bag home every day a little heavier than it went forth. Even school itself had its consolations; for the very teachers that scolded me for insolence and conceit liked the way I picked up my lessons, and began to give me prizes, and told the priest what a pity it was that so good a student was so trouble-some.

Meanwhile they poured religious instruction into us, and taught us many pretty prayers and sweetly sad hymns. They hoped that these lessons would mould us, however slowly, out of our natural barbar-ism into some measure of consideration, honor and kindness; and perhaps in most of us the seed was not planted without some pretty growths. After all, we are at birth mere animals, dirtier and uglier than the puppies in the litter; our parents alone can tolerate us (after a while), or nurses who have become hardened to the native human form. Only that great school, the family, and that great family, the school, have been able to debrutalize us, by forcing upon us the accumulated decencies of group life. If they have used, in this process, an abundant amount of legendary lore, let us remember that they believed these legends true, and thought them indispensable to the salvation of our souls. Perhaps, in an earthly sense, they were; and these marvelous myths were like milk teeth—doomed to decay on contact with the rough realities of the world, but useful until such time as stronger structures could take their place.

To me, in those impressionable years, these myths were a great delight, and filled me with awe and poetry. Indeed it was as poetry that they won us; we listened to the story of Adam and Eve in much the same mind as when we heard tell of Jack the Giant-Killer and little Cinderella. We did not ask were these stories true; they were interesting and wonderful, and that was enough. And then when the figure of Christ stepped into the legend we were thrilled as by no other story ever; here was a hero greater and nobler than any, who had been the fearless foe of tyrants and the unjust rich, who had died not for one fair woman only, but for all mankind; and who

through all his adventures and his sufferings had
been as beautiful as Hoffmann painted him, and as
gentle as a maiden's love. We saw pictures of him,
chubby and rosy in his mother's arms, standing unshaken among the learned doctors, lashing the merchants out of the Temple, feeding the multitudes,
welcoming the little children to him, forgiving the
fallen woman, sitting at the last supper to break
bread with his betrayer; and then on the way of the
cross, scourged and mocked and wearied beyond
bearing, crucified between thieves, pierced with a
lance, and taken down into the arms of his mother,
dead. What stones we should have been not to be
touched to the depths of our hearts by this noblest
story ever told, this finest flower that has ever blos-
somed in the jungle of the human soul, this magnificent symbol of genius crucified for daring to redeem
mankind!

Was it any wonder that this entrancing narrative
became for years the core of my idealistic imagination? I was always a hero-worshiper; and I think it
was as a hero, rather than as a God, that Christ ap-
pealed to me. I accepted intellectually the dogma of
his divinity, but I did not feel it in my heart. What
I saw was the young preacher reciting the Beati-
tudes, or the pale, stern leader mourning over the
unrepentant city, or the emaciated corpse lying limp
at the foot of the cross. I was filled with a great love
for this man; so much that to this day, when I should
be ready to admit the historical uncertainty that en-

shrouds him, his figure gathers round it, in my mind, a thousand tender memories, and endless emotional reverberations. I thrill yet at the mention of his name, and hunger yet for the ideal life he wished mankind to live; if to love him and hear him gladly is to be a Christian, then, sceptic and pagan though I be, I am a Christian too, and Christ is still my God.

It was around this poetic personality that Catholicism wove itself into the substance of my mental and emotional existence. I began to say my prayers with more feeling and understanding; the lines of the *Pater Noster* and the *Ave Maria* became for me not phrases any longer, but heart-felt aspirations. Suddenly I became pious as I had never been before.

Strange to say, I did not cease to be a miscreant at school, or to give my mother trouble at home; I continued to gather in the marbles of other boys, and took eagerly to all the sports. I remember the beating my father gave me once, for stopping half an hour on the way from the store to play marbles with some chance-encountered enemy. It was well deserved, for I had been explicitly warned against delay, and the entire household awaited my return with the edibles for the evening meal. But it was the last time my father ever struck me; and he might not have struck me then had I not added insolence to disobedience. He ruled us, after our youngest years, only with a stern look and a just life; his example of silent industry and quiet kindness meant more to us than hard words or birch rods. None of us has come near him in modest strength of character and simple nobility of soul.

My father did not bother very much about the religious side of our development; he wanted us to be clean and capable lads; and for the rest he entrusted us to our mother. To her, on the contrary, our religious life was of supreme importance; she labored tirelessly to teach us the doctrines and prayers of the Church so far as she knew them. She added example to precept, prayed long, went to Mass many times a week, and gave to the Church with a wild extravagance that made my father frown a little, though he never said a word. Consequently my attack of piety impressed my mother much more than it did my father; he saw no evidence that the change within me was making me more of a man; but my mother walked with a new pride when she found that her teachings had sunk into my heart. I do not know, but I suspect that it was with her connivance, and perhaps at her suggestion, that old Père Dubois sent for me one day, and took possession of me in the name of the Church.

Père Dubois was the most majestic figure in the town. Tall, straight, white-haired, he walked through the streets in his cassock and broad-brimmed hat, and there was none, of whatever faith, who did not admire and respect him as he passed. The dignity of a great institution gave measure to his gait; and the memory of a great tragedy gave tenderness to his actions and his speech. Story had it that the old priest had not always belonged to God; that in his youth, in far-off

France, he had loved a fair maiden with all the enthusiasm of inexperience, and had been bound to her for many months in happy troth. But one day he had heard her voice crying wildly from the river; he had run down and plunged recklessly, coming to her only as she sank for the last time, out of his reach; he had himself been rescued by a friend; and then, an hour later, he had seen the body of his beloved, all bloated and blue, lying at his feet. The world had become meaningless for him, and he had fled into a seminary as a refuge from insanity and despair. Ordained, he had gone to Canada to put space as well as time between himself and that bitter scene; and from Canada he had followed his migrating parishioners into New England. Prayer and routine and somber ritual had healed him; and though he could never learn to preach well, he had a soft hand for every childish head, and a soft word for every soul. A broken heart is kind.

I did not know why he had sent for me; surely it was to scold me for my latest disobedience. And it seemed so when he spoke.

"My boy," he said, "You have given your teacher much trouble."

I bowed my head; it was true enough.

"Yes, Father," I said.

"Then why do you do it?"

I had no answer for such a simple question.

"I don't know, Father."

"I will tell you, my son. You are proud. You disobey because it seems to mark you out as a hero. That is shameful."

I wilted under this ruthless analysis, and almost crouched as I saw the Abbé rise and come towards me. When he raised his hand I was prepared for the worst; but he merely put his arm around my shoulder.

"My son," he said, "you must not behave badly any more. You are going to be a good man, and a good student. Tell me, would you like to be an altar-boy, and serve my mass every morning?"

I trembled at the unexpected honor.

"Yes, Father; I would be glad."

He put his hand on my head and muttered a blessing.

"I will tell Sister Rose Mary to teach you," he said. "You will come to the sacristy every day at seven o'clock. Each morning you will be near God, and His spirit will fill your heart with happiness. Perhaps if you study hard the Bishop will send you to college, and you will prepare yourself to join Holy Mother Church as one of her priests. Would you like that?"

I was overwhelmed.

"Yes, Father, I would like it very much."

He led me to the door with his arm still around my shoulder.

"Remember, then," he said, "this must be your ambition. From now on you are not to be just like the others; you must study more, and pray more, and always bear in mind that the Church has chosen you to be one of our servants. Hereafter you belong to Christ."

I went home exalted and wondering. When I told my mother what had happened she embraced me silently, and tears shone in her eyes.

CHAPTER III

I GET A BLOODY NOSE

THEN suddenly the scene shifts to New Jersey. I remember nothing of the change; nor of my intermediate domiciles in North Adams and other Massachusetts towns. My father had been offered an improved position in a new factory at Arlington, and after a month's trial without us, he had had us all shipped to a very modest house in Kearny. The rents in Arlington were too high; and to avoid them my father trudged two miles to work and two miles back, morning and evening, in sunshine and rain and snow; for trolleys had not yet made legs obsolete in those Jersey days. One of my oldest memories of this new environment is a picture of my father setting out for work through a wild storm, lunch-pail in one hand and the other hand keeping the driving snow out of his eyes. How he struggled for us during that painful readjustment! There were eight children now, all of us great eaters and great wearers of clothing, and only one of us old enough to work. Harry brought his earnings faithfully to the little mother; but despite her economy and care, the family treasury was always low.

27

There were no rainy days in the sense of workless ones; I can not remember my father being ever out of work. But there was misfortune. One of my older brothers took sick and died. The sadness that for a long time darkened our household left a vague impress upon my memory. It was my first encounter with death, but I was too young to take it seriously. Never since then has death taken any of our immediate family, so that I have missed one of the major provocations to philosophy.

How different things were, here, from the noise and movement of Readsboro. There were no factories near us, no churches, no schools, hardly a store within a mile; only one institution was at hand, indispensably, and that was Roche's saloon. It was strategically placed on the road to the Arlington factory, and offered itself as a gentle suggestion to the workers as they passed in the evening to their homes. My father too would stop there, on pay-nights, and have a glass of foaming ale; perhaps, on holidays, a glass of wine; it never kept him long, and it warmed and cheered him so that he came to our table in a jolly mood despite his toil. I never remember seeing him take too much. He was happy in his wife, and though he did not idealize his children, he loved them intensely in his silent way. When I think of it, I marvel that I cannot recall his giving our mother the slightest cause for jealousy, much less for any doubt as to his absolute loyalty to her. In short, I dote on my father.

I have reason to, for like my mother he denied himself a thousand pleasures that we children might have
an education. He had received none himself; he had
never had a day in school; and if within a few years
of our arrival in New Jersey he reached the position
of superintendent of the largest department in the
new factory, master of three hundred men, it was by
native ability and tireless industry, against the
handicap of utter illiteracy. That was an achievement beside which this paper-scratching of mine
seems a little thin. As if he suspected that we could
not do so well with so simple a start, he poured all
his wages into our mother's hands, and agreed with
her that they should stint themselves to give us as
much schooling as we wished. I have often reflected
on this impulse, which seems to be so deeply rooted
in every parent's heart, to give the children a finer
rearing than their own. We are not such a bad lot
after all, we funny theological apes; we utter a regrettable amount of nonsense on our parabola
through the world, but we can love with a magnificent devotion. When I wish to renew my faith in
progress, I consider the working and the power of
this instinct of parental aid; how it lifts the children
upon the shoulders of the parents, generation after
generation, and raises life to higher levels of enterprise and thought. All laws, actual or proposed, can
be only a modest force beside this lever through which
love moves the world.

It sorely grieved my father and mother that there

was no parochial school within reach of us. My
mother in particular was horrified at entrusting our
immortal souls to the godless schools of the state. She
was glad to hear that a chapter of the Bible was
read at the general assembly of the pupils every
morning, and the "Our Father" recited; but it was
the Protestant "Our Father," with that gratuitous
and patriotic British phrase at the end, about
"power and glory." Reluctantly she let us go, Leo
and Fred and myself. As for us, we were rather
pleased at the prospect of finding out what sort of a
place a godless school might be.

I have no vivid memories of P. S. No. 1; as usual,
my mental pictures are chiefly of misadventures with
the rules and regulations of the world. I remember
the Principal, Mr. Bascom, spanking me in his
portly and dignified way, and frightening me into
Christian humility for a day or two; but that is all.
Then we changed, for some forgotten reason which I
hope was not disgraceful, to P. S. No. 2. Here again
I seem to have spent my time breaking laws instead
of learning lessons. Yet I must have done something
scholarly, for I found myself promoted into the same
class with my brother Fred, who was nice enough not
to hate me for it. He too was a villain in school;
I can still see him and myself tied to our seats for
misbehavior, and suddenly astounding the teacher
and the class by getting up and marching about with
the seats attached to our sedile organs. We were
given a generous allotment of slaps on the hand with

a hard rubber ruler, and for a week we had swollen palms; but that was not too great a price to pay for the distinction of being the worst boys in the class. When will some subtle reformer find a way of making us as proud of virtue as we are of deviltry? Perhaps we should prohibit virtue by an amendment to the Constitution?

The little mother was unhappy in those days; not only because one of her dearest boys had died, but because the rest of us were apparently going from bad to worse. She was worried especially about my loss of piety. I did not care to pray as much as before; I had quite forgotten that I belonged to Christ; and I behaved more like a little ruffian than a future saint. In the midst of this demoralization my mother's labors and cares so increased that she had no time to give us any of that religious instruction which had heretofore been the staple of our mental lives. She cooked and cleaned and washed and ironed for the family of ten, with only such help as Delia could give. She rose at five and went to bed at twelve, always after long prayers. Once she broke down utterly, and was near death. I remember a handsome young priest coming from afar, galloping up romantically on horseback, whispering a moment with the physician, and then entering the sick room with him. I slipped in behind them, just in time to see my father bending over the bed, holding my mother's head in his arms, and covering her haggard face with kisses.

"Mary, my Mary," he said, over and over again.

31

TRANSITION

Then he saw the priest, and stood aside reverently
while Father Morley held my mother's hand and
spoke to her.

"Do not fear," said the young pastor; "you are a
strong woman, and you will get well. The doctor has
told me so. Let us pray together."

And then, unabashed, he knelt beside the bed and
prayed, silently. His stern ascetic face showed his
absolute sincerity; and our courage rose under the
suggestion of his confidence. My father knelt, and
we others knelt too; all except the doctor, who left
the room quietly, having a theology of his own.
Whether because of the prayers or the pills, my
mother improved from that day on; and within a
week she was at her duties again. Her labors, having
failed to break her, made her; she grew strong and
resolute by the tasks she did, and was always able to
do a man's work when there was need.

The coming of the young priest proved a har-
binger of happy changes for my mother. Another
priest, Father Kernan, a fine masculine organizer,
collected from the Catholic families of the neighborhood enough money to build a church; when I was
eleven or twelve a parochial school was added, and
Fred and I found ourselves once more under the
wings of "the faith." I liked the change well; the
nuns were good teachers, and I could forgive them
their theology for the almost supernatural patience
they showed with our stupidities and misbehavior. I
remember with sorrow Sister Cecilia, a delicate
32

woman who suffered from a nervous disorder that brought her to an early grave. A Stoic of the most phlegmatic temperament could not have been more tolerant of our rascalities. She begged us, gently, to be quiet and considerate; but we took a vile advantage of her weakness, and played upon her every manner of harassing prank. I have the consolation of remembering one youngster still more villainous than myself; but there was not much to choose between us. I recall with unwelcome clarity one disturbance in which Jimmie Calmar and I co-operated bloodily.

Jimmy was my favorite enemy because he was in the habit of winning from me most of the marbles which I had captured from lesser experts than ourselves. One noon we quarreled over our game; and we were making up to each other in the most Queensberry style when the bell rang for the afternoon session. We hesitated, and Jimmy suggested that we should wait and fight it out after school. This was considerate of Jimmy, who quite literally preferred fighting to eating. We entered the class-room like old friends, and behaved exceptionally well that afternoon, lest we should be kept after school and forfeit the chance to show what mighty warriors we were. Of course the class knew of our arrangement, and anticipated a happy hour watching our noses bleed.

All went well till one little girl, either for love of us, or from one of those acute attacks of virtue to which young ladies used to be subject, went to the teacher's desk and betrayed our murderous plans. Sister Cecilia was duly horrified; she called Jimmy to her, and asked him was this report true. Here my memory balks; I quite forget what Jimmy said, and what I answered when the same question was put to me. Sister Cecilia sent to the rectory for Father Kernan; he came in stern majesty, took Jimmy and myself into the sacristy, and dragged out of us the proud confession that we had planned to go behind Smith's barn as soon as school was out, and settle our difficulties like men of honor. I suspect that Father Kernan did not take the matter as seriously as the good Sister. He called us little fools (there is no word like that to get under the skin of a boy), laughed at the cause of our quarrel, bade us shake hands, and made us promise to be friends. We went back to our seats deflated and reduced, while the class silently mourned the loss of a Roman holiday.

No doubt I felt relieved at this sudden treaty of peace; for Jimmy had never been known to lose a fight. I think I should have gone home like a law-abiding citizen when class was dismissed, had not Jimmy come up to me and whispered fiercely:

"Say, we promised to be friends, but we didn't say nothin' about not fightin', did we?"

I saw the warlike implications of his diplomatic note, and my heart beat a little faster. But I showed a brave front to the world.

"What's the matter?" I asked, very harshly. "D'ye want to fight?"

"Sure," said Jim. "Nobody's got to see us, and nobody can tell on us. I'll go down into the wood where the burnt spot is; you make believe you're goin' home, but when nobody sees you you go round the other way and meet me at the place. All right?"

We went, and there, alone in the woods, without the anesthesia of applause, we fought. It was the hardest fight of my life, in a physical way; certainly it was the longest. I enjoyed it for a while, because it seemed that I was getting the better of the redoubtable Jimmy; and Jimmy confessed that he was operating under unprecedented difficulties. But his wind was better than mine, and his nerve better; he punched and punched and punched; and at last I was rolling on the ground, while Lord Jim stood over me with blazing eyes and clenched fists, ready to make me horizontal as soon as I should dare to be vertical. I climbed wearily to my feet and tried to meet his onslaught. But he beat me down again and again. My clothes were torn, my buttons were scattered over the battlefield with geographical impartiality, and my nose, mouth and blouse looked like the multitudinous seas incarnadined. Finally Jim refused to knock me down any more; repetition had dulled the edge of victory.

"Say, Jack," he gasped, "you're beat; why don't ye give up?"

"All right," I said, dully; "I give up."

He held out his hot and swollen hand.

"We're friends, ain't we?"

"All right," I said, "we're friends." I was in a mood to agree to any abstract proposition. No doubt I would have knocked him down if only I could have raised my arm. But I had never disliked Jimmy; I admired his audacity and skill, and I knew that he had overcome me in a fair fight.

Then my memory gives me a laughable picture of Jim and myself, all bloodied o'er, clothes dirty and hair flying, trudging arm in arm out of the woods to the road that led to my home. I had a mile to walk, and I could hardly stand. A grocery wagon passed in my direction, at a rapid pace. I succeeded in lifting myself upon the tail-board, but in the process my school-books fell out of their strap into the street.

"Stay there, Jack," Jim called out; "I'll get them." He gathered my learning together, and with his last breath of wind caught up to the wagon and handed me the books.

Then I fell into the cart senseless, and slept peacefully until it stopped at its destination and the jolt brought me back to consciousness. I returned to the world, found the use of my feet, and walked apathetically home. I would have agreed heartily with Cæsar then,—I had lived enough.

What my mother did to me when she saw the condition of my clothes, and judged therefrom the condition of my morals, I will leave to the Reader's pleasant imagining. The gods were rather cruel to me on that occasion; I was almost dead, and had received instruction enough for one day. But perhaps, being provident gods, they were offering me an advance payment for my later sins.

CHAPTER IV

I FALL IN LOVE

ALL the evidence of my behavior in those years from eleven to thirteen drove my parents to the reluctant conclusion that I had every disqualification for the priesthood. I was a little rowdy,—dirty, disheveled and disobedient; and though I was precociously clever in my studies, my brilliance was of a conceited sort all the world apart from that willing submissiveness of mind which makes a perfect servant of the Church. I continued to be outwardly pious at the altar, and to skip less words in my prayers than the other boys; but it could not escape even the parental eye that I liked marbles better than Holy Mass, and was more interested in Jimmy Calmar than in God. In short, for a brief interval I was a normal and terrestrial boy.

And then I fell in love.

Since the escapade of the button I had almost forgotten the sexual dichotomy of mankind. I had kept away from girls, and had seen so little of them that until the age of eleven or thereabouts I presumed that both sexes had been made on the same anatomical plan, and that the essential difference between them was one of petticoats vs. pantaloons. I had sisters;

38

but I had been too young to observe Delia's transformation through puberty into a young lady with
passions and tragedies and steady callers of her own;
and Edna and Evelyn were tots in arms. Baseball
and a hundred forms of sport absorbed me.

I don't know just when I became conscious of sex
again. I think it was through the teasing of some
older lads with whom I had gone wading in the tra-
ditionally forbidden pond that always marks the map
of boyhood. I went home with a head full of specula-
tions; and from that time I had an X-ray eye for the
structural differences between boys and girls. I
hunted eagerly for anything that could enlighten me;
I worried my inadequate little dictionary for definitions of the mysterious technical terms which tried to
conceal the truth from me; I took solitary walks,
and once more, as in the forgotten past, brooded
alone in my room over the sacred tabus of physiology.
I gave less of my time to sport, and more to reading.
I passed through the usual difficulties of adolescence.

Almost simultaneously with these troubles, and no
doubt associated with them, came one of the most
spiritual experiences of my life. We call it calf love;
but though a calf is a pretty animal indeed, and I
would not for anything offer insult to its placid
grace, I protest against such a name for the loftiest
and most ethereal relation that youth can know.

Near me in school sat a fair-haired, rosy-cheeked,
gentle-eyed girl whom we shall reverently conceal
under the name of Irene. She was a quiet lass, whose

modesty was a lesson needed by my flamboyant soul. She was a well-behaved pupil, but she had a mind of her own, and could make it up when she had to. She led the girls in studies, as I led the boys; and there was a certain rivalry between us until this strange feeling of love crept into my wondering soul. Then I gloried in her successes more than in my own. I found myself admiring every move she made, and every word she spoke; I observed with stealthy and inexplicable interest her hair, her neck, her hands, and her knees (she was young enough to have visible knees). I spent many moments thinking how glorious it would be to kiss her knees.

Yes, I know quite well that it sounds ridiculous in these days when knees are no longer romantically remote. Nevertheless I record it with mad, glad candor, so grateful am I for that redeeming interlude of disembodied love. For mind you, though I was at this period all overcast with sexual imaginings, I never thought of Irene in that light at all. I longed for a thousand kisses; and beyond that only to do her every service that she would receive. I brought her pailfuls of berries that I had picked; I helped her with her lessons; I stole off, when the boys were not looking, to walk with her to her home. I was subdued and made gentle with an unprecedented happiness.

Where is Irene now? What a shame it is that I do not know, that I allowed the chaotic currents of our diverse lives to make us strangers in the world! I am told that she became a nun, and disappeared into the anonymity of the convent. Perhaps if I saw her now I should not recognize her—though I am sure that she is beautiful still. No doubt these profane pages will be hidden from her pious eyes, lest she should remember that she once had kissable knees.

It was Irene who introduced me to literature. Till I met her I had known only such pleasant romancers as Alger and Henty; and I had fed voraciously on a five-cent weekly that told of Frank Merriwell and his glorious band, who won so many ball-games in the ninth inning, broke so many hearts, had so many lives, and made so many nickels for Messrs. Street and Smith. Even to the age of twenty I was not quite emancipated from these splendid fairy-tales. I am not sorry; for I had a happy time reading them, and they served to give me a lust for books which naturally demanded better and better things as I grew. Their heroes were incredibly heroic, and their plots fantastically impossible; but not more so than the heroes of Dumas, or the plots of Will Shakespeare.

And then one day I saw in Irene's hand a book called *Pickwick Papers*. I opened it and was at once allured by the abundance of conversation it contained; here was a lively book and a juicy one. And it was so immense—seven or eight hundred pages; surely the author had been paid by the page, and had had an extravagant wife. I thought it would be quite a feat to read such a volume through; perhaps I should be the first boy in the world to accomplish it. But what moved me most was that it was Irene's book; it must be good if her soft hands had touched it and her bright eyes had traveled along its lines. I begged it from her; and that night, against the protest of my parents, I burned the midnight oil over the adventures of the Pickwick Club, and Sam Weller, and the fat boy who always fell asleep. O happy and undisillusioned Victorians! maligned and misunderstood, what a delight it must have been to watch the creation, week after week, of that incomparable imaginary world! What a delight it was even now, across a thousand obscuring differences of land and speech and time, to know this vivacious style, this inexhaustible humor, this endless chain of exciting incident! I read every word, and marveled that I had lived twelve years without discovering this book. I returned it to Irene, and begged her for more.

"It's all I have by Dickens," she said, sorrowfully. "But papa says he will get me *David Copperfield* for Christmas."

Christmas was several months away; I could not wait that long. Within a week I had managed to accumulate fourteen pennies; and armed with them I walked the three miles between our new home in Arlington and Dressel's book-store in Newark. I asked the grouchy old gentleman behind the counter for his cheapest edition of *David Copperfield*. He went into a rear room, worked his way precariously among stacks of broken-down books, and emerged with a copy that might have rivaled Ulysses' wanderings.

"I will let this go for twenty-five cents," he said, munificently.

My heart broke temporarily.

"But mister," I said, with a politeness which I seldom achieved, "I've only got fourteen cents."

He was unmoved, and turned away to another customer. I looked longingly at the book, and helplessly at space in general. Then a tall handsome gentleman, whom I conceived as a millionaire philosopher but who turned out to be a butcher, came over to me and put his arm around my shoulder.

"What do you want, sonny?" he said.

"*David Copperfield,*" I replied.

"How much do you need?"

"Eleven cents."

"Is that all? Here you are; when you get rich you can pay me back."

I should have thanked him. But I was so grateful then that I could not speak. I accepted the eleven cents as a gift from God, and walked out of the store in a daze. I trudged home in ecstasy over the kindness of Providence, the goodness of human nature, and the pleasures in store for me in the 860 pages which I carried under my arm.

From that day I became a tremendous reader. When everybody else in the house was asleep I would read on, despite a thousand admonitions about the injury I was doing to my health, and the cost of gas. It is true that I lost something of my taste for sport,

and more of my skill in it; I could not play ball with
"Dots" Miller, or "shoot" marbles with Jimmy Calmar, any more. But what a new universe I had found!
I no longer lived in prosaic New Jersey; I wandered
around the world with my heroes and my poets. I
discovered Byron, elocuted his address to the ocean,
and went through every word of Moore's biography.
I did not understand all that I read, and what I did
understand shocked me agreeably. But I liked the
poetry and the sentiment, and admired Byron pro-
fusely. I remember the day when I finished Moore's
account of the poet's death at Missolonghi: I was
overwhelmed with emotion; and kneeling, I begged
God to let poor Byron at last out of the Hell to
which, presumably, he had been condemned. I forgot
that this was contrary to Catholic theology, and that
(as the pope told the protesting cardinal who found
himself pictured among the damned in Michelangelo's "Last Judgment") not even God can get a
soul out of Hell once it is in. But I was horrified to
think that the handsome and melancholy poet had
been burning there for three quarters of a century.
I felt that that was enough, even for an Englishman.

These new developments—sexual irritability, first
love, and a passion for books—combined to mark my
transformation, at puberty, from boyhood into
youth. There was still another change, difficult for
me to remember in detail, but quite as pervasive and
profound, and of crucial importance in my life. It
will seem absurdly out of harmony with the erotic and

44

literary awakening that accompanied it; and yet it
too, no doubt, contained an element of sex and poetry. I became pious again. I don't know just how it
happened; partly it came, I think, from the turning
inward of my mental life in books and love; partly
from the effect of these in stirring up the fund of
sentiment within me; and partly from my sudden and
passionate admiration for Father Morley.

He had succeeded Father Kernan as pastor of the
little church in Kearny. He came to us from several
years of graduate study in Italy; and though he had
gone an Irishman he had returned looking almost
Italian,—dark and fiery and full of energy, like another Corsican. What a vivid picture he made as he
galloped through the parish on his prancing horse!
He rode like a gentleman born to the hunt. He had
the small feet and hands of an aristocrat, and the
alert and mobile face of a poet; yet in his thin lips
and sparkling eyes there was an omen of anger and
power which enabled him, despite his boyish stature,
to dominate almost every one who came into his life.
We did not know then that a painful disease was
weakening him, and shutting him out from that high
career for which his energy and his intellect had
fitted him.

Sometimes he would come into the class-room and
relieve the teacher for a while. Those were lively
minutes, in which we did more thinking than usually
in whole days. He would sit or stand at the desk and
aim question after question at us by startling and

incalculable turns; if we could not answer at once he passed ruthlessly on, until we were all trembling with alertness and anxiety. What a mind he had!—as rapid as an electric spark, and as bright; you could almost hear the crackling of the fire of his thought in the incisive sentences of his speech. I was just at the age when I relished these acrobatics of the intellect, this leaping logic, these sudden demands for precise definitions, these frankly tricky questions, these challenges to detect the fallacies of a subtle argument. I did my very best for him, and thrilled more under his praise than even at the smile of the girl I loved.

I was happy in those days when it fell my turn to serve him as acolyte at Mass. He was so genuine and complete: a man of mind, and yet obviously aflame with feeling; a man of spacious knowledge and yet of the most intense devotion. He did not hurry through Mass like so many priests, who seem to be thinking of their postponed breakfasts when they are changing bread into the body of God; he gave us every word distinctly, so that the sonorous Latin became a stately chant as he pronounced it. He seemed absorbed as he went through the acts of the solemn ritual; and when he prayed, no hypocrite dared join in the response. He was such a priest that if every priest could be like him I would the world had become all Catholic. Kneeling beside him on the altar-steps, I felt almost physically drawn to him; I longed to embrace him and be one with him.

Under his influence I began to take religion seriously again. The Mass became a vivid drama to me, and I saw the Crucifixion anew at every elevation of the Host. I prayed so fervently that people took it for granted that I would become a saint. I listened intently to every word of Father Morley's sermons; I thrilled under his chastisement of human imperfection; and I began myself to yearn for the privilege of preaching, the austere delight of denouncing man and praising God. How eloquent I would be when my turn came, and how I would draw all the world to Christ!

One day Father Morley came to see us in our Arlington home. He was not at his ease with women, and had little of the graceful geniality with which the Abbé Dubois had warmed the feminine hearts in his flock. But the fire of a serious mission shone in his dark face, and the women trembled with reverence as he spoke to them. My mother was all a-fluster as she sat before him, grieving silently over her unpreparedness to receive her visitor as she would have wished—with every inch of the house immaculate, herself in the neatest dress, and the children groomed as if to enter heaven.

"Your boy," he said, "is doing very well in school."

This was handsome of him, for only a week before I had been reported to him for misconduct. I stood in awe near my mother, unable to meet his eye; for this was the same man to whom, in burning shame, I confessed every week my burden of sin.

47

"I'm so glad to hear that, Father," said my mother humbly; "I always had great hopes for him."

"I knew you had," he said; "and that is why I came to see you to-day. Would you like to have him become a priest?"

"I'd thank God every day for it if it could be, Father. I've prayed for it these last ten years."

"And you, John," he asked, "would you like it?"

I hesitated; I vaguely realized that I was being asked, very suddenly, to make a momentous decision. I could find no other words than simply,——

"Yes, Father."

He put both hands on my shoulders, and spoke in a way which aroused in me vague memories of the similar words of Père Dubois five years before.

"Some day you will be a brilliant servant of the Church. We are going through great changes. The enemies of the Church are very powerful, and she needs new champions. Perhaps you will be one of these. Come to me Saturday morning, and I will take you to Jersey City, and enter you for the scholarship examinations at St. Paul's College. Meanwhile study hard, and remember, in your behavior everywhere, that you are called to the priesthood, and the hand of God is on you."

He went out to his horse, and disappeared down the street, trailing clouds of glory. My mother smiled on me proudly, and celebrated this second epiphany by baking an incomparable pie. As for me,

I FALL IN LOVE

I went up to my room and sat staring out of the window for many hours, wondering what I had done with my life. This time, I felt, the decision was irrevocable. Once again I belonged to Christ.

CHAPTER V

I MEET DARWIN

I was graduated from parochial school that spring with a medal for "general proficiency," which (they explained to me) did not include good conduct. All summer I came to the convent near the church, and studied algebra with Sister Margarita. She had the best qualifications of a good teacher; a little knowledge, and much patience. I shrink with shame when I recall how many times I made trouble for her. Once her patience gave out, and she took me to Father Morley with tears of anger in her eyes.

"Father," she said, "I can't teach with this boy in the class. I can't control him. Either he must go or I must."

But within a few minutes he had soothed her and sent her away reconciled to my existence. Then he turned upon me with a volcanic eye that shriveled me into half of my natural self.

"Let me never hear any more complaints about you. Go!"

I went out crushed, with my tail between my legs. I was a better-behaved boy after that; and Sister Margarita came to think of me as almost her favorite pupil. Now she spent an hour with me every day, rewardless, to fit me for the examinations at St. Paul's; teaching me algebra, correcting my compositions, and going over with me the subtler mysteries of the catechism.

Late in August I went to Jersey City, and sat at a desk all day in one of the hardest tests I have ever taken. When I received notice a week later that I had been one of the three victors, I wondered whether the sly Jesuits had not passed me at Father Morley's request, on the ground that I belonged to Christ, and had to be put through.

So in September I entered college. I commuted daily from Arlington by railroad, and then walked a mile and a half through the vilest part of what I may mildly term the most unfortunate city in the United States. How strange it is that the metropolis of America did not develop there, on the west side of the Hudson, accessible by land to all the continent, and washed by the same majestic river that buffets Manhattan's shores! In place of that proud destiny the city of my first Alma Mater had become merely a railway terminus for New York, breathing the fumes of ten thousand locomotives that brought freight and passengers to the lordly Isle of Towers. Perhaps some day, when clean electric current will do the work of the world, turning its machines and moving its trains, this unhappy and discouraged city will be redeemed, and its sooty wastes and huddled hovels will flower into gardens and palaces. But I shall never quite forgive it for being what it was when I knew it, and filling my lungs with poison for the better part of seven years.

Once arrived at college, I was content enough. I found the lessons easy, and did so well that I was projected, in mid-term, into a higher grade. There the work was harder, and I had for many years to remain satisfied with something considerably less than leadership. Ultimately I became quite an expert in Latin, and achieved the useless distinction of being able to converse, fitfully, in a dead language. I studied Greek for six years, and taught it for three; and yet its classics never came to mean for me, in the original, anything but a task, a struggle with syntax and unreliable verbs; like any man, I must read them now in translation. Why should we torture our boys and girls with these once noble and now extinct forms of human speech?

The Jesuits were good teachers, and of course good disciplinarians. I have known some thirty Jesuits intimately; and all were men of superior intellect, all but two were magnificent teachers, and all but one were men of golden character. There was Father Judge, emaciated and theological, made gentle by consumption, and reconciled to an early end; never did I hear him utter an unkind word, or do any unjust deed. There was Father Ziegler, who made even Greek palatable with his bubbling good humor; and Father McLoughlin, who bore with me so patiently in the years of my mental chaos; and

Father Collins, perhaps the most capable of them all, a strong, stern man, saddened (I suspect) with an unfulfilled romance. And there was Father Gillespie, nervous and satirical, jolly and kind, who took the sails out of my conceit and helped to tame me into a socialized animal. I remember once mispronouncing "Æneas" by accenting the first syllable.

"Any ass would know that it's not 'Æ'-ne-as,' " said Father Gillespie.

"That's why I didn't know it," I answered, implying a related reason as to why he did.

He said nothing; but one day, when he entered the class-room suddenly and surprised me in some nonsense, he pulled my ear with no consideration for my dignity, and for many days I was an inverted hero. That single resort of my Jesuit teachers to direct action helped me to a better perspective of my modest place in the world.

John Moore helped me too. John was a tremendous fellow, tall, stocky and muscular, several years beyond me in age, and quite out of my reach in stature, strength and height. One noon, in the playground, a snow-ball struck me in the temple, and for a minute laid me low. When I came to, and saw the crowd around me, I could not forego the opportunity to crow; and I announced magnificently that I would thrash the thrower of that snow-ball whoever he was, and no matter how big. Moore heard me, and informed me that he was the gentleman I sought. Inwardly I groaned; outwardly I flew all my flags, and

invited him to settle the matter after class. I will not
go into further details; I have been humiliated often
enough in this history. At four o'clock that afternoon
I was in a condition of dilapidation that rivaled the
aftermath of my disagreement with Jimmy Calmar.
I never had to fight again at college; apparently the
boys felt that I had had my share of physical education.

The reader will be relieved to know that this is the
last time I shall regale him with fisticuffs. After this
second slaughter I thought it wise to restrict my exploits to the realms of the intellect. I had not abandoned, even in the turmoil of college studies and college sports, my passion for the literary world; I
pestered the College librarians more than any other
student; and soon ran through the novels of Scott,
and Thackeray, and Jane Austen, and Hugo, and
Dumas. Indeed, that little collection of harmless au-
thors was not enough for me; and by a kind of intellectual gravitation I found the Jersey City Public
Library, and hauled away books at a greedy rate.

I doff my hat (or should I humble my head?) when
I pass that Library to-day, or the similar institution
in Newark; it was in those treasure-houses, rather
than in college, that I found an education. I liked
the Newark Library best, because there we were permitted to roam about among the books, and select
them for ourselves. It was an admirably managed institution, offering every incentive and every aid to
the student. The only tragedy was that a limit had to

be placed on the number of books which one might take out at one time. As I passed among the stacks my hands reached out hungrily for this or that alluring volume; I was overwhelmed by the riches about me, and could hardly bear to leave any of the discovered masterpieces behind me when I went. I must have been a familiar figure there in those days,—at once timid and proud, bold with heresy and hesitant with thought, looking wistfully and lovingly upon those glories of literature and science and philosophy, for which I knew that my little lifetime would not suffice.

You are to picture me at this stage as a slightly round-shouldered lad of eighteen, already bending under the weary weight of this unintelligible world. I was short and almost thin, fated to be one for whom the body was merely the tolerated and neglected vehicle of a transcendental ego. I was not ugly; a prejudiced friend might have thought me presentable, had not my nose suffered a declination of its axis in some heroic football game. The lure of books had begun to pale the pristine ruddiness of my cheeks, but it had put a wild lustre into my eyes, giving me the aspect of a hunted and seeking soul. Not for many years now would I know the healing touch of peace.

One day an old Jesuit met me on the porch of the college hall, and saw from the bindings that some of the books I carried were city property. He reproved me gently.

"Don't you know, my boy, that you must not read without the guidance of a priest? Perhaps some of these books are on the Index; and you may be endangering your immortal soul in reading them."

I forget what I replied; but my curiosity continued to prove greater than my respect for my immortal soul. I was resolved to know every famous author; and when I read somewhere that Charles Darwin had written the most important book of the nineteenth century, I made up my mind that, Index or no Index, I would read that book.

In those days I was in the habit of visiting Father Morley in his new domicile as Vice-President of South Hall College. He used to wait for me on the shaded gravel walks of the campus grounds; and we promenaded together while he poured into my ears words of affectionate counsel and inspiration. I sometimes think that a priest is called "Father" because he has no children. His heart hungers like ours for the pleasures of paternity; and inevitably he finds some youth to whom he can be at least *pater in spiritualibus.*

"What are you reading?" he asked, taking up the book I was carrying under my arm.

"The Origin of Species," I answered, innocently. He frowned.

"So that's the track you're on. Do you know that this book is an attack upon your holy religion?"

"No, Father; I didn't know that."

56

"It is. Are you not afraid that such a book will destroy your faith?"

I answered with my usual conceit.

"It would take more than Darwin to shake *my* faith."

"Let us pray to God that it will," he said. "But your very pride is your weakness; it is in just such minds as yours that unbelief grows. You are too young to think of these things. That is why our Holy Mother Church forbids books of this kind except for those who are old enough to stand unshaken by them. It would be better for you, John, never to read another line of Darwin until you have been graduated from college."

He exacted no promises, and I went home unbound. At one moment I vowed I would follow his advice faithfully; and then I wondered what it was all about, and why this dull book should be so terrible, and what hurt could come to me from reading just a bit of it.

Nevertheless, *The Origin of Species* went back to the library half unread. Even with the stimulus of prohibition I found myself unable to grasp the argument. I had looked for proofs of man's descent from the ape; and I found, instead, an intricately detailed discussion of every animal except man. I was disappointed, and smiled with superiority at the unnecessary fear with which my masters viewed this dryasdust biologist. I decided to give *The Descent of Man* a brief trial, and if it proved no better than its predecessor I would leave Darwin virtuously alone. But I had only to read the table of contents to see that this book was to prove much more interesting, and perhaps more damaging, than the other. Very soon it dawned upon me that according to Darwin man was an animal differing only in degree from other animals, born like them, hungering like them, associating like them, loving like them, reproducing like them, and fated to die as completely and irrevocably as the lowest.

I was not easily convinced; and I made every effort to keep my footing against the undertow of doubt. I sought out the Catholic contributions to the question; I read reply after reply to Darwin; and found the refutations much easier to understand than the theory. But my pride automatically made me the antagonist of every argument I heard or read; and the more direct the argument, the sharper my hostility became. Darwin wrote quietly, without controversial animus; he had a universe of facts, and put them down dispassionately; he did not argue, and one could read him without anger. But the theologians had more logic than biology; they started from theoretical premises, and worked their ways by the most marvelous syllogisms to the most respectable and foreordained conclusions. Very often the premises were open to doubt, or the conclusions were wider than the proof. Like the theologians, I was poor in facts but had a keen nose for fallacies; I did not know enough science to refute Darwin, but I was clever enough to find a sieve of holes in the arguments of his adversaries. It was these refutations that made me an evolutionist.

One day I went with a pious friend to the Museum of Natural History. There the evidence for evolution was made so visible that even a theologian might understand it. My companion was horrified at my suggestion that perhaps, after all, Darwin's view was correct; he responded with tropistic inevitability:—

"What kind of a monkey was *your* father?"

He had no doubt that this settled the matter definitely. A few minutes later I heard him calling me.

"Jack, come over here. Good God! Look at this gorilla."

He was standing amazed before a glass case containing a stuffed gorilla, which stood almost erect, a forelimb grasping the branch of a tree. It looked for all the world like some hairy savage groping towards humanity.

"Jack," said my friend, "I give up. Darwin is right."

A month later he had almost forgotten the incident; and when he saw me with Spencer's *Principles of Biology* under my arm he sniffed superiorly.

"Are you still bothering with that nonsense?" he asked.

It was bothering me a great deal. I had by that time read half a dozen of the great protagonists of the evolution theory. I was happy to find that St.

Augustine had interpreted Genesis in evolutionary terms, and that Alfred Russell Wallace, the amiable rival of Darwin in discovery, had defended evolution without losing God. I struggled to protect this position against the agnosticism of Spencer and Huxley; I wished to be an evolutionist without abandoning my ambition to be a saint.

Indeed, I was at this time more pious than ever. I read Father Faber's devotional works, and Cardinal Newman's books, and over and over again I went through, in Latin and in English, *The Imitation of Christ.* I left home early every morning in order to hear Mass at St. Paul's; several times a week I knelt at the altar-rail to receive Holy Communion; and on Sundays I served as chief acolyte in Arlington. The little parish of ten years before had spread out from Kearny now; and while Kearny built a fine new church, the growing Catholic population of Arlington bought a little chapel that had for a generation resounded with Methodist hymns. Apparently, while the Church was losing me it was winning thousands.

I prayed, as devoutly as a young sceptic could, that God would keep me loyal to the Faith, and accept me at last, cleansed of doubt, into his service as a priest. I made novenas of many kinds, and broke all records for the number of rosaries I mumbled. Meanwhile I gave my teachers the most generous opportunity to resolve my difficulties. I pestered them with argument about it and about; with only this result, that they put me down as a nuisance, and set me

aside with the comment that when I was older I
would understand these matters better. I do.

Unable to get a sympathetic hearing from my
teachers, and finding the other students at college
suspiciously hostile to every mention of evolution,
I sought out other ears, and began to mingle with a
group of boys and men who met in the telegraph
office in Arlington. Most of these boys were non-
Catholics; some of them had *risqué* stories which attracted me; and one of them was as eager as I to discuss theology. He was a tall handsome lad, about
twenty-one years of age, named Harvey Keap; in
later days he came into considerable repute as "the
tramp poet." He had apparently gone much further
on the road to the Everlasting No than I; and when
he heard that I still believed in God he laughed up-
roariously.

"God?" he said; "why, God is just a joke played
upon kids by their mamas. He's only a bogey-man
to frighten children with. It saves a lot of spanking,
and, later on, a lot of policemen."

I began to argue learnedly, but he stopped me
short.

"Look here," he said, sharply; "we can settle this
matter in a jiffy. I'll show you what I think of your
God." He raised his right hand and looked at the
ceiling. "If your God exists," he said, "let him strike
me down dead this minute. He can't, you see. He isn't
born yet."

Perhaps I do Harvey injustice in reporting this.

He has found God useful in his poetry, and may find him useful, later, in his philosophy; he may resent this immortalization of what was perhaps a transient bravery. But if I know him well he is still as careless as ever of what the bishops think. I tell the story because his challenge made a profound impression upon me. I pretended that his defy only proved that God was busy and had no time to play with poets; but I went home worried into sleeplessness.

It was just like me that having seen Shelley's poems in Keap's hands, I should feel impelled, at the first chance, to see what this poet was who could satisfy so bold a mind. Almost at once I came upon the story of Shelley's expulsion from Oxford for circulating his pamphlet on "The Necessity of Atheism." I tried to get this essay, and failed; but the very title of it damaged the remnants of my faith. Then I heard of Swinburne's thanksgiving to "whatever gods there be,"

> That no life lives forever;
> That dead men rise up never;
> That even the weariest river
> Winds somewhere safe to sea.

I arrived at Fitzgerald's *Rubaiyat*, and found atheism, determinism and epicureanism beautified beyond resistance. I went back to Byron, and understood his deviltry a little better than before; I read *Don Juan*, and though I never finished it, it finished me. I concluded that almost every independent spirit of the nineteenth century had been an agnostic or an infidel.

One night I had been reading some of this heretical literature until a single stroke of the clock aroused me into the realization that it was time for sleep. My parents had begged me not to read to so late an hour; unconsciously they understood that these books were like a virus in my blood; but my greed for forbidden knowledge was stronger than their gentle dissuasion. So on this night every soul in the house was asleep but myself, and all was as quiet as in the nursery rhyme. My reading through at last, I knelt by the bed and began to pray. Dimly I saw my faith slipping from me, saw myself left standing as if naked on some lonely shore, with the darkness falling down around me. Even more dimly I saw my whole generation, thousands and millions of youths, passing through the same ordeal, and as unwillingly as myself. I did not want to abandon my Church; I loved the fair creed that had given me the story of Jesus and the gentle face of the Virgin; I liked every priest I had met, and remembered gratefully the kindness of the nuns; I did not want to lose my father's respect, or my mother's love. I begged God to tell me how to answer these books, how to be strong against this blasphemous poetry.

I prayed a long time, and then fell wearily into bed. Even as I passed into sleep I had a vague feeling that my prayers were useless, that there was no one in the skies to answer me. The next morning I did not

pray, and I did not think; a dull certainty had settled down upon me. As I went to school I kept whispering to myself, in horror, the word which I had
been taught to dread beyond all others in the world:

"I am an atheist. I am an atheist."

CHAPTER VI

CONFESSIONAL

THAT first year of independence was one of pride, unhappiness, and hypocrisy. I felt like a man adventuring into a dangerous wilderness alone. The thought that other young men everywhere were going through the same slow change from belief to unbelief was too vague to comfort me. I was marked off from my fellows as one darkly unlike the rest, a Byronic hero of the intellect; and I bore my solitude in majestic silence. I could say nothing of my theological puberty to any of my family; they would not have understood me, and would have looked upon me as a leper. I could say nothing to my teachers, for excepting Father Collins they knew too little of science to be able to discuss the matter fruitfully. For months I carried the demon of unbelief in my breast like the Spartan boy with his stolen fowl.

Because of this mental isolation my life turned inward more than ever. The ball-fields saw me less and less, the libraries more and more. Now that Providence had fallen out of the cosmos the world seemed a strangely chaotic thing; and I yearned to know the laws that, apparently without mind or purpose, had made and kept it one. In those years when I was passing through the sophomore and junior grades of the college course I did an unhealthy amount of reading. I found Spencer's essay on the classification of the sciences, divided the world of knowledge on its lines, and mapped out for myself a schedule of reading that would have overwhelmed a Stuart Mill. I kept fairly well to that program; in two years I read nearly nine hundred volumes;— how thoroughly, the mathematical reader may judge. By the time I was a senior at college, I felt myself the intellectual equal of any stripling on the planet. I no longer argued with my teachers, being convinced that they were irretrievably distanced by the advance of my mind. I pursued truth unaided and alone.

Meanwhile I continued to go to church, to confession and communion; I left no stone unturned, nor any lie untold, to conceal from my parents the loss of my theological innocence. That year of hypocrisy cost me a great deal in self-respect; but I am not sorry I chose so devious a course. I think I would have lied and pretended to this very day if it could have kept the sad fact from my father and my mother. I felt as yet no call to inform or reform the world; it was entirely a matter between myself and those whom I loved a little better than the truth.

Later on I found relief in the sympathetic friendship of Dave Howatt. I was astonished and piqued to find that he had lost his faith at an earlier age than I, and had made no Shakespearean tragedy of the change. We had long walks and talks together, played ball by our emancipated selves, made raids upon the Newark Library, and grew in heresy and sophistication. The gap between the old religion and our new philosophy widened with every day, until at last the task of pretense became intolerable.

One Sunday I took the long trolley-ride out to South Hall, and entered, unexpected, the office of Father Morley. He had now become president of the college as well as rector of the seminary, and his quick success in every field would have warranted him in stretching his pride to a higher notch than before. But he was as kindly as ever to me, and gave me without stint the time which he so badly needed for other visitors and his work.

"Sit down, John. Is anything wrong?"

I have not had a harder minute in my life. Where was I to begin? Could I tell a part without telling all? And surely, when all was told, this man, whom of all men I loved next to my own father, would send me away in anger and scorn. I floundered about for introductions, intimations, gradations; and then in despair I blurted everything out in a word.

"Father, I don't believe in God any more."

I sat taut, prepared for lightning and storm; but for a long time he said nothing. He merely looked at me in growing astonishment and pain, while the meaning of my simple announcement burnt itself into his mind. It was a severe disappointment to him, though no doubt he had had other irons in the fire than myself. He looked almost appealingly at me for a time; and then suddenly hardening, he spoke words which fell upon me like tongues of flame:

"If you are an atheist we can have no further business together. Go your way, and may God have mercy on you."

I walked out as proudly as I could. At the door I turned back to him, and managed, before my voice broke, to say:

"Good-bye, Father. And don't tell my mother; it would break her heart."

Suddenly his arm was around me and he was pressing me to his breast. I burst into wild sobbing, as if all the suppressed emotions of a year were finding voice; I lay limp in his arms while he let me cry to my heart's content. Mingled with my scepticism of a man was the sensitivity of a high-strung girl. Out on the campus students and visitors strained their eyes to see through the windows what this strange commotion was in the office of the President. Meanwhile he was quietly comforting me, talking gently as I cried, until, as I understood his words, the full nobility of the man flooded my soul like an unexpected dawn.

"You're not a bad fellow," he said; "and I know that this isn't altogether your fault. Half the educated world is going through the same trouble. You'll get over it. You were wrong, you see, when you said Darwin couldn't shake your faith. But it is only shaken; deep down in your heart it is still there, and will always remain there. Perhaps it is better that you should pass through this period of doubt; it will deepen you and make you stronger. You will pull yourself up out of this silly notion that the world is a ball of dirt; and your faith in a Divine Intelligence will come back to you. It may not be just the same faith as before; and it needn't be. We are passing through a great change, John. Our Holy Mother Church will adapt herself to the new knowledge, as she has done in the past. We need young men like you, who have tasted modern science, to answer modern science. We will send you to the best Catholic university in Europe—Louvain—and there you will learn the old theology thoroughly, and be ready later to share in making the new. No; I am not sorry that you have gone through this; you will come back to us."

I said nothing. I was exhausted; and I did not quite share his confidence. But how grateful I was for that confidence, and the kindness of heart that could offer me such honors at the very moment when I had made utter shipwreck of all his plans for me! I wanted to embrace him, but he looked so strong that it would have seemed absurd to offer him love. Men can love only what is weaker than themselves, and women only what is stronger.

"Go back to your studies," he went on; "and go back to your prayers. Promise me this, that even if you do not believe, you will pray."

I promised gladly. It was so little to do for him. I

had almost lost him, and here he was, more generously mine than ever. But I asked him:

"You will not consider me hypocritical if I go to church and to communion as I used to do?"

"No. Tell your doubts frankly to your confessor; but so long as you wish to believe again in God and Christ he will absolve you. You do wish to believe in God and Christ again?"

"Yes, Father, I do. I was happy when I believed; nothing could make me happier than to believe again, and be a priest, like you."

He saw the affection that halted my speech, and his confidence in being able to reclaim me sparkled in his eyes.

"Go home and be happy," he said.

As I went down the corridor from his office a score of waiting visitors looked in astonishment at my swollen eyes, and made me understand that I had chosen a very inopportune time for my little tragedy.

CHAPTER VII

LOVE AMONG THE RUINS

For some days I was at peace. I felt myself partly
cleansed of hypocrisy, and I knew that a great and
good man loved me. A second innocence came to me:
I went to Mass every day cheerfully; and though I
did not pray as much as in younger days, my prayers
were honest, addressed quite frankly to an unknown
God. I begged the Almighty, if he existed, to restore
my faith in his existence. After a while it seemed a
little ridiculous to me, and I found it increasingly
difficult and unnatural. I was of a wicked generation
that demanded a sign; and no sign appeared. Perhaps if I had been patient for a year I might have
recaptured the old faith, on Pascal's principle that
one should cross one's self frequently with holy water
—*celà vous abêtira*. But now two experiences came
to me which drove religion into the neglected back-
water of my life. One was socialism, the other was a
girl.

During my annual vacations I had become a proletaire. My career at high school and college (St.
Paul's included both) cost my parents very little
directly, since my scholarship gave me free tuition
throughout the seven years; but it cost them much

indirectly, as I brought nothing whatever into the family treasury, though I insisted on eating every day. My older brothers did not grudge me my good fortune; and they felt that they were making a necessary sacrifice to give a priest to the Church. But it would have been an unpardonable imposition upon them all if I had idled my summers away.

In those vacation periods I saw the world of industry. One of my earliest occupations was as grocer's clerk. For the sum of three dollars a week I weighed out sugar and butter and flour and cakes, drove the delivery wagon, and wrote the advertisements. I remember the difficulty I had persuading my master to change the spelling of a sign he had written, announcing to his "costumers" a fall in the price of beans. I had a great time that summer driving the wagon around, at a reckless speed which in this legless age would seem intolerably slow. I can still see before me, as I write, the broad back and steaming flanks of that old horse; though I suppose he has long since gone to the equine paradise. In those days competition was sharp and real; we were always scheming to undersell the store across the street; and the margin of profit was so small that in a short time my employer became bankrupt. After fifteen years of hard work, his successful rival was rich enough to buy his own house and mow his own lawn. The business of "going in for one's self" has never since suggested any delusions of grandeur to me; I know that many are called, and few are chosen.

My hardest summer was spent in a little gold-foundry in the rear of the City Hall in Newark. I forget my employer's name, though he was very good to me; while I remember with bitter distinctness the name of the jeweler who exploited both of us. Always I found that behind the man who drove me to arduous toil there lurked a more sinister and stealthy figure who drove him. It might be the landlord raising rents as his tenant's profits grew; or the wholesaler forcing inferior goods upon the retailer as the price of letting him have goods at all; or the New York office threatening to discharge foremen or superintendents who did not keep their "hands" working as fast as possible for the lowest possible wage. It was just where personal contact was missing that the greatest injustice grew.

So old Boulanger (let us call him that, for he was French, and looked like a general) was as easy with me as his own safety would permit. I worked from eight to twelve and from one to five. During the noon hour, when Boulanger went home to eat, I walked down Mulberry Street to a saloon where, if I bought a five-cent drink, I was privileged to stand and eat at the lunch-counter to my stomach's content. It was good food, properly cooked, and, under the circumstances, remarkably clean. With the rest of the fifteen cents allowed me for my noon meal, I would go to a news-dealer and buy some paper edition of a famous novel. It was in those hot days that I discovered Zola, and sat alone in the shop from twelve-thirty till one, prowling for pornography. Once Boulanger came in too soon, and I had no time to put the book away. He looked at it, saw that it was Zola, and instead of berating me gave me a friendly rap on the head.

"Villain," he said, in French, which was the only language he knew; "you are anxious to know the worst about the world, aren't you?"

This was not quite the proper analysis, but I let it go uncorrected. The old man was something of a pagan, and did not grudge me the sins of youth. He never went to church, and laughed when I told him I was studying for the priesthood. Yet when the summer was over he gave me a pretty gold cross, and wished me as much happiness as he thought possible to a celibate. He too must be in paradise now, poor fellow.

The next summer I worked in the factory where my father superintended the "Specialty." It was characteristic of him that he did not want me to get a place merely as his son; he advised me to stand in line with the others at the employment gate, and take my turn and my luck. I was handed over to Mr. Burke, a man after the type of my father, bookless and letterless, but belonging to nature's nobility. (The Reader will be tired, by this time, of finding every man in this story a nobleman, and every woman half a saint; he must not look for villains here, because I have found none; and I believe they are as rare in life as they will be in my book.)

LOVE AMONG THE RUINS

I put my new employer's kindness to the severest
test a few days after entering his shop. Saturday
was cleaning day; and each man splashed his working quarters with a hose, washing the celluloid shav-
ings from the comb-sawing machines into a drain in
the floor. Occasionally the hose would be turned in
sport upon some unsuspecting employee; and on my
first Saturday, it seems that I was listed for this
christening. I tried to dodge, but received my cleansing nevertheless, and from head to foot, till I was wet
with rage. When the hose came into my hands I
turned it fiercely upon my enemy. He fled towards
the door, and I pointed the hose in that direction; so
that Mr. Burke, who entered just as my prey dodged
aside, stopped the stream of water with his breast.
My reaction-time was too slow to avoid the mishap.
When I saw what I had done I dropped the hose in
paralyzing consternation, and awaited my discharge.
Mr. Burke frowned, turned off the water, did the
various tasks he had entered to do, and then went off
without saying a word to me. I would have toiled
eighteen hours a day for him after that, for a week
or two.

I learned many things that summer. The workers
were a rough but good-natured lot, who knew no
other topic of discourse than sex and sport. We had
a baseball "pool," and spent the morning discussing
the prospects of the "Giants," the "Yankees," the
"Dodgers," the "Cubs," the "Reds," and the other
tribes of athletes through whom the cities of Amer-

75

ica have become known to our college students. What talk remained after that went to the anatomy, physiology and pathology of the reproductive system. Each morning heard boasts of the adventures of the evening before, even to a list of nine resorts which one of our heroes had patronized in one night; and each week had its exhibitory extravaganzas. The one thing these men were proud of was the luxurious abundance of their seed; they were always ready to help a childless parent, and boasted of their accomplishments in paternity as if children had never been made before. They were all good church-goers; and yet their favorite joke with me concerned the great sport I would miss by vowing myself to chastity.

While my instruction in anatomy and physiology progressed, I learned something also of industrial economy. At first I managed (I think) three machines, slipping thin plates of celluloid into them, cooling them with water while they sawed teeth into the plates, and then taking out the resultant combs. I was paid $1.50 a day, and thought it fair enough. But towards the end of the summer my three machines were taken away, and some twelve machines were installed in their place. The twelve worked much more efficiently than the three, and with greater speed; my production was multiplied ten-fold. My rate of movement, and the strain of the accelerated work, were so increased, that I asked to be changed to piece-work, so that I might get a higher reward for greater industry. I earned on the new plan some two dollars a day, which averaged a quarter of a cent per comb. One Saturday, as I walked through a department store in Newark, I saw the same combs, blessed product of my hands, offered for sale at fifty cents a piece. I calculated the expense of plant, depreciation, power, shipping, book-keeping, finance, advertisement, and swivel-chairs, and concluded that I was receiving about one-tenth of my due. I understood the subtleties of "surplus value" before I had ever heard the words; and I was a Marxian before I became a socialist.

I am surprised that socialism had not come to me before. Perhaps, as one who knew factories only in his summer vacations, it took me some time to realize the difficulties of the workingman's lot; and perhaps Arlington, as a little out-of-the-way town, was slow to discover the new gospel, just as the *pagani* were the last of the Romans to hear of Christianity. Several times I had seen a young orator addressing an open-air meeting in the square near the railroad station; but as I was a better orator myself, I passed on in disdain. Occasionally I stopped and listened for a while, to have the pleasure of exposing the speaker's fallacies to my friends. Finally I chanced on an "agitator" who really caught my interest. I forget his name, I forget even his face; but I remember very well the topic of his address—"Why Must the Poor Be Always with Us?"

The speaker astonished me by discussing Christ not as a god but as an economist. He brought together certain selected quotations which seemed to make Christ a communist. He took it blithely for granted that Jesus had been put to death not for any pretensions to divinity, but for these communistic inclinations. I suspect that scholars would not bear out this view; but I was willing to accept the suggestion as within the realms of possibility. The anomaly was, said the speaker, that a man who seemed to side entirely with the people against priests and merchants and kings should have so reconciled himself to poverty as something ineradicable and everlasting.

"*Must* poverty last forever?" the young orator asked, passionately. "Are we not ashamed to let that problem go unanswered? Is there no way out?"

I did not quite agree with his solutions, but I felt the stimulation of his questions. I began to read economics, and within a week after that street-corner speech I discovered the literature of socialism. Almost overnight my interest in theology faded away. I came down suddenly from heaven to earth, and instead of asking any longer, "Is there a God?" I began to rack my brains over the question, "Is there any way out of poverty?" I fed with great appetite on the various Utopias—More's, Campanella's, Bacon's, Harrington's, Bellamy's, and the first of Mr. Wells's succession. My loss of the theological heaven left me, like my generation, hungry for an earthly paradise.

Then I grappled manfully with the three volumes of Marx's *Capital*. I finished the first volume in ten years. I became almost a reactionary through disgust with the formlessness and obscurity of this nineteenth-century Bible. I tried Spargo's *Life of Marx* to offset my dislike for the man's style, and to sharpen my understanding of his ideas; but when I found that he had let his children starve in order to write a book which had been a public nuisance for fifty years, I denounced him as a heartless doctrinaire. I turned with relief to the romantic career of Ferdinand Lassalle, the bright and sociable pages of Wells, and the insolent prefaces of Bernard Shaw.

I was near the voting age now, and began to take a tremendous interest in politics. Of course I did not mention socialism to my family; my father was an hereditary Republican, who insisted that the Democrats had always brought hard times; and I knew that in his mind socialism was not a political theory but a form of irreligion. My confidant in this field, as in so many others, was Dave Howatt. He was working at that time in New York; and he brought me exciting tales of the campaign which Mr. Hearst was making for the mayoralty. I began to read Brisbane's editorials, and concluded that Utopia would be just around the corner if "we" could only elect the famous editor. Dave and I went to New York several evenings a week in the last month of the contest; we waited for hours in crowded halls to see and hear the candidate himself; and we applauded every sentence that fell from his lips. On election-night, when the returns were thrown upon a screen at Times Square, and our hero's mounting votes promised to give us victory, I shouted myself so hoarse that for a week I could not speak. I have long since made up for that week.

This speechlessness was a boon to me as well as to others, for it convinced my mother that I was really playing politics in New York, and not doing something still worse. She had observed, with the sensitiveness of love, a falling-off in my piety and devotion, and had mourned my sudden absorption in such alien and unintelligible affairs as a campaign for the mayoralty of a villainous city in another state. She begged me not to come home so late, and touched my conscience by waiting up for me every night till twelve and one, which were late hours in those days. On the night before the election I was more delayed than usual. I found my mother asleep in her chair; and as I looked at her pale face I understood for a passing moment that there may be something more important than politics. I woke her and asked why she had waited up for me. She replied strangely:

"I can't tell you."

I was a bit startled; why should there be so much mystery about my platonic affection for Mr. Hearst? I insisted on the reason.

"John," she said, hesitantly, "where do you go these nights?"

"Why, to the Hearst meetings, of course," I answered.

"Ah, yes, you tell me that, but——"

80

She stopped, and began to cry quietly. I bent over her and begged her to tell me just what it was that worried her. At last she found words.

"Tell me, John, you wouldn't go to——?"

Poor little mother! What a mess of worry I had given her! I put my arm around her, and told her that the thing had never entered my head. She dried her eyes and let me lead her up to her room. In the darkness near her door she caught my hand.

"You promise me, John," she whispered.

I promised.

A few months later love sang me its second song.

It was a great mistake of my parents to let me join the choir. If I remember rightly, I served as acolyte at early Mass on Sundays, and then returned to sing at the late Mass. That was well enough, and my singing was not much worse than that of the others. But it escaped the notice of my family that I was turning twenty-one, and that the organist was a pretty girl. Her name was Esther, and her hair was liquid gold. She was a wild Irish rose, coy and sprightly, and as ready for romance as I.

If we had not had so many rehearsals there might have been less mischief. The rehearsals were held in the homes now of one, now of another, member of the choir. At one of these I had an experience which produced some posthumous illumination. All the work had been done except the preparation of a duet between myself and Clare,—a woman considerably older than myself, and unwillingly intact. Her family were out for the evening, and when the rest of the choir had gone, we were left alone. For a time we practised our duet. Then, to my surprise, Clare rose, and went up stairs. Half way up she turned and beamed upon me.

"Want to come up with me, Jack?"

I had no suspicion of her meaning; obviously my mother's solicitude had exaggerated the precocity of my development. I answered with laudable simplicity:

"No; I'll stay here."

Very soon she came back, a little flushed and angry. She made no objections to my going home; I could be of no further use to her. Not till I lay in bed, safe from her charms, did I understand what she had meant. A year later a young man who had proved more responsive was compelled by law to marry her. When I saw him passing to his punishment I whispered to myself:

"There, but for my innocence, go I."

It was shortly after this that we met for rehearsal in Esther's house. I took in observantly the superiority of her home to ours, the grandeur of their piano, the depth of their upholstery, and the removability of their rugs; even their cat looked more prosperous than the lazy old Maltese who used to lie on her back on my reading board and shamelessly invite me to tickle her nipples. I noticed the business-like ability of the father, and the modest culture of the mother. I also noticed Esther.

Irene had been too immature to arouse me to passion with her physical charms. But this was a different story. Some inexplicable increase of hydraulic
pressure was driving me to a blind erotic hunger. As
I stood beside Esther and sang to her playing, I
had all I could do to refrain from biting her rosy
flesh; and perhaps I was saved from this atavism by
the fact that I could not make up my mind whether
her neck or her arms were the more desirable. The
Reader will perceive, from this indecision, that I was
already something of a philosopher.

Yet I would not let this confession of the rising
tide of sex within me give the impression that my love
for Esther was merely physical. When I looked into
her eyes, or heard her voice, or watched her simplest
actions, I fell into a trance of admiration. Even in
her case the last lust never came to me; and I was
fairly content to talk with her or hold her hand. But
when she let another candidate hold that hand I
smiled bravely to hide a heart full of jealousy and
rage. I was such a fool one evening as to take to her
home two of my handsomest college chums, Kevin
Lynch and Tom Meaney; Kevin as clean and finely
built a youth as ever Greek sculptors knew, and Tom
as clever and as charming as Mephistopheles. If memory kept all details, and readers had a fund of patience like Fortunatus' purse, I could tell a Dan-
tesque tale of hellish sufferings that evening, as we
three lads vied with one another for Esther's smiles,
and she divided them among us with that subtle wis-

dom which nature gives prenatally to women. But
let me inform Kevin and Tom, wherever they are,
that as I bade Esther good-night she whispered into
my ear (I hope not also into theirs) these deliriously
delicious words:

"Mother says I may keep steady company now if
I like."

What an innocent and simple thing to say!—or
am I innocent to suppose it so?—and yet what rainbows of happiness it flung around me! I hardly slept,
those nights; and instead of racing through books
in my room when I was home from school, I sat on the
porch looking for hours into the unresponsive air.
Wherever I turned I saw Esther's face, her glorious
hair, her full lips, her bright blue eyes, her radiant
smile, the alluring softness of her throat,—and more
with which the Reader need have no concern. Already
I pictured her as my wife. I wondered how, after my
coming graduation, I could find work that would
support us in a condition consonant with my dignity
as a Bachelor of Arts. I covered many sheets with
calculations of the cost of rent, furniture, chinaware,
food, clothing, and the other necessary evils of married life.

What could a college graduate do anyway? There
were so many things that an ordinary man could do;
but the more educated one became, the fewer the fields
that were open to him. I could not study medicine or
law; for these required fond parents making post-
graduate sacrifices, and I might rather expect exile

than further aid when the truth came out. It would be a fine thing, I thought, if I could earn a living by writing; but I had already tried that and failed. Had I not written "A History of English Literature," and a novel, and some odds and ends of poetry?—and were they not lying now in the attic, tagged with rejection slips and enjoyed only by mice? What could I do?"

I wrote bravely to Arthur Brisbane, and asked whether he could give me work on the New York *Evening Journal.* He answered that there were eight hundred applications ahead of mine, but that if I really wanted a place I could have it. Nevertheless, I should be warned against the profession of journalism, for (he wrote) "reporting deforms more men than it forms." I accepted the offer and ignored the advice. I suspected that it was true; but how could I get Esther if I had no job?

What had happened, meanwhile, to my ecclesiastical vocation? It had dissolved in the light of knowledge and the heat of love. Though I kept my promise to Father Morley and prayed like a tempted Anthony I found the figure of Esther getting mixed up with the Virgin, and the economics of marriage entangled with my rosaries. I tried as long as I could to postpone the day when I should have to break the news to mother and father that I could not enter the priesthood, being drawn now towards a more normal and popular vocation. The happiness of my new love was mingled with the torture of the impending crash.

I quite forget how at last I made my mother understand that I had fallen from the pedestal upon which she had placed me. The ignoble truth was that she discovered the fact for herself before I could say a word. I remember that on returning from school one day I found her sitting quietly idle,—an unprecedented attitude for her at any time.

"Tired, ma?" I asked.

"No; only here"; and she laid her hand on her breast. "Are you going to rehearsal to-night?"

"Yes."

"Are you going to take Esther home?"

"If she would like me to."

"You are in love with her."

It was no question, but a statement, a resigned acceptance of fact; my mother had come to understand my humanity. I said nothing; and she went on.

"You don't think any more of becoming a priest and serving God. You forget all that we have sacrificed to let you go to college. Now that you have your education you don't care for the mother and father and the Holy Church that brought you up and kept you pure and sent you to college all these years when your brothers were working."

It was so nearly true that I could make no answer.

"You are young," said my mother, "and you don't know what you're doing. You love her now, but it won't last. You are not old enough to understand how hard marriage is. Oh, my dear John, you are only a boy, and you want to throw yourself away so soon."

"I don't want to do anything in a hurry, ma," I said. "I promise you I won't."

"Do you love me enough to stay away from her for a month, just to see if she means so much to you as you think?"

"But, mother, I'm so happy when I am near her. I don't want anything more than that, just to see her every now and then."

She did not ask again. We went about our separate tasks in equal misery; I torn with the old dilemma of two loves, she sad with the eternal tragedy of a mother who realizes that her son has found someone dearer to him than herself. How unreasonable it is (if we set aside the racial needs that underlie the categorical imperative of love) that a man should leave the mother and the home that have cherished him for twenty years, and fly to some strange face whose loveliness lies not in remembered kindness but in an imagination that burns with the hunger of the flesh! How absurd it is that every woman, to fulfil herself, must hate an older woman, and tear away from her the son whom she has made with her sufferings and her cares!

My conscience was with my mother, but all the rest of me yearned for the sight of Esther's smile. I spent a hot hour writing a letter of farewell to her; I wept over every line of it, and when I signed my name and sealed the envelope I was sobbing so loudly that my mother might have heard me downstairs. I did not know that she had left the house and was taking his-

tory into her own hands. I opened the envelope, re-
read the letter, and saw that it was good; I improved
some phrases, corrected the punctuation, and sealed
the envelope again with the tearful conviction that I
had written a masterpiece. Then I put the letter in
my pocket and went out and did not mail it.

By the time evening came I had convinced myself,
with all the arts of logic at the command of a Jesuit
product, that my mother had asked too great a sacrifice of me, and that my feeling for Esther was of so
pure a character that there could be no harm in my
seeing her occasionally. I dressed carefully, walked
downstairs with my heart in my mouth, and went to
the rehearsal.

I had done better to stay home. All through the
evening Esther looked away, and said no word to me.
I fretted over the explanation of these contemporary
storms in regions presumably so unconnected as my
mother's heart and Esther's. Her own mother was as
cold to me as a spinster, and as polite as an enemy. I
sang as poorly as possible, seeing question-marks instead of notes. When the rehearsal was over I asked
Esther's mother if I might have the usual honor of
taking her and Esther home. She cut my heart in two
with her reply:

"No, we'd rather not."

I went off in a stupor, forgetting to say good-bye
to the other members of the choir. I walked down the
street, sat on a park bench, and looked at the earth.
I was too vain to think that Esther no longer cared

for me; something else had gone wrong. I vowed to kill the person who had stepped between us.

That night I, age twenty-one years and seven months, cried myself to sleep. The next day was Saturday, and I was free from school. As soon as I had eaten breakfast, silently before a silent mother, I took my hat and walked up the hill to Esther's home. A great dog came growling at me. I patted his head respectfully and propitiated him into letting me go up the porch and ring the bell. Esther's mother came to the door, but did not admit me.

"Your mother," she said, angrily, "was here yesterday and asked me not to let you see Esther for a while. I think it might be a good thing too."

There was nothing more. I thanked her, and came away crushed with defeat and yet stiff with rage. I was not through with rejections. That afternoon fate sent Esther along a street where I was prowling and moaning. I almost ran to her.

"Esther," I asked, "are you willing that we should not see each other again?"

She threw her golden head back proudly.

"People think I am taking you away from the priesthood. I won't have them say that of me. Please do not speak to me any more."

This time I was quite broken; even the "abominable pride" which Father Morley had denounced crumbled in me like a shattered spine. I went away and wandered in deserted fields, calling passionately upon God to help me, and quite forgetting that I no longer believed in his existence. I might have gone to pieces had it not been for my brother Ben. I shall never forget how Ben found me walking aimlessly about, and listened to my rage and my love, and comforted me with peanuts, and took me home. What a brother he was to me that day! May I be near to comfort him, if his world should ever fall about him as mine fell about me then!

CHAPTER VIII

I COMMIT SUICIDE

FATHER McLOUGHLIN, teacher of our diminutive graduating class at St. Paul's, took this highly inopportune season to suggest that I should become a Jesuit. He invited me into the little room where he studied and slept,—a room just big enough to hold his tiny cot, his rude reading-table, and his books. I was impressed—though not to the point of imitation—by this simplicity of life, and this ascetic self-denial, in one of the finest scholars and gentlemen I had ever met. He was kinder to me than such a trouble-maker as I was had any right to expect.

"John," he said, "I can tell from your questions in class that you are passing through a dangerous condition. I have seen other cases like yours, and unless the trouble is caught early it leads to a general disintegration of mind and character. If you would only humble yourself to accept a little guidance you might become one of the most favored sons of the Church. Let us send you to the Jesuit Novitiate at Woodstock; you will have a quiet and regular life there; and you need not make up your mind for several years whether you wish to join our Order or not. If you do join it we will send you to Oxford and give you every chance to become a great scholar. What do you say?"

The idea made not the slightest appeal to me. I should have been glad to study at Oxford; but even Oxford was not worth such a price. And what would Oxford be without Esther? And without faith? I was surprised and flattered to see how well I had concealed from my teacher the extent to which scepticism had entered my soul. I told him that I was not such stuff as Jesuits are made of. He sighed, and let me go.

A week or so after that I betrayed something of the change that had taken place in me. Some famous English priest had come to Jersey City to lecture on socialism, and the boys in the higher grades at St. Paul's were invited to attend, on the theory that they needed a general vaccination against this political disease. The lecturer was eloquent, and carried his audience with him easily. He took up, one by one, the socialist leaders from Marx to Bebel, and showed convincingly that some of them were agnostics, and that many of them were Jews. He concluded, amidst great applause, that socialism was impracticable.

It seemed to me shameful that a serious economic theory, having the highly laudable end of abolishing injustice and poverty and establishing the brotherhood of man, should be done away with so easily. I wrote a letter to the Jersey City *Evening Journal* in which I suggested that the religious beliefs of socialist leaders had as much to do with the practicability of socialism as the religious beliefs of Republican and Democratic leaders had to do with the correctness of their views on tariff or free trade. I protested against the unfairness of such sophistry, and urged that the next time the reverend lecturer spoke against socialism he should invite some socialist to answer him. Secretly I pictured myself as receiving such an invitation.

The letter was printed, and I thought it read very well. The morning after its publication Father Collins, Vice-President of the college, sent for me. He showed me my first public effusion.

"Did you write this letter?" he asked.

"Yes," I answered.

"Very well. Unless you write a letter of retraction and apology, you can never graduate from this college."

I paid the strictest attention. Graduation was only three weeks away. I had written a magnificent commencement address; I could not bear the thought that it might never be delivered. I did not care much about the degree; but the disgrace? And the blow to parents who had already borne so many disappointments from me?

"Will you give me a day or two to think it over?" I asked.

"You may have till Friday."

I went off brooding on the insolence of office and the spurns that patient merit of the unworthy takes.

When Friday came I adopted the favorite policy of wise men—I did nothing. On Monday I was summoned again to Father Collins' office.

"Well, sir," he asked, "have you made up your mind?"

Pride, rather than honesty, dictated the answer.

"I think that what I said in that letter is perfectly true, and I don't see how I can be such a liar as to take it back."

"Very well. That will do." And he showed me the door.

The sympathetic reader, who may recall how momentous his graduation days were to him, will understand how I fretted in the days that followed. I expected dismissal from college any day; and my brain burned when I pictured the consequences at home. I thought I might get some word of consolation from Esther, if only I could speak to her and explain things in general and particular; I had not clarity of mind enough to reflect that the girl had probably never heard of socialism, and would have no sympathy with any defiance to a priest. One day I saw her coming down the main thoroughfare of our little town, and I marched up to her with brave face and fearful heart. In the sight of several friends, she turned squarely about and walked away from me. I was bewildered rather than enraged; this was the culminating misfortune of a miserable month, a final blow that dulled me almost to insensitivity. I made up my mind, without deliberation, and without enthusiasm, to leave home and town and college and go to the virgin West.

The next morning I started out with five cents, the usual nickel given me for my daily lunch. I took the train to Jersey City, and then the ferry to New York. I had pleasant thoughts, for a moment, of how everybody would miss me, and what a failure the commencement exercises would be without my speech. I did not stop to think how my mother and father would feel, or whether my liberty was worth the sorrow my disappearance might cause them. I resolved to write to them that afternoon, and to assure them that as soon as I had become rich I would return to them and make them happy. And then black doubts came to me, whether so temperamental a lad could ever succeed, anywhere?

I stood at the stern of the ferry to avoid the crowd, which always moved towards the front. I leaned over the side, and watched the waves swirling up around the boat. Suddenly the thought came,—Why not drop over the railing and be done with it? Everything would be simplified, every problem would be solved. I do not remember thinking then of another world, or even for a moment fearing hell; it is remarkable how thoroughly the belief in hell or heaven had dropped out of my life. What stopped me, of course, was the fear of pain: the horror of choking, and swelling with water, and feeling the hammer-strokes of an exhausted heart and a snapping consciousness.

"O God!" I moaned, turning away; "I can't do it."

And so I reached New York, and wandered aimlessly about, debating what I should do with my nickel. Instead of buying a morsel of food, I spent it on the Elevated, and rode up Ninth Avenue to 72nd Street. There, for no reason that I can recall, I left the train, and went west to Riverside Drive. I walked along the Drive to the neighborhood of 137th Street.

At two o'clock I was sitting alone on a bench in the Park. I had not eaten, but I was not interested enough in life to recognize that I was hungry. I stared darkly in front of me, so demoralized that I believe I had even abandoned the effort to think out what I should do next. A well-dressed, white-haired gentleman sat down at the other end of my bench, and occasionally looked at me with evident concern. At last he spoke to me.

"Anything wrong, my lad?"

I resented his intrusion, and answered, briefly,—

"Nothing." Then suddenly I blurted out: "I've run away."

"I knew it was something like that," he said, smiling. "Every spunky boy does it some time or other, you know. I did it myself."

"Did you?" I asked. "Where did you go?"

"Oh, I came all the way across the ocean. I lived in England, you know. I had a quarrel with my family, and left them in a huff, and came to New York. When I got here I worked like the devil, saved up everything I didn't wear or eat, and then took

96

ship back home. I found that my mother was dead."

He stopped, and looked far away across the river. I looked too.

Suddenly I stood up. "I think I'll go home," I said. He held out his hand.

"I'm awfully glad. Can I help you?"

"No, thank you."

Foolish answer! Penniless and lunchless, I had a hard time getting home. I walked down to the 23rd Street Ferry, and there my monthly ticket won me admission to the boat that connected, at the Erie Station, with the train for Arlington. The little town did not seem half as stupid a place as it had appeared to me the afternoon before. And the house which my family had bought looked very pretty and inviting, as if everybody that lived there must be fortunate and happy. I arrived just in time for supper; and though that was late for me, no questions were asked and no lies were told. But I think my mother wondered a bit at my unusual appetite.

CHAPTER IX

ON THE NEW YORK *JOURNAL*

STRANGE to say, I never heard more of the proposal to refuse me my diploma. When I saw that the commencement programs had been printed, with my name entered as one of the speakers, and observed the solicitude with which Father McLoughlin trained Kevin and myself for the ceremony, I concluded that Father Collins had relented. The great occasion came, I received my diploma, made my speech, and the world went on as if nothing had happened. I was a bachelor of many arts, and master of none.

A week later I presented myself to Arthur Brisbane. He had a little office partitioned away from the noise and confusion of the editorial rooms of the New York *Evening Journal* in William Street, near Park Row. He sat before a typewriter; apparently, he composed so rapidly that only a machine could keep up with him. He was a tall, strongly-built man, with a large head already for the most part bald. He looked less like a writer than a successful business man; and one would never have supposed that this highest-paid editor in the world was as well-read as any professor in the land. His salary had not quite spoiled him; he still cracked his editorial whip, when he liked, at the legs of the rich, and was far ahead of the country in his political opinions. It was not for nothing that he had been the son of a great socialist.

He gave me hardly a minute.

"So you want a job as a reporter? Remember that I warned you against it. If you insist, hand this note to Mr. Hastings."

He clicked off a message on his machine, and passed it over to me. As I stepped out I could hear the typewriter rattling with the next day's editorial. He never spoke to me again; he saw me sometimes, but he was engrossed in large affairs. I had been only a punctuation point in his hurried life.

I was sorely disillusioned when I saw how a newspaper was made. The presses that printed the news were far more romantic than the men who wrote it. In a corner of a large, poorly-ventilated room sat the city editor, with four or five telephones before him; all day long he talked into those telephones, quietly, easily, and without excitement, as if he were addressing some friend at his side; and yet he was speaking to a hundred different parts of the city, and beyond, to a hundred different men, about a hundred different things; it was through him that the chaos of daily fact became a newspaper. The remainder of the room was occupied by tables and chairs and human beings; the tables were almost covered with typewriters or with the morning newspapers from which so much of the evening news was pilfered. The floor was filthy with scraps of paper, dirt, cigar-stubs, cigarette-ends, and poorly-aimed tobacco juice. Imagine the provocation to good English and clear thinking in a room where fifty typewriters filled the air with their racket, and a hundred telephones were buzzing, and a hundred men and women were talking. Here a base-ball reporter was writing some story over the name of a famous player; here a hard-faced young man was writing the "Beatrice Fairfax" column; here the sporting editor was interviewing some lumbering bashful pugilist. The walls were lined with telephone-booths; in these the "re-writers" received the findings of reporters sent out for news; some typewrote their articles as they listened, others took notes and then came back to their machines. Five minutes after the news had come in, it was on the city-editor's desk in a form ready for the compositor. Some of it the editor threw into the waste-basket; some of it he curtailed to fit into the interstices of advertisements. What remained was rushed down to a lower floor, where great linotype machines transformed molten lead into news. Then the forms were fitted into the presses, the thousand wheels moved, the mighty iron arms rose and fell, and the white sheets came out blackened with crime and alive with sport. Finally, out of a wall on the ground floor, bundles of news-papers were shot into red-and-white wagons; the wagons rattled to every quarter of the city, and the insatiable metropolitan appetite for news was quenched for an hour.

Here was the dizziest business I had ever seen. And all in a minute I was plunged into this life and left to drown or swim. The city-editor glanced at Brisbane's note, eyed me rapidly, and said:

"Go into Booth 10 and take a story from Mc-Manus. Write about sixteen lines."

I fumbled around for paper and pencil, and rushed to Booth 10. I hated telephones, and here I should have to live with them.

"Hello!" I shouted.

"Hey, you," came some advice from the next booth; "don't talk so damned loud."

"Hello," I heard a voice over the wire. "Who's this?"

"A new man," I answered.

"O Hell! Why didn't the boss give me Smithy? Well, kid, take this. Girl twelve years old found naked in coal-bin; bloody, dirty, raped; 2222 Second Avenue. The body's still in the cellar, waiting for Coroner Warburger. Six detectives are looking for a suspected Italian coal-dealer. Girl's name is Maria Carlatti—C A R L A T T I. Got it? Good-bye."

I rushed to a typewriter, and achieved the apparent miracle of writing sixteen lines of correct English in the center of Bedlam. I handed it to Holloway. He read it as I would have read a line, and then turned to me.

"Always put the main item in the first line," he said. "Introductions and explanations later. Take a newspaper and study how it's done. Now go up to

2222 Second Avenue and report to McManus and do whatever he tells you. Call me up if you find out anything worth printing. Call me up again at four and I'll tell you when you can go home. Do you know how to get up there?"

"I'll find it," I said.

"Take the Second Avenue 'L,' at the Bridge."

I took my hat and hurried off. I was happy to be out of that stuffy turmoil; and enjoyed the isolation of anonymity in the long open-air ride uptown. I sat up straight and breathed deeply in the way which I had learned from the magazines of Mr. Bernarr Macfadden. Suddenly my straw hat, which I had just bought to impress the New York *Journal,* flew off my head, and sailed down into the street. I meditated with painful rapidity, as the train approached the next stop, whether I should get off and go back for my hat, or ride on heroically to my assignment. In the one case I might regain a precious hat; in the other case Mr. Hubbard might write a "Message to Garcia" about me. I decided that since the girl was dead, she would not mind waiting a few minutes. I recovered the remains of my hat.

I found it difficult to get access to the home of the tragedy, for I had neither the card nor the face of a reporter. But I had enough of boyhood left in me to elude the police who guarded the entrance against the curious crowd. Refused admission, I went into the house next door, climbed to the roof, and descended almost like Santa Claus into the dingy

102

tenement where the Carlattis lived. I learned that the dead girl was still in the cellar. Sped on by sex curiosity I leapt down the stairs; and in a moment I was behind the Coroner himself, gazing upon the corpse.

I shall not describe it; I am not concerned to show that rapes are committed in New York, and that the raped bodies of young girls are ghastly and pitiful things to look at. The evening papers were featuring rape that summer; not because there were more of such cases than before, but because some enterprising editor had seen in these cases a chance for extra circulation, and the others had had to take it up. As my slumming progressed I became more disgusted by the lubricity of certain editors than by the rapes themselves; nevertheless the sight of that torn and blackened and bloody body was a heavy item in my education. The difference between book-learning and the sharp tuition of life itself gaped suddenly before me; with all my literature and science and philosophy I felt myself an innocent and helpless novice in the presence of these brutal realities. To pass in one week from scholastic disputations to murder and rape was a severe strain upon a mind already racked with religious doubt, family discord, and the pangs of despised love.

The body was taken upstairs, and we followed the Coroner into the little crowded room where he was to examine the relatives of the child. Mr. Warburger had no respect for my innocence; he asked the mother and the father a number of insistent questions which

103

finally drew from them the confession that for a long
time they had not lived as man and wife. Gradually it
dawned upon me that the Coroner suspected the father of having raped and killed his own daughter.
I was horrified; but I listened with an almost patho-
logical intentness to every question and every answer.

I did not eat much that night, and I did not dare
tell my parents what sort of life it was that a reporter
led. I hardly slept, and faced with revulsion the prob-
ability that for a long time I should be dealing with
matters of this kind. And it was so. All week I had to
report to McManus on the Carlatti case; and I spent
a day in the almost breathless task of accompanying
a detective through the bar-rooms and back-rooms of
the vilest saloons in the effort to locate a suspected
man. On the following Monday I was assigned to another rape case, with instructions to get an interview from the mother. I found this task unexpectedly
easy. The mother was a widow; and in the midst of
her description of her daughter's troubles, she offered, in the plainest of broken English, to teach me
the art of love. I fled from her in ungallant haste,
while she stood in the doorway and cursed me as less
than a man.

There was another case where a man had raped
and killed his own daughter. I was sent up to the
Bronx apartment house where the murderer had
lived; and as I went I rehearsed the instructions
which I had received from the city editor:

"We want a picture of the girl. Remember that

any reporter can get the news, but it takes a *Journal* man to get the picture."

I found myself, an hour later, at the house I wanted. I went to the janitress, and offered her some money for permission to get into the room which the girl had occupied. She refused; the police had evidently spoken to her a language more international than that of gold,—the language of fear. A few minutes later I made my way into the building, climbed to the roof, and as my luck would have it found a sky-light over the apartment which I sought. I forget how I opened it; I remember only that I jumped down and found myself master of all that I surveyed. How a mere intellectual could have mustered up such audacity I can now hardly understand; but there I was. I went through all three rooms and gathered up every female photograph I could find. I unlatched the door from within, let myself out quietly, and escaped with my spoils.

Instead of worrying about being jailed for illegal entry, I thought only of my achievement in securing the pictures; I swelled with that pride of action which book-worms know when for a moment they have lived. Surely the editor would lift his eyebrows, praise me, and raise my salary. But when he learned how I had taken the pictures he shook his head.

"We can't use them," he said.

"Why not?" I asked, angrily.

"Because if the police found us out we'd be subject to a fine, and you'd be liable to imprisonment. We have to keep in the good graces of the police department, or else they'll shut us out from all sorts of news that we must have."

That was the sum total of my Nick Carter afternoon.

My last case was a murder in 42nd Street. A storekeeper had made advances to a sales-girl, she had rejected them, and he had shot her. When I worked my way to the inside of the crowd the dead woman still lay where she had fallen. A trickle of blood wandered from her breast along the cracks in the floor. She was a beautiful girl, with a fine profile and a great wealth of blond hair; only that morning, no doubt, she had thought of a hundred niceties of toilette, and of the lover to whom she would be true, and of the home she hoped to have. It was all gone now; a little slip in the routine of life had destroyed her, and left her helpless there, like a worm crushed by some hurrying foot in the rain.

"Have they found the murderer?" I asked a policeman.

"They're chasing him. I hear they've got him cornered in Spalding's store, down the street."

I ran out and looked for Spalding's. I made out the place at once by the crowd that besieged the doors. Within, four policemen were on guard, with drawn revolvers.

"Where is he?" I asked.

"He ran upstairs," answered one of the officers.

"Why don't we chase him?" This was an inverted

editorial "we," not intended to include the first person.

"Go ahead," was the reply. "Who's stopping you?"

I regretted the "we," and having spoken, I began to think. Evidently in interesting events there were other aspects than that of news. These policemen were thinking not of the story, but of their lives; they preferred to be outside the headlines reading them, rather than in the headlines dead. The murderer, presumably with several shots left in his revolver, was, it seemed, standing at the top of the stairs; he would make an easy target of anybody pursuing him, while he himself could remain almost unseen.

We stood there, excited and ridiculous, for half an hour. Meanwhile the prey had slipped the net; he had gone through a window and down a fire escape into an alley. The policemen detailed to guard the rear of the building arrived just in time to see him pass into Forty-third Street. They pursued him bravely, though he turned upon them and shot one dead. A driver jumped down from his truck with that public forgetfulness of danger which so often conquers the "first law of nature," and sank his great hook in the murderer's brain; but at the same moment the hunted man sent his last bullet into the driver's body, and captive and captor fell dead together. Ten minutes later the news was brought to us as we crouched anxiously beneath the stairway in Spalding's store. Three men and a girl dead; here was story enough for a reporter; and tragedy for half a dozen homes.

I was unfit for journalism partly because I had not the boldness which pierces the privacy of human hearts and ferrets out their secrets, and partly because behind every column of news I saw the suffering of men and women. Brisbane was right: these experiences were deforming me, making me hard and cynical; my idealism was passing into a "realism" just as untrue to life as my dreams had been, because the nose for news smells out the bad and ignores the good; virtue has always been less interesting than vice. Within a month of my interview with Brisbane I felt that I had enough of this work; to continue it would turn me into either a lunatic or a criminal.

It was Father Morley who rescued me. When I supposed that he had driven me out of his thoughts, when I had given him every reason for believing me irretrievably a worldling and an atheist, he still kept faith in me, and held me guiltless of my sins of doubt and love. He did not know how loathsome my work as a reporter had become to me; but almost as if he had known, he held out his hand to save me. Fool that I was for not keeping his letters!—they were all so simple and perfect in expression, and so simple and perfect in feeling; they would have given substance and fragrance to these bits of the past that I would snatch from a fading memory.

Would I come and teach in South Hall? The remuneration would be small, but the work might prove

congenial, and be a stepping-stone to higher places
later on. I could have laughed aloud with joy as I
read; never had I had so much reason for believing in
Providence, even in a Providence prejudiced in my
favor. I wrote a grateful acceptance; and I hastened
to tell my father and mother that though I could not
be the priest they had wished to make of me, at least
I was to be a teacher in a Catholic college, under the
man whom, of all the priests we had met, we admired
and loved the most.

I blush to relate that I was dishonest with the
Journal after that. Instead of working conscien-
tiously on every assignment, I occasionally imitated
the trick of older reporters, who went to a show, or
dozed off in the lobby of a minor hotel, and then
called up and sent in, from their imaginations, a
much better story than the facts themselves would
have made. And like them I stole off an hour or two
every day before my time. I felt that I had only a
week or two left with the *Journal*, and that these de-
linquencies were peccadilloes. But I am ashamed now
when I look back upon that fortnight; and I wish
the Reader to set me down as a man capable of a sentimental idealism, but capable also of lies and greed.

I was punished by what was in effect a dismissal.
One morning towards the end of August the city editor called me to his desk.

"Look here," he said, "are you sure you like this
sort of work?"

"Fairly well," I answered. I was not due at South

Hall till the middle of September; I could not afford to be idle for three weeks. But I failed to deceive the editor.

"I don't think you do," he said. "You're not the man for newspaper work. You're too soft and literary. I'll keep you on for a while if you wish, as a courtesy to Mr. Brisbane; but I know you'll be more comfortable elsewhere. Suppose you take two weeks off with pay, and try to find something more congenial. Then come and tell me what luck you've had."

I thought this a very happy solution, and agreed to it with what must have seemed a suspicious readiness. It meant that I was to have several weeks' rest before taking up my tasks at South Hall. I went out into City Hall Park as happy as a child let out of school. For the first time in a long while, I spent more than a nickel on my lunch. I took an early train home, and from the upper deck of the ferry I waved a glad good-bye to rape, murder, theft, divorce, prizefights, and Beatrice Fairfax. I walked the streets stiff with the dignity of a professor.

CHAPTER X

I CONVERT THE CHURCH TO SOCIALISM

SOUTH HALL was a paradise. You approached it by wide gravel walks that ran apart and then came together before the entrance of the administration building. Every inch of the walks was shaded by generously spreading trees. To the right lay great fields of corn and wheat, which fed the college tables; at the left was a spacious playground where happy lads were tossing baseballs, basketballs, and handballs, and the other paraphernalia of youth. The buildings were of gray stone that had taken on the mellow shades of age; the chapel particularly was picturesque with its fine rose-window and its graceful lines. Behind the administration building were dormitories, class-rooms, recreation rooms, and the sleeping quarters of the teaching staff.

I spent a day fixing up my room, and finding shelves for my accumulating books. I met my fellow-teachers, and found them a rather uninspiring lot. Some of them were encyclopedically ignorant; none of them had any of my passion for literature or philosophy; and they looked upon me, I am sure, as an innocent lad who had no business on this rough and

111

material globe. Yet these same men, unlettered as they appeared to me, were capable teachers, skilled disciplinarians; and discipline was a subtle art in a school where the students, on whose tuition fees the institution depended, could seldom be severely punished, and could never be dismissed.

Some of the teachers stand out individually in my memory: Cummings, who dressed like a millionaire on fifty dollars a month; Zaccarelli, the fiery Italian, who swore like a soldier despite my dubbing him "Cardinal," and who wished to kill us for laughing at his *staccato* English; and timid old Daly, who indulged in alcoholic amnesia once a week, and spent the other days worrying whether Father Morley had heard about it. I liked Zaccarelli best, because I relish pride and passion in a man; but the only one with whom I could have any stimulating mental intercourse was Daly.

We used to go out together for long constitutionals; and inevitably I let slip some hints of heresy. I remember how once we traveled out to Midland Beach and paced the boardwalk while we exchanged philosophies.

"You frighten me with your doubts," he said. "Aren't you afraid of Hell?"

"Would you," I asked, "damn anybody to everlasting punishment for even the worst of crimes?"

"No, I'll be damned if I would." Daly sometimes covered the pale timidity of his thought with a scarlet vigor of expression.

112

"Well, why should you think God less decent than yourself?"

He did not answer; instead, like Socrates, he asked another question.

"So you don't believe in Hell?"

"No," I replied, magnificently. "It would be an insult to God."

Daly was impressed.

"Hum," he said, "I never thought of that before. Do you know that ever since I was a child I have suffered from visions of hell and its tortures? To this day that awful fear grips me." He hesitated. "Listen: I have a terrible craving for whiskey. If I go a week without it I feel that I am dying of thirst. Every cell in my body cries out for it. When I go to confession I promise not to drink again; but I always break the promise. I can't get rid of the idea that some day I shall die in drunkenness and go to Hell."

I laughed at him.

"First of all," I said, with the confidence of youth, "there's no hell to go to. Secondly, drunkenness isn't a sin, it's a mistake. Sin is injury to others."

"Oh, it's a pleasure to hear you say that," Daly sighed. "If you can rid me of the fear of Hell I'll be a happy and a grateful man."

In my simplicity I thought that a life-time's belief could be eradicated by a minute's argument. I was astounded to find that on the following day Daly shunned me. I followed him to his room, opened his door, and asked what was the trouble. He almost pushed me out.

"Look here," he said, excitably, "you're an infidel, and you're doomed to everlasting Hell. For my own soul's sake I don't want to have anything to do with you any more. And I think that Father Morley has a right to know what kind of a man you are."

"You're an old fool," I retorted. Then he shut the door in my face.

So I was in hot water again. Every day I expected to be summoned to the President's office for a severe reprimand, at the very least; and every day that passed without this summons strengthened my resolution to remember, hereafter, that I was an instructor in Latin, Greek, and French, but not in theology. I did my work as well as I could, and felt happy when the President asked me to take, in addition to my contracted tasks, a class in geometry.

Instead of scolding me, Father Morley gave me unstinted friendship. After nine o'clock in the evening, when all the teaching staff were in bed, he would often come to my room and invite me for a walk. They were substantial walks—sometimes to the center of Newark and back. The sturdy little President was a redoubtable pedestrian, with wind enough for absorbing speech as he strode along. On these trips he became my private tutor, and gave me his philosophy of this world and the next. What he saw in the Catholic Church was not a body of doctrine, much less of scientific knowledge, but an organization —the greatest that the world had ever seen—for the moral improvement of mankind. He recounted in vivid episodes the struggle of the Church with the poverty and disorder of Rome in the age after the Antonines, with the moral and ethnical degeneration of the Greeks, with the ignorance of the Huns, with the militarism of feudal chieftains and the greed of medieval emperors. He saw the Protestant Reformation as the beginning of an individualist disintegration; these petty princes, jealous of the Peter's Pence that financed the Renaissance in Rome, these sensual monks restive under discipline, had broken down such international order and peace as the world had never known before or since, and would never know again until some great moral force, rooted firmly in ancestral faith, should stand above the warring states and tame them into harmony.

"Modern civilization?" He questioned both the adjective and the noun. Civilization, that began with the Anabaptist riots and ended with a Europe armed for suicide? "Modern" thought?—which began with individual judgment in religion, passed to individualism in politics, and was ending in an orgy of devil-may-care immorality, childless marriages, and capitalistic greed? "Modern" science?—which changed its dogmas in every century, made pontiffs of its guessers, and exacted from a credulous people belief in immaterial electrons that made matter, and material atoms that made mind, and a mechanical clock-running-down universe in which there would never be anything new, never anything but what had been decreed by the gases of the primeval nebula? It was not Milton, then, that had dictated "Paradise Lost" to his daughters; it was this nebulous nebula, whose constitution had fatally determined every line of the epic, and every punctuation point. What a Gargantuan comedy it was, that a man could believe all this, and then strain at the story that Christ had walked upon the waters!

It seemed to Father Morley that the principle of private judgment was as wrong in religion as it was in science. The puzzles of mind and body, of life and death, of morality and peace, were surely as subtle and abstruse as the problems of atoms and masses and strata and stars; if the uneducated individual bowed to the scientific specialists in science, he should bow with equal readiness to the theologian in matters of religion and morals. If the educated individual found his uncertain knowledge in discord with the doctrine of the Church, he would, if he were a man of judgment, maintain his loyalty to the Church in the trust that when time and thought had established the new opinion beyond the reach of doubt and controversy, the Church would adopt it and remould her theory accordingly. How absurd it would be that an organization nineteen hundred years old, caring for three hundred million souls, should accept new-fangled philosophies on the recommendation of a few men temporarily enthusiastic about a temporary hypothesis? How many "truths," the Church had seen come and go, how many sciences, during its life, had been born and passed away; what guarantee was there that the favorite guesses of modern thought would not seem to a later age as ridiculous as the star-reading of the astrologers, the head-reading of the phrenologists, and the gold-making of the alchemists? Science, like most history, was a fable agreed upon—for a while.

No; these matters of theory were not the important things. What counted was the tremendous effort to humanize and socialize the race; to curb the greed of the strong and comfort the sorrow of the weak; to frighten evil-doers with the fear of hell, and hold out to the unhappy or bereaved the solacing hope of paradise; to preach to all men incessantly the virtues of gentleness and kindness, and fill their dull lives with the poetry of the Sacraments and the Mass. This was the mission of the Church; and one who understood it so would put aside his frail individual judgment, and accept the teaching of the Councils as he accepted, in physical science, the reports of the savants. Individual judgment would be the end of the discipline and the co-operation which had given to mankind, in the Church, its most powerful instrument for the elevation of the race.

That (unless I am mingling later thoughts with memories of those days) was the philosophy of my friend the President. He brushed aside such difficulties as the cruelties of the Inquisition, the burning of

117

Bruno or the condemnation of Galileo, as the inevitable mistakes of an organization divinely founded
but manned by imperfect men; he would not apolo-
gize for these bloody errors; and he would no more
abandon the Church on their account than he would
leave his country because it had been unjust to
Mexico in 1848. Ah, a man should be loyal to his nation, should love it even if it erred; but how much
more should he love and be loyal to the country of his
soul, to the great faith that had built the cathedrals
and painted the Sistine Chapel, the great hope that
had held up countless millions of men and women in
distress and misery, the great charity that had
turned Europe from a wilderness of marauding
beasts into an ordered home of letters and the
arts!

I can imagine now what a Voltaire or a Diderot,
a Lecky or a Buckle, a Schopenhauer or a Nietzsche,
might have said to such an argument. At the time it
had an effect upon me proportioned not to its logic
but to the moral nobility of the man who uttered it,
and the love I had for him. Any theory that could
make it easier for me to work with him, help him,
and please him, met in me the co-operation of a
will-to-believe. Perhaps the material and moral filth
that I had encountered in my slumming as a reporter
inclined me to react away from the cynicism and
scepticism of my *Journal* days. Meanwhile the almost weekly visits of my parents to South Hall, or of
myself to them at Arlington, and their renewed and

118

infinite kindness to me, affected me in the same direction. In this almost sexless atmosphere I had begun to forget the very face of Esther. I found myself wondering whether my unbelief was so vital, or my negations so certain, that I could not don the cassock and realize the hopes of those whom I loved.

At the same time a new factor entered my life, whose name was Charley McMahon. Next to Tom Meaney he was surely the brightest of the lads I had known at St. Paul's; and he was beyond all comparison the most brilliant of my friends at South Hall. He was in senior class when I joined the teaching staff; and though Father Morley looked askance on such intimacy between a student and an instructor, Charley and I used to pace the paths together for many a disputatious mile. He was a handsome boy; a little younger than I, but quite capable of following whatever lead I might open in our conversation. I was astounded, on one of our walks, to hear him mention Karl Marx.

"What?" I asked. "Have you read Marx?"

"Sure," he answered.

"Read him through?" (These questions always go together.)

"Not on your life. I left the second and third volumes for later incarnations."

"What do you think of socialism?"

He looked at me quizzically; I suspect he was a little uncertain how far he might go with a friend of Father Morley.

"I think it's interesting," he said. "What about yourself?"

I was willing to pay for confidence with confidence; it was so hard to keep all my advanced thought to myself.

"I think it's the hope of the world," I replied.

He was not so enthusiastic, but he responded favorably enough.

"I'd like to see it tried," he said. "But you know the Pope denounced it in one of his encyclicals, don't you?"

"Yes; but in the same letter he said many pretty things about the workers of the world. Most of the Catholics in this country belong to the working class, while most of the capitalists are Protestant."

"That's right; the large industrial cities usually have Catholic administrations. The Protestants get the money, and we get the people."

"Well, if our Church is the Church of the poor, why shouldn't it cast in its lot with socialism?"

He looked a little frightened, and made sure that we were not overheard.

"That's a large order, Jack," he said.

"They say that in 1889 Father McGlynn came near carrying the Catholics of New York into the camp of Henry George and single tax."

"What the deuce is single tax anyway?" Charley asked.

We lost ourselves for a while in the bogs of eco-

nomic theory, and then returned to the poetry of
socialism.

"There's not much chance of the Church going socialist," said McMahon.

"There is a chance," I argued. "With the right
leaders, socialism would sweep the world. The Church
and the workers together would be irresistible. We'd
have again a united Europe—perhaps we'd have
Europe and America united—under the papacy; war
would stop, and there'd be such prosperity and happiness as never before in history. What a glorious
thing it would be all around!"

"You're reckoning without the millionaires.
They'd buy up every paper, poison the editorial and
news columns and make every respectable ass in the
country turn up his nose at you. You know the power
of 'holy script.' The people believe anything if they
see it in print."

"That's the whole point; socialism can't succeed
so long as press and pulpit are both against it. But
if the Church were with it, the press would be power-
less. There is only one force in the world that can
cope with money, and that is religion. The priest is
stronger than the editor. It would be a simple thing
for the priest to show that the New Testament
preaches a socialist, even a communist, ideal."

"Phew! You're going fast. You're not in for equal
division, are you?"

"No; of course that's impossible. All I want is that

121

the Church should come out definitely against exploitation, and on the side of the under dog. I want to see the Church declare a holy war against poverty and greed; I want her to make it shameful for a man to squeeze rotten wealth out of the filthy misery of factory slaves. I want her to stop idealizing poverty and meekness, and begin to stigmatize the hard-faced, ruthless money-maker, and the safely-elder war-maker, as types a thousand times worse than the drunkard, the harlot, or the atheist."

I have always enjoyed making speeches, and have always postponed to the end of my speech any consideration of the trouble I might be brewing for myself. Oratory is such an orgy that one may willingly pay a price for it. Now that I had shouted my piece, and phrased my dream, I resigned myself to having my friend turn against me, as Daly had done, for the safety of his immortal soul. But McMahon was made of sterner stuff.

"Jack," he said, enthusiastically, "I'm with you. For such a Church I'd be willing to lay down my life. I've been hesitating about entering the seminary; but if you think there's any chance of our getting some of the new blood in the priesthood warmed up to this idea, I'll go in with all my heart and soul."

"Let's think it over," I suggested, with very uncharacteristic caution. "We have half a year yet. If we feel, in June, that the thing is possible, I'll put on the cassock with you. It will be a long and patient grind; but it's the only way in which socialism can come. Once we get into battle we may find the younger clergy anxious for the move. Then, by God, we'll rebuild America, and renew the Church."

In the fall of that year we entered the seminary.

CHAPTER XI

IN THE SEMINARY

IT was, for me, an act of hypocrisy, generosity, idealism and egotism. After two years of effort I had had no success in recapturing either the old piety or the old faith. I found some response in my heart when I thought of the lonely figure of Christ; but it was impossible for me to conceive a personal deity. I entered the seminary trusting that faith would come by osmosis, by the contagion of the environment. For the time being I accepted the Church as a great moral institution, and was willing to put aside my private opinions in order to work with her. I thought I was behaving like a statesman; but when I look back upon those years I see myself walking under a mountain of lies. Ah, if we could only relive our past as we would make our future; and if we could only live our future as we remake our past!

In the deceptive enchantment of retrospect the pervading motive of this new move presents itself as a desire to please my family and my friends. Strange to say, I had forgotten love; and the thought that I was foregoing the delights of marriage no more entered my head than the thought that I was also escaping its responsibilities. Here I was at South Hall, surrounded by priests and seminarians on every side; there was but a step between them and myself; and by taking that step I should with one act redeem all the injury I had done my mother, and fill her heart with an intense joy such as she might never have known had my progress toward the priesthood been undisturbed. And she loved me so much (or so I thought); she was so gentle and tender with me; never reproaching me, never even uttering a word of her hopes. But I knew that she had been praying, morning and night, for this dénouement to my devious youth. I could not disappoint her any more.

The idealism and the egotism were inextricably mixed, as they so often are. I took with Quixotic seriousness the mission I had assigned myself, of working within the Church to ally it with socialism; and I was prepared for a life of warfare to that end. But this was theoretical: what actually moved me was the vision of myself making fiery speeches for the cause, suffering contumely for it, and at last getting credit for its victory. In that dream of the future I saw my path as a Way of the Cross, with success arriving just in time to prevent a crucifixion. I would be the Pope of American Socialism, the Second Savior of the World.

So you picture me now in the flowing cassock and the square biretta, looking a little more pompous and learned than before, walking with the consciousness of my augmented importance in the history of mankind. Though I continued to teach some of the innumerable languages in which I had been instructor, I lost the privileges and emoluments of a professor. Instead of receiving a salary for my work, I found it necessary to consume nearly all of my savings to keep myself in clothing and theological texts. Instead of eating the cannibalistic meals that had been served at the teacher's table, I had to accustom myself to the ascetic diet of the seminarians' refectory. Instead of a spacious chamber and a luxurious bed, I had to share with another young saint a small bare room directly under the roof, where we suffocated in summer and shivered in winter. Many a day found the water in the wash-bowl frozen to the bottom. It required a great deal of religion to get out of bed on those icy mornings; and as I had a little less than the others, I suffered accordingly.

We rose at five, washed in a minute, dressed in two, and then hurried down to the chapel for first mass. Very often we stayed for a second mass, making an almost continuous hour on our knees. Every knee in the seminary was calloused with devotion, and almost every back was bent with the humility of prayer. Then we were free till breakfast time, which came at half-past-seven, and found us ravenous. At nine we crowded into a little room on the top floor, and Father Farrell instructed us in dogmatic theology. He had just returned from a long stay in Austria; and he combined with a Teutonic patience in study and teaching, a tendency to speak English with queer

126

Teutonic idioms—ending every fifth sentence with "the same." But there never was a purer heart or a kinder one.

At ten I hurried away to teach a class in Latin. My cassock made the problem of discipline easier; but my penchant for bad puns tempted the students to exercise their wit upon me occasionally. At eleven we had Father (or, as he was now called, Doctor) Morley in moral theology; this was by all odds the severest hour of the day. He was a teacher who quite came up to Nietzsche's ideal, of exacting much and praising little. He assigned huge lessons of the most abominable subtleties, and expected us to recite and discuss the lesson in Latin. We had a terrible time of it; and if any of us had not begun to hate Latin yet, we learned to hate it now. I had the advantage of having kept my Latin fresh by teaching it; and when the others failed to hold the Doctor's pace he would appeal to me as the forlorn hope of the Latin tongue. I did my best; but I remember vividly the day when I too fell down, and he turned to me like a dying Cæsar to his Brutus, with the stern words: "*Neque tu hanc rem melius studisti*"— "Neither have *you* studied this matter too well." So deeply did they burn into me that to this day I can hear him biting out those words.

At 11.45 we passed into the chapel for prayer; and at noon into the refectory for lunch. While the sinful business of eating went on in silence, a seminarian read Alzog's *History of the Church*, or some

127

similar sedative. After that, for a happy hour, we
were free to play billiards, chess, checkers, or the
piano in the recreation room—most of us smoking
furiously while we had the chance; or to play hand-
ball or baseball with due seminarian dignity, holding
up our black skirts as we chased the ball over the
field. At two we had a class in ecclesiastical history,
taught by a charming young priest whose name I
have forgotten (health to him nevertheless!). Then I
went into the college rooms to teach—sometimes
French, sometimes English. At four o'clock we were
free again for an hour. At five we met on the gravel
paths and recited the rosary together as we marched
slowly along under the trees. This was one of the
pleasantest parts of the day, for it gave us a chance
to think of the things we had had no time for during
the other hours. Then we entered the chapel for more
prayers, and at six we had a modest supper. After a
half-hour for the pipe, we retired to our rooms, and
prepared our studies for the next day. At nine we
filed down to the chapel again. At nine-thirty we were
in bed.

I sometimes wonder whether this arduous schedule
was not designed in part with a view to meeting the
problems of sex. Here were forty vigorous young
men, just at the age when the sex secretions break
the dams and don'ts of morality: how were they to
be prevented from falling in love with the chamber-
maids? The answer apparently had been: Tire them
out. When we struck bed we were so exhausted that

even the visions of St. Anthony would have had no charms for us; had Thaïs herself appeared we should have turned our faces to the walls and slept. As it was, the chamber-maids had evidently been selected with a view to discouraging enthusiasm. I have no doubt that all but a few priests in America keep their vow of celibacy; in the crucial years of their development the energy of sex has been ruthlessly channeled into other fields, and the habit of indifference then acquired remains.

Perhaps we should explain in a similar way the unquestionable sincerity of priests. The early twenties are the age of religious doubt; if a man does not learn to doubt then, he will believe to the end of his life. And doubt requires energy; it is unnatural, uphill work; acceptance is much easier. Most of us are as willing to let others think for us as we are to let others work for us; here it is the mass that exploits the few, and surrenders to them all the risks of innovation. Now in the strenuous life of the seminary no time was left for doubt; one believed because one could believe without thinking, while doubt demanded thought. In those formative years the mind of the future priest took on the habit of belief; and all the assaults of later experience would hardly dislodge the dogmas there absorbed. Time and again, hungry for intellectual companionship, I suggested a doubt or two to the brighter men; they looked at me with uncomprehending eyes, and thought me "queer," and "not quite sound." The seminary saw to it that, barring an occasional alcoholic deviation, these men should be faithful sons of the Church to the day and hour of their deaths. It was a remarkably thorough operation.

On Sundays we prayed twice as much as usual; but also we had an afternoon's holiday. In the morning, besides our early mass or two, we knelt within the altar-railing, in our starched white surplices, to sing High Mass in all the grandeur of its ritual. The dinner was especially good that day, and we were allowed to eat it without the distraction of exciting literature. Then we were trusted with three full hours of comparative freedom. We dressed in our finest black suits, our stiffest Roman collars, our shiniest boots, and our best derbies, and went out in pairs for an extended walk into the magnificent country that surrounded the college site. All through the two winters of my seminary life I took these walks without the protection of an overcoat; partly to save expense, partly to show the others what a brave and hardy fellow I was. At five we were back for the rosary.

Then (on Sunday evenings) came Vespers; a glorious ceremony for the eyes and ears, but dire torture for a young seminarian who always had, in public, a painful consciousness of his legs, and who could never accustom himself to go through with grace and ease the complicated ritual that flourished at South Hall. Some of the boys liked these dramas, and became proud experts in liturgy; but I looked forward and backward to them with horror. Once, in the midst of

Vespers, as I was swinging the censer before Father Morley, I became confused, trembled, and stopped, utterly unable to think of what the ritual called for next. For a moment the universe stood still.

"What's the matter with you, John?" whispered the astounded Doctor.

I could not answer. I handed the censer weakly to another seminarian, and took refuge in the sacristy behind the altar. I could have cursed the man who had invented so elaborate a ceremony, turning religion into a puppet-show, and priests and acolytes into actors. It never occurred to me that perhaps most people, participants as well as congregation, liked this colorful pageantry. I sat there brooding until the services were over; and then, when I expected my fellow-seminarians to laugh me down as a dunce, they comforted me with sympathetic smiles, and two or three of them took care to engross me as soon as possible in a game. The kindly President never mentioned the matter to me, and remained as gracious as ever.

I did better when it came to the annual sermons which we were allowed to preach. I selected a difficult subject, wrote a brilliant paper in which I shocked both students and faculty with my knowledge of profane literature and philosophy, and spoke my speech with the passionate eloquence of one who hungered for admiration and praise. My only reward was a gentle reprimand from Father Morley for the doubtful orthodoxy of my views.

"John," he said, "I notice that you chose a philosophical rather than a moral subject. That's a wrong lead. . . . Your congregations will not care a whit for your subtleties and your historical allusions, your hypotheses and refutations and interpretations. What they want from a sermon is a guide and stimulus to good conduct. After all, what are all the theories in the world beside a word of comfort or an act of kindness?"

The good Doctor used to honor me, in those days even more than before, by choosing me as the comrade of his walks, and even of his prayers. Though I had not reached the stage in which the candidate for the priesthood begins to read the Breviary, he instructed me in its use; and on many an evening we read the day's assignment together, verse by verse in turn. I liked the music of the Latin, and caught occasionally the majestic metaphors and the noble simplicity of the psalms and songs we read. I went to bed, on those nights, with a heart filled with happiness over his affection for me, and yet tortured with the thought that I was guilty of unpardonable deceit. Sooner or later, I felt, I must tell him everything.

CHAPTER XII

I RE-ENTER THE WORLD

TOWARDS the end of my first year in the seminary a
midnight fire destroyed the college dormitory. I was
alone in my room at the time, and did not awake till
I heard rather unusual noises outside my door.

"What the devil are you doing with that hose?
Bring it here, damn you!"

"Hose"? And "devil"? And "damn"? I passed
from sleep into amazement. I peered out into the corridor, and found it filled with firemen. Apparently
they were letting the building burn while they dis-
cussed ways and means and displayed their vocabulary; it turned out later that the fire-alarm had in-
terrupted their weekly exhilarations. I smelled smoke
and whiskey, and heard the shouts of seminarians
and students on the campus below. I dressed, hurried
down into the open, and saw that half the institution
was in flames. I must have been sleeping well, for a
seminarian vowed that he had knocked at my door to
warn me. Everywhere the question was whispered:

"Is the place insured?"

"The Doctor says it is," answered someone in the
crowd.

I put off all worry, and permitted myself to see the fire as an esthetic spectacle.

"It looks like Hell, doesn't it?" I observed to a fellow-seminarian.

It was a foolish remark, inopportunely frivolous and profane. While it yet echoed in my ears I found myself looking into the stern face of Father Morley himself. In the dark I had not noticed that he was directly in front of me. I bowed my head and shrank into silence for the rest of the night.

It was a relief to us all when, a few weeks later, the insurance companies agreed to pay the total loss. The little Doctor, amid the thousand worries of a college without class-rooms or sleeping quarters, had energy enough to go out and raise a fund which, with the indemnities, made it possible to erect a splendid structure for an enlarged college. In a little while the new building was going up, and we seminarians joined the masons and carpenters in the task of having the place ready for the next term. Led by a tireless and almost omniscient seminarian—Blair of Paterson—we made cement, and hammered nails, and built chairs and desks, and painted walls and floors, and for a month or two exchanged the intellectual for the practical life. After the minutiæ of moral theology it was a pleasure even to hammer one's thumb. When the building was finished we looked upon it as our co-operative product; and to this day I pass it (safely anonymous) with a strange feeling of affection and pride.

All in all, my year and a half in the seminary were a tolerably unhappy time. Theology was an abomination to me. I managed to "cram" the lessons in ten or fifteen minutes before class, and to keep them in my head till the hour was over. When, in January and June, we were examined by the seminary faculty and the bishop, I reduced each text-book to my own summary, and escaped the ordeal with comparative success. My evenings, which were the only time left me for study, went not to theology, but to profane philosophy. I had been made librarian, and passed many reverent hours among the books which lay almost unused in one of the prettiest buildings on the college grounds. I came upon unsuspected treasures in the midst of those dusty tomes of dusty thought. There I first discovered Anatole France, represented only by *The Crime of Sylvestre Bonnard;* the book was so objectively written that I presumed Anatole was a good Catholic and a highly respectable Academician, who had confined his knowledge of women within the proper numerical limits. And it was there that I found Spinoza.

Why Hale White's translation of the *Ethics* should be in that pious little library the Lord only knows. But there it was; and as soon as I opened it I realized that I was reading one of the great books of the world. I was of a logical turn of mind, and liked rigid argumentation; it was at least a novelty to have a philosopher offer no blinding rhetoric, but a sternly ascetic structure of definitions, axioms, propositions, and proofs. I took the book to my room, and read every word of it, though I understood less than half. I questioned every definition, and scrutinized every demonstration; I rejected some with lordly independence of mind, and jotted down in the margin what I thought Spinoza should have said. But when I had finished the book, and then finished it again, I knew that the *Ethics* would be one of the strongest influences in my life.

The first result was a renewal of my negations. Never had the case for determinism been expressed with such scornful and apparently irrefutable logic. "Men think themselves free because they are conscious of their volitions and desires, but are ignorant of the causes by which they are led to wish and desire." Free-will was an egotistic delusion. Determinism appeared to me, in the context of Spinoza, to have a certain majesty and courage in it; man was at last strong and brave enough to face himself without lies, and see himself as part of an irrefragable web of cause and effect and inviolable law. The very thoroughness with which this view erased all possibility of miracle or effective prayer, the ruthlessness with which it reduced proud man, dressed in a little brief rationality, to the level of circles and stones, the short work it made of heaven and hell,—since it would be ridiculous to save or damn people for actions not really their own,—all this attracted me, as one must admire a blow or a word that annihilates an enemy. And this sublime interpretation of God as the sustaining structure of the world, the impersonal and unchangeable order and law that bound the Many into the One and made almost audible the music of the spheres,—how puerile beside it was my youthful picture of a bearded patriarch seated precariously in the clouds and leading his orchestra of angelic sycophants!

While I was abandoning all notion of ever believing again in the freedom of the will, I began to hunger for my surrendered freedom of speech and thought. I envied this man who had refused a professor's honors and a monarch's subsidy in order to think unhindered in his attic room. What courage, and what sincerity! What a lesson to one who was deceiving himself, by every subterfuge of sentiment and heroics, into a lifetime of hypocrisy and intellectual abdication! The vision of the gentle philosopher polishing his lenses, writing his heresies, and dying modestly and almost alone, with his life hardly begun but his masterpiece safely bequeathed to the world, came as an uplifting revelation into the darkness of my confinement. He too had been disowned by his friends and cast out by his family; but he had not flinched for a moment; and in the face of every temptation he had held up his head and scorned to lie. How could I have looked such a man in the face?

As I review those unhappy days, it seems to me that in one moment of awful clearness I saw the dishonor of my course, and realized that I must leave the seminary before I could become a man. I knew, in that moment of light, that nothing could be more terrible for me; that it might cost my mother's life, and forever darken and ruin my own. I knew what a crash of many hopes it would be for my father, and in a lesser way for my spiritual father in the President's office down below. And I loved them, these three, with that same intensity of feeling which made me nervously sensitive and rebelliously proud. How could I ever tell them that I had absolutely lost the faith which they had so zealously taught me, and which they were expecting me soon to preach? How all the elements of my life would tumble down about me, leaving me motherless and fatherless, homeless and friendless, in a world that would see only my hypocrisy and my ingratitude, and would never know anything of my struggles and my doubts!

For though I had sensed it before, it did not occur to me then (so far as I can recall) that many young people were enduring the same difficult transition. I had not the imagination to pierce through the walls of my room into the souls of these other youths; or beyond those walls into the other seminaries of the world, to see the future Tyrrells and Loisys tearing their hearts out with questioning and bewilderment; or into the colleges where young men and women were reading with wonder the findings of anatomy, and physiology, and embryology, and biology, and paleontology, and physics, and were slowly and unwillingly passing into a cold agnosticism; or into a hundred thousand homes where the ancient

138

battle of young and old was being fought anew between honest doubt and ancestral belief. In my egotism and my ignorance I did not realize that I was merely one of a vast number of souls caught in this sudden flood of change, crushed in the conflict of two faiths and two generations.

And yet there was Charles—my fellow-conspirator —who, immured in an Italian seminary, had been separated from me for a season, but had now become, like me, a second-year seminarian at South Hall. Was he not going through the same fermentation? What was it that made Charley a little less vivacious, in these days, than he had been? Was he hesitating too?

One day we paired for a long walk, and when we had climbed the hills beyond Maplewood, and sat on a cliff that overlooked Newark and gave a dim view of Manhattan's man-made peaks, we talked very frankly to each other.

"Look here, Jack, how do you feel about this seminary business?"

"It isn't as clear as it used to be."

"Still believe in socialism?"

"Yes; more than ever."

"And a socialist church?"

"We're up against a stone wall. The Modernist movement is dead in Europe, and it isn't even born in America. I never realized until I got into the seminary how absolutely the priests believe in every word of the defined faith."

"Why," he said, "they believe every line of Butler's *Lives of the Saints*."

"I'm beginning to lose hope," I sighed.

"So am I, Jack."

We looked down over the cliff as glum as owls.

"It's a hell of a joke on us," said Charley, with the profanity which, in these years, he had to reserve for me.

I felt a little guilty.

"I got you into this mess. I'm awfully sorry, old man."

"No you didn't, Jack; I got myself into it. I did it to please the folks. This socialist side of it was just a bluff to fool my brains. If I hadn't had that little bluff I'd have invented something else not half so magnificent."

Silence.

"What the deuce are we going to do now?" he suddenly burst out.

"I've been trying to answer that question for a week. Every night I decide I'll quit, and then the next morning I try to think where to begin, and what will be the result at home, and I shoot billiards and teach Latin, and forget all about it till night-time comes."

"I guess we've got to get out sooner or later."

"Yes. We've wasted two years of our lives here; we've been running around in a circle while the rest of the world has been moving ahead."

"I don't know but the world's been running around

140

in a circle too. But I'm tired of the circle; I want to
try the straight line for a while."

"That's just it, Charley. I feel as if I've been the
rottenest liar on earth. I'm going to buckle up soon
and get the whole matter cleared away. There's no
use."

I could see his last straw of hope leaving him.

"Not a damned bit," he said.

For a while we lay down on the rock, face to the
earth, as despondent as only youth can be. It was
uphill work to pull ourselves down from that
mountain-top and go back to our prison and our
lives.

In the end I decided, weakly, to send the news to
Father Morley by note. I had faced him once before
with my confessions; I could not rise to the ordeal
again. I told him that after much thinking I had
come to the conclusion that I was not fit for the
priesthood; and that I would leave as soon as I could.
I begged him to forgive my failure to live up to his
belief in me, and I thanked him from my heart for
the kindness and friendship which he had lavished
upon me. Wherever I went the memory of him would
be with me as my greatest incentive to live an honor-
able life.

The next morning he sent for me.

"I'm glad you're doing this," he said. "I've known
for a month past that you were slipping away from
the Church. Some of your fellow-seminarians have re-

ported to me the books you were reading, and various bits of conversation which they overheard. I had hoped that your prayers might save you for us; but perhaps you did not pray with your heart."

For a long time we were silent. He looked at me sadly.

"Where are you going?" he asked.

"I shall try to get a room in the Y. M. C. A. on 23rd Street, New York."

"Have you found work?"

"No."

"Why don't you go back to your family?"

"They wouldn't want me."

"How much money have you?"

"Thirty dollars."

"And you are going into the hell of New York with that?"

"I'll get along," I said, hopefully.

He took out his bill-folder and emptied it.

"I have only twenty dollars here. Take it. When you get a start you can repay me."

He offered it three times, and I refused it twice. I held his hand a long time as we said good-bye, for I felt that we would never see each other again. And he had meant so much to me; life would be empty without him.

"My poor boy," he said.

I went up to my room dull with misery. I packed my books, put on my only suit and my one civilian collar, and then, with the help of my room-mate, carried my trunk down-stairs to the front door. When the seminarians saw what I was doing there was a commotion among them. One or two of them seemed glad to be rid of so suspicious a character; some of them were sincerely sorry; one of them came secretly to me and said into my ear:

"I wish I had your courage. I never wanted to come here, but my people egged me on till I couldn't resist them. I wish you luck, Jack."

And Charley said, quietly:

"I'll be with you in a few days. We can't afford to let it look too much like a busted conspiracy."

The expressman was in the habit of calling at a certain hour every morning. I sat on my trunk and waited for him, expecting to ride with him to the station, and take a train for New York. But suddenly Father Morley's maid called me.

"The Doctor wants to see you."

I anticipated another difficult good-bye, but I was glad he wished it. He was pacing up and down his room.

"Sit down, Jack," he said. "I've been wondering whether you'd like to have your old place as a professor again. We need another teacher, and there's plenty of work here if you're willing to do it. You would receive sixty dollars a month and your board. Meanwhile you could be looking around at your leisure for better things. Would you care to do it?"

Was all this work, waiting to be done, merely an invention of his kindness, by which he hoped to ease

my exit and entry into the world? I saw at once that
this plan would go some distance toward softening
the shock which my withdrawal from the seminary
would give my mother. I grasped at the opportunity.
I thanked him, and returned his twenty dollars. He
smiled as he saw the old tears blinding me, and put
his arm affectionately around me.

"Some day," he said, "you will find a good wife,
and you will have a child. Then you will be happy
again."

I have never known a greater or a finer man. May
the years be gentle with him.

CHAPTER XIII

ALL SORTS OF THINGS

I HAD re-entered the world, but the navel-string of my second birth remained uncut. For a month I stayed within the precincts of South Hall, shirking the unpleasantness of a visit to my family, and feeling no hunger as yet for the city-life to which, somehow, I knew that I was destined. The long struggle I had had to make before breaking the bonds that had drawn me towards the priesthood left me weakened and apathetic; and for a while I merely drifted with the days.

My room now faced the recreation hall and the athletic field; for hours I would sit looking through the window at the vivacious students and the grave seminarians moving along the walks or playing their various games. I envied them their unity and peace of mind, the simplicity of their souls, the quiet content of their secure and limited lives. I foresaw that the same restlessness of thought which had broken down my belief in Christianity would not leave me for long the devotee of any faith, that I was doomed to pass through many negations before rounding the Everlasting No and moving up again to light and affirmation. The world would exact a heavy price from me for the privilege of doubt.

At last I mustered up enough courage to go home for a brief visit. All my older brothers and sisters were married now, and I was spared the ordeal of facing them; while my younger brother, Ben, gave me such sympathy and understanding as leaves to this day a fragrance in my memory. My father was silent for the most part, and not unfriendly. My mother was kindest of all to me, but with a sadness of face that made her kindness the sharpest cut of all. I made no effort to explain; for it seemed impossible that I should ever make my parents understand my doubts. To their direct and simple minds it appeared as an evident truth that any Catholic who left his faith must be either a sensualist or a fool.

Assuredly I was a sensualist; for in a remarkably short while after I had recovered from the nervous exhaustion of my escape into the world, I fell in love again, and less ethereally than before. Memory refuses to picture my first meeting with Rose; but there she was, suddenly within my orbit; smiling, lively, sociable, kissable Rose. Before I knew it I was in her home, playing for her singing as three years before I had sung for Esther's playing. What queer organisms we mortals be! So long as the fatiguing life of the seminary held me, sex had been only a faint curiosity and a word; now that the routine of life was easier, and I could rest and spare some energy from my immediate tasks, at once the imp of erotic imag-

ination and desire appeared, and led me a merry and
varied dance.

Rose was a good girl, with a temper that seemed
almost unwomanly in its even calm. I liked her for
that; I liked her for her simple ways; and I liked her
for her old mother, who filled me with cakes and
candy whenever I came, on the old theory of the relation between the male stomach and the male heart.
But I am afraid that I liked Rose chiefly because I
was hungry for the more substantial aspects of love.
I had been content to look at Irene; and content to
kiss Esther's hand; it would have been a sacrilege, I
felt, to ask for more. Now I was not so easily satisfied.
I kissed Rose's hand, and when I saw that she did not
take it too much to heart, I kissed her mouth; but
though her lips were as sweet as any that I had ever
pressed, they left me thirsty still. I kissed her hair,
her eyes, her ears, her neck, her arms, and as much of
her in general as she would permit, searching passionately for some point of satiation, like Ponce
de Leon seeking the fountain of youth. And always
the areas that I had not yet kissed seemed more luscious than those I had, though surely they were of the
same material. What villains we are, that only the
forbidden or withheld is sweet to us, and the most
generous woman is soonest left unloved.

Alas, poor Rose, I helped to wither you, did I not?
—sipping your honey greedily and then passing on
as coldly as the wind that blows a petal from a flower.
I did not hurt you, and I left you as when you first

discovered love; but I was shamefully unkind to you. When I met a lass still fairer than yourself, I tired of you, not understanding yet the joy of honor and fidelity; and to free myself I told you that I was an unbeliever, so that you might send me away. You did what I wished; but I know that you would have come with me had I asked you even once more; and it was brutal of me not to ask that once again. I wonder where you are now, and if you are happy? Perhaps in your modest way you are happier than I, happier than any man can be who has read the books of the philosophers.

While this love-life of mine swept on, the old lust of knowledge and experience rose in me again, and at last seduced me from South Hall's virgin soil. I had begun again to read the daily paper,—a habit which in my seminary years I had foregone without pain or loss; and day after day now the chaos of the world knocked at the door of my mind and begged for a little attention. At that time I read the Newark *Evening News;* it contained rather less of literary gossip than I wished; but I owe it one great boon—the friendship of Henry Alden.

This item of news, unlike most such, was really news, romantically and incredibly novel, and yet transpiring in East Orange, within walking distance of my room. Mr. Alden had established in his town a forum for the open discussion of various public issues. Although he was a rich man, he had so steeped himself in the lives and times of the founders of the

Republic that he had come to believe in liberty of thought and speech as the very essence of Americanism and democracy. When he organized a series of lectures, by different leaders, on rival theories of law and government, he discovered that there was a group, as ancient as it was small, which held that government did more harm than good, and had better be abolished. These people were called anarchists. It was a terrible word, and I think even the courageous Alden must have shivered over it for a while. Most of the leading anarchists, fortunately, belonged to Europe; but there were two famous ones in America, —Emma Goldman and Alexander Berkman. It occurred to Alden that merely as a matter of fairness and thoroughness his symposium on government should include an exposition of the anarchist theory by the redoubtable Emma.

You will imagine what the white collars of East Orange said when they saw Miss Goldman's name on the expensive announcements of their forum. Every man who had cheated his customers or deceived his wife acquired a new and easy respectability by joining in the cry against the invasion of a peaceful town by this unladylike advocate of dynamite. The forces of law and Constitutional order began to work, and the owner of the hall where the lecture was to be held was persuaded to announce that he could not permit the use of his property for anarchistic propaganda. Alden, angered at this civic cowardice in the face of one woman and an easily refutable theory, announced that the lecture would be held at whatever cost.

When the scheduled evening came I left the college and walked to East Orange. The trip took longer than I had calculated, and I spent some time inquiring about the location of the hall. But I found it unnecessary to go to the lecture, for the lecture was coming to me. A crowd of about two hundred people approached; and when I saw in their van a strongly-built and masculine woman escorted by a slim, grey-haired aristocrat, I knew that the location of the hall was now a matter of no importance. I waited for the two leaders to pass me, and I had a chance to observe them carefully.

I did not like the woman. Her face was hardened by years of suffering and intellectual isolation; her manner was assertive, and her carriage as utterly without grace as her speech was without charm; I missed in her all the elements which make a woman attractive to a man. She would have told me, in her sarcastic way, that a woman may have other purposes and functions in life than to please a man; and I suppose that would be true. But I did not like the lady.

It was rather unreasonable of me, for I was at once attracted to Henry Alden, despite the fact that he had none of the physical characteristics of a masculine hero. He was not strong; he was so slight that but for the even ruddiness of his face and the energy and courage of his actions, you might have thought that he was struggling with some congenital bodily weakness. He walked with a quick and nervous step and when he spoke it was like a Frenchman—with his whole body, and with indescribable animation. Yet, with all this vivacity of speech and movement, there was something quiet about him; he moved quickly but noiselessly, and though he spoke rapidly, he never raised his voice, and never forgot the perfect manners which revealed, through the disguise of his democratic dress, the born gentleman.

Behind them walked several policemen, and behind these the crowd. I fell in, and found that we were being led to a large barn in the rear of Alden's home. He had foreseen all difficulties, and had set up a platform and several chairs in the most spacious part of the barn. It was as spick and span as any home, though the neighing and stamping of a horse could be heard from another end of the building as we entered it.

The great agitator and her host mounted the platform, followed by some intimate friends, and by the zealous blue-coats. The seats on the floor were soon taken; and behind them the rest of us stood, uncomfortable but absorbed. Then Emma Goldman spoke, and the illusion of grandeur was dispelled. We had expected a fiery denunciation of official tyranny and popular bigotry, with an exposition of what anarchism meant and how it could operate; instead we found that we were listening to a lecture on the modern drama. The speaker seemed ill at ease and certainly (as I concluded on later occasions) not at her best.

"What do you think of her?" I asked the man who stood next to me.

"She's an old hen," he answered.

"I should say," said another, "that she's more like a rooster."

Nevertheless I had to concede her courage. With her ability this woman could surely have opened many doors to respectable comfort and position. Yet she had chosen a hard lot as the exponent of a theory which, through its unnecessary association with violence, had aroused against it every established power in American life. It was laughable to see four tremendous policemen solicitously noting the words of this one woman discoursing on Ibsen, Hauptmann, and Shaw. No doubt these names sounded suspicious to the gentry of the law; surely these unheard-of foreigners were criminals and anarchists, and the officials of Ellis Island must be warned against their entry.

I walked home with an evening of experience added to my little store. It was interesting to know that there were women like Emma Goldman, and pleasant to know that there were men like Henry Alden. Gradually the life of the outside world drew me magnetically away from South Hall. The old lust of living and of literature burned in me again. I wanted to know. I longed for every stimulating contact, every educative environment, every deepening experience.

I wanted to read every good book ever written, see every good play, hear every good composition; I wanted to feel the feverish flux of a varied life around me. I began to do my work at South Hall carelessly, and to run off, at night and at week ends, plucking at the fruit of the tree of knowledge.

One of these expeditions brought me as far as Coney Island. I had heard that there were indecent side-shows there, and I looked for them. Not finding any, I had to be content with slot-machines, which promised more than they performed. Then I walked restlessly from street to street, asking myself which of these women belonged to Mrs. Warren's profession. Suddenly a girl touched me on the arm and said to me quickly:

"Say, kid, do you want a good time?"

She was rather dilapidated and uninviting; obviously the color in her face belonged to synthetic chemistry. But I was anxious to know just how good a good time was. She took me into a saloon and ordered a drink. She drank, and I paid.

"Come with me," she said.

She passed through a door into a hall that led at the left to a stairway, and at the right to the street. She started upstairs, thinking I was behind her. But I turned precipitately and fled through the exit to freedom. I saw a policeman, and trembled. Then almost breathlessly I walked to the train-shed at the Brighton end of Surf Avenue and hid myself in an obscure seat of the next express for New York. Three hours later I was again at South Hall, safe in my room, but still hot with shame.

If the lust for experience remained curbed by fear, and by the afterglow of the Christian ethic still alive within me, the lust for literature was free. I found the libraries again, and could even afford, occasionally, to buy a book. In this queer world those who read books cannot buy them, and those who buy them cannot read them. At Broad and Bridge Streets, Newark, in those days, stood Burgess's book-shop. Burgess was a handsome Southern-looking fellow, with the frame of an athlete and the beard of a Shavian. He did not insist on his visitors buying his books; and he loved discussion more than a sale. I sat on his counter and exchanged ideas with him vivaciously. After a while other book-lovers joined these chats, and our lonely heretical souls thrilled with the new joy of intellectual comradeship and mutual admiration. It was out of this little group that we formed the Social Science Club of Newark.

Assuredly a big name for so small a circle—twenty young men and women who had never taken any systematic instruction in economics, sociology, or history. Some of us were teachers, others were clerks, others were in business in a minor way, and one was a minister. We loved him best of all the group, for "Uncle Tim's" wit was almost as infinite as his kindliness. I remember how once, when we were reading

Ghosts together, and we were all keyed up to Ibsen's sombre seriousness, he sent us into convulsions by interpolating a clause of his own into the passage which it fell his turn to read. The passage was a direction to the players, and Tim quietly made it run: "Mrs. Alving walks to the centre of the room, stands on her head for five minutes and says . . ."

After a while we tired of reading other people's books, and decided to begin each meeting with a paper on some learned subject, by one of ourselves. I forget, of course, all the papers read there except my own. We met on that occasion in an East Orange home, and our host invited Henry Alden to sit in with us. The paper went well, and won me some friends who kept my coming tragedy from being absolutely fatal. I outlined plans for a great monthly magazine, which should be the expression of liberal thought in religion and politics; and Alden volunteered to support it financially if we secured enough aid from other sources to make it a practical venture. I went home with my head in the stars.

Part of my pleasure lay in the impression I had made on the prettiest girl in the group. In the apparently accidental way in which such things happen, I found myself taking this girl home after our meetings. She lived in the finest section of Newark, in a luxurious apartment, and was apparently heiress to a modest fortune. After a few weeks I was sitting on her sofa with her, all a-thrill with the touch and warmth of her body, and tempted, as usual, to bite

155

into the soft and scented flesh of her neck and her arms. Things might have gone to matrimonial extremes, had she not snatched the initiative from my hands. One night, as we looked into each other's eyes, and pretended to be talking about Wells and Shaw, she suddenly changed the subject.

"Do you know," she said, "I think the greatest mission a woman could have in life is to marry a genius and support him."

"What did you say?" I asked, startled.

"Yes, marry a genius and support him. If I thought a man highly gifted I shouldn't think of letting him work for a living. If necessary, I would go to work myself rather than let him work for me."

As she had assured me, on various occasions, that I had all the ear-marks of genius, including those which Lombroso had listed as common to geniuses and idiots, I suspected that I was involved in this sudden turn of her thoughts; and she looked at me with such expectant tenderness that I felt called upon either to propose or to take to my heels with the better part of valor. Instead, I ate another piece of cake. I never went to see her again. She was too anxious, and destroyed the necessary illusion of male initiative.

A week or so after the reading of my paper I received an invitation from Henry Alden to spend an evening with him. I dressed as I had not done even for my set-to's with Rose; for just as every Englishman loves a lord, so every socialist loves a millionaire. I am sure I was ahead of time, or insufficiently late, but he welcomed me in high spirits. Within a minute or two we were talking with the intimacy of old friends. He filled me with candy and ginger ale, and then we went out and lolled in the hammocks on the porch. Darkness came upon us as we talked, but we turned no lights on; it seemed pleasant to hear only each other's voices in the stillness of the night.

That talk was an inspiration and a comfort to me. It was a comfort because this man, secure and confident, asked me to go out into the world and fight for the truth as I saw it, with the assurance that if ever I needed help he would not fail me. It was a comfort to hear a man of the broadest culture and the widest travel describe the pains of my intellectual puberty as part of a great change that was transforming the thought of the educated world from supernaturalism to naturalism; it was good to know that I was not alone in my heresies and my negations. And it was an inspiration to see a man descended from the oldest New England stock, and born into wealth and influence, using his position and his means to help the poor in their struggles for a better life, and standing up with polite tenacity for the absolute liberty of mind and speech.

"So you thought, when you gave up the old faith, that you were quite alone? But you were just one of millions and millions. The whole world is undergoing the same change that has nearly broken you. Copernicus began it, Voltaire carried it on, and Darwin completed it; it is the main line of the thought of Europe in the last three hundred years. No mature mind in the western world can ever believe in the old theology again. Hypocrites will pretend to, and fools will try to; and I suppose the great masses of the people everywhere will not feel the change as keenly as we. They, perhaps, will pass gradually and insensibly from one supernaturalism to another; the change may be painless for them, one form of anesthesia acting before the other has lost its effect. Notice the wild growth of new religions all around us; some of them are growing faster than our own religion grew in its first few hundred years. For sensitive young fellows like yourself, of course, the change will be like a birth, a tearing of the new life away by force from the walls and tissues of the old. There may be great bloodshed; we may have to fight for the privilege of suffering this change. But for us who read, the change is unavoidable; we'll have to go through with it."

We were silent for a while, hearing only the swaying of our hammocks and the chirping of the birds in the trees.

"And after the great change," I asked,—"what then?"

"I have often thought of that," he answered, "but who can tell? Perhaps the educated people will become sensual Epicureans, having many *liaisons* but no children, while the uninformed will breed large families and bring them up in ignorance; the same work of education may have to be done all over again, both for generations and civilizations, in a vicious and futile circle. I suppose that the idea of a better world on earth will for large classes of people take the place of the hope in heaven, and we shall have great waves of Utopian aspiration. I think it will be a wonderful age, a renaissance not only of the intellect, but of all the powers of man. Remember what Voltaire said in his old age?—'Young men are fortunate; they will see great things.' But you, what do you think of it all?"

It was very courteous of him to ask me; but I had not thought of the matter yet in impersonal terms; I had been absorbed in my own little part of the great change.

"I am still thinking," I said, "of the suffering the change will bring. Not merely to disappointed parents, who will rear some of their sons to be priests only to find them becoming apostates and atheists. I am thinking of the apostates and atheists themselves. They will always have within them some seed of the faith they have left; they will feel a strange emptiness of soul when they look into the skies that once held a loving God, or into graves that once meant resurrections. I think some of them will go back to the old faith after a while, unable to bear the world without fiction. But even those who do not go back will secretly yearn for the poetry and comfort of the old beliefs. If we had never had the idea of a Father in heaven, and a happy life after death, we

159

might bear this world cheerfully enough. Perhaps our children, or their children, will learn to be happy without lying to themselves about death. But we won't. We'll find it harder to die, I think; a little harder to leave life when we can never hope to taste its sweetness or see its colors again. The age of the great change will also be for many of us the age of the great sadness."

"I imagine that people have always found it difficult to die," he said, with the trace of a smile in his voice. "Napoleon remarked that every man who feared death was an atheist; and if that's so, atheism is the most universal faith. Even for the poor, God is not a belief but a hope; and I think they are a little suspicious of it all. That is why they fight bitterly any man who questions God; it is hard enough that their own souls question him, when they would so like to believe in him as they believe in the things they touch and see."

"But their hope is something."

"Never mind; we have our religion too. Let them make their sacrifices to the unknown God; we shall 'love the earth,' and build our modest heaven here. We too have our charity, which is not of alms alone but of social justice. We too have our faith, that some day all men may be brothers. And we have our hope, that we may write our names among the builders of a better world."

We walked arm in arm down the street before we parted. When he turned back, with a cheery "Come

again soon," it was as if I had left a portion of myself behind. But I marched home with my heart full
of a new courage. Perhaps I too might write my name
among the builders of a better world?

CHAPTER XIV

CATASTROPHE

WHEN June came I bade Father Morley a last good-bye. In those final months we had drifted far apart, and now we seldom did more than exchange the courtesies of the day. He knew that I was being drawn into the vortex of what seemed to him a vain and useless life. When we parted it was almost coldly, as if we understood, by some vague fatalism, that we would never see each other again. We had been together for so many years as teacher and pupil, spiritual father and half-spiritual son; now the hostile tides drew us apart mercilessly, and we turned and followed our divergent fates. Friends are so precious, and friendship is so brief.

He had helped me, with characteristic generosity, to secure an appointment as summer session teacher in the public schools of Newark. The new work was difficult, but I went through it diligently, and won an engagement as substitute teacher for the fall. I was ineligible for a regular appointment, since the rules required either a year in Normal School or two years' work as substitute.

I had moved from my comfortable room at South

Hall to a narrow den on one of the upper floors of the Y. M. C. A. building in Newark. It was an irksome and lonely life; and I was glad when my mother asked me to come and live at home. There were now six in the household: my parents, my younger sisters, brother Ben, and myself. Edna was then (if I may betray such secrets) about fifteen, and Evelyn about thirteen; they were the sweetest and loveliest girls in the world at that period of its history; and they endeared themselves so much to me that when the crash came it was almost impossible for me to resist their tears. Ben roomed with me, and brightened my life with inexhaustible good-humor and undiscourageable loyalty.

The summer session over, I went with Dave Howatt to spend a week at Physical Culture City, where Bernarr Macfadden was at that time making athletes out of intellectuals. Dave had converted me to vegetarianism, even to a highly ascetic form of it which virtuously avoided all cooked foods, and exalted the calories of nuts and fruits. I spent half of every day cracking nuts, nibbling away at vegetables, and washing my face with pears, peaches, and watermelons. Part of the day went to those debates about God, soul, immortality, socialism, anarchism, single tax, vegetarianism, free love, and sex, which are the eternally-resistant material on which the adolescent mind sharpens its teeth. The rest of the daylight hours, and something of the night, I gave to flirting with the girls. Once a fair lass and I lost our way in the pine forest; after hours of wandering we concluded that we should have to play Babes in the Wood, and I was all a-flutter with questionable expectations. Then we stumbled out into a road, and found ourselves unromantically close to home. I shudder to think what would have happened had we not come out upon that road. No doubt the whole course of history would have been changed.

In the fall I entered upon my work as substitute teacher in the Newark schools. If the theologians had known about substitute teaching they would have been spared the necessity of inventing hell. A substitute had no regular class; he (or she) was called in at any time to replace a teacher who was temporarily unable to appear. These assignments lasted sometimes for a day, sometimes for a week, once, in my case, for a fortnight. It was hard work from every point of view: the teacher had to fall in with a new grade of studies, acquaint himself with new types and individuals, and discipline forty or fifty youngsters who seemed to have saved all their potential misbehavior for his unlucky stay. There was no time to gain respect or affection; and very little opportunity to show any ability as a teacher. I found that five hours of this work were as exhausting as anything that I had ever done. The remuneration was two dollars for each day of actual teaching; my earnings for the first three months averaged eight dollars a week; and out of this I reimbursed my mother for room and breakfast, ate lunch and supper in cheap restaurants, clothed myself, and paid my fares. I tried to add to this income by taking night-school work; but the task of disciplining a group of nocturnal barbarians after five hours of work with diurnal barbarians proved too much for me; I made a failure of the extra work, and after the fall term I was dismissed.

I went on for several months under these conditions, until I began to wonder whether I could bear a year of it. I lived the most abstemious life, and yet I could save nothing, and could never think of buying a book. I was eating too little, and had to content myself with inferior foods. I became pale and nervous, and for the first time in my life I worried about my health.

I thought to add something to my income by lecturing; but the audiences I could attract would never have sufficed to pay for a hall. "Uncle Tim" Cairns came to my aid by offering me his parlor for one evening every week. With this encouragement I issued an invitation to the members of the Social Science Club to attend a series of twelve lectures on "The Philosophy of Herbert Spencer," at a cost of three dollars for the course. "Uncle Tim" was the first to accept this invitation; and when nineteen others followed him, I set out on my career as a modern sophist, carrying my little university under my hat, and peddling my wares wherever they would sell.

It was out of this lecture-course tha⁙ my little tragedy grew. One of my hearers recommended me to the Freedom Association of New York; and they sent me an invitation to come and address their Sunday evening audience on "The Origins of Religion." The fee was to be five dollars. It was a rather small sum for a lecture that was to cost me the hardest month of my life; but the Association probably felt that the financial reward would be sufficiently rounded out by the pleasure I would have in hearing myself talk. I accepted the invitation without imagining that anybody in the quiet precincts of Arlington or South Hall would ever hear of my remarks.

If I remember rightly, that lecture fell on the first Sunday evening of the year 1912. The hall was a small room in East 12th Street, seating some one hundred and fifty persons. It was crowded beyond its legal capacity when I came; people sat even on the edges of the platform, and looked around at me with eager constraint. What was it in religion that had irked these people so, and made them so anxious to hear it reduced to natural and earthly terms? Were they too caught in the throes of transition, and hungry for companionship in rebellion? Or was it the spectacle that drew them, the spectacle of a young man, just out of a seminary, standing up to renounce his faith? How many such groups, the world over, had gathered together this same day to declare war on the fables that had lightened and darkened their youth? How many such groups had met on other days, and in other years, and in other centuries? I saw Protagoras reading his essay "On the Gods" in the home of Euripides; I saw Bruno preaching passionately his rebel faith to little circles in Italy, and Switzerland, and France, and England; I saw the youthful Spinoza whispering his heresies to his unsympathetic friends; and I thought that I had become one of their glorious and endless dynasty.

I had prepared myself diligently, and had read every authority that I could find,—though I remember that Frazer's many-leaved *Golden Bough* was strangely out of the list. I was at the age when sex mingles itself with every enterprise, and I had been drawn overmuch to those books which dealt with the phallic aspects of ancient faiths. Certainly I stressed that side of the subject a great deal more than I would now. My hearers liked the exaggeration, and were delighted to learn that almost every symbol in religious history, from the serpent of paradise to the steeples on the churches in nearby Fifth Avenue, had a phallic origin and significance. They asked me a hundred questions, which I answered with unhesitating assurance. They acclaimed me a great scholar, an impassioned orator, and a courageous heretic. I went home confirmed in the opinion I had long since formed, that I was a great man, and that the world would hear from me soon.

Part of the world did. I think it was on the following Friday that I was called to the telephone in the office of the principal of the Montgomery Public School, where I was serving as substitute. I had had better fortune there than in most of the schools; the regular teacher was gracious enough to send word that she would be ill all season, and I had every prospect of being allowed to continue with the class till its graduation in June. The principal had prevailed upon the Superintendent of Schools to promise me, beginning with February, the license and stipend of a regular teacher.

It was my brother Ben who was calling me from the architect's office in which he worked.

"Jack," he said, "you're in an awful mess. The Newark *Evening News* has a story, on the front page, about the Bishop excommunicating you because of your lecture last Sunday."

I dropped back from the telephone, and came near passing into another world.

"Good God!" I exclaimed, "what if that paper gets into our house?"

"It's the first edition," said Ben; "perhaps you can get the *News* to keep it out of later editions."

I asked him to meet me at five o'clock and go home with me; and then I called up the *News*. It was too late; all editions had been printed. I went back to my class and pretended that the population, capital cities, industries, and exports of the South American republics were matters of crucial interest. Not till an hour later did I see just what the *News* had said about me. The horror of impending events was mixed in me with a vague pleasure at seeing myself so prominently in print. The item, half a column long, and inescapably conspicuous, informed the public that the Bishop had learned of a lecture given by me, in which I had reduced the origin of religion to sex worship; that since I had recently taught at South Hall it was desirable that the people should know that I was no longer connected with that institution; that by my actions I had placed myself outside the pale of the Church, and Catholics should have no relations with me of any kind.

I was stunned into a sort of insensibility. When my friend Monte came upon me as I sat in a lunch-room waiting for Ben, I joked about the matter, and classified myself with Bruno, Huss, and Servetus. Then Ben appeared, and his worried face restored my perspective of the situation.

"There'll be hell to pay," he said, briefly.

We traveled home in silence. I was prepared for a violent scene; there was every reason to expect that my father would at once order me from the house. But I was greeted with comparative calm. Neither my father nor my mother had seen the *News*; but my mother had received a message from the parish priest asking her to come and see him the next morning.

That evening Ben and I went to Father Eastman, and begged him to keep the matter from my mother. Without defending either my behavior or my opinions, Ben struggled valiantly to make the priest see the matter from the human instead of the ecclesiastical point of view.

"It may kill her," he urged.

But Father Eastman did not take that seriously.

"You are an enemy of the Church," he said to me, bluntly, "and the Church must protect herself against you."

I tossed about all night trying to think of some way out. Could I keep my mother from going to the priest? Sooner or later he would get to her. Could I ask my older brothers to prevent their fellow-workers in the Arlington factory from showing the *News* to my father? But they lived in Belleville and Newark; I could hardly reach them in time; and they would have scant sympathy with me anyway. Could I go to the priest and offer him a retraction? I would have done even that if it could have saved the peace of my family; I felt that my freedom of speech was a little thing beside the happiness, and perhaps the life, of my mother.

The next day was Saturday, and I had no work. I ate breakfast with Edna and Evelyn, and found it hard to play up to their usual innocent and worry-less chatter. My mother had gone to Mass; I knew that when she came back I should have the unhappiest hour of my life. I went up to my room, and tried to read.

I did not hear my mother return; but I heard on the stairs a step which I knew to be hers. The door of my room was closed, so that I could not see her enter her room, which was at an angle adjoining mine. Then suddenly there came a dull noise, as of some one falling on the floor, and a cry that for a mo-

CATASTROPHE

ment hypnotized me into a breathless immobility.

"My God! My God! Give me back my son!"

I opened the door, and saw my mother lying face downward on the floor, her grey hair disheveled, her hands clasped and stretched out before her. I went to her and touched her arm. She stared at me with wild eyes that seemed to be looking through me at something beyond, and then she cried out again:

"My God! My God! Give me back my son!"

I talked to her, but she did not seem to hear me. My sisters came in, horrified, and tried to lift her from the floor; but she shook them off; and when she looked at them she showed no sign of recognizing them as her daughters.

"What is it, mother?" they asked her. "Why are you crying?"

Instead of answering them she burst out again in her weird appeal to God. My sisters turned to me for help.

"Jack, what's the matter? What does she mean?"

I could not answer. I tried to say something, but failed. Then I muttered:

"I'm going to get pa."

I ran from the house to the factory, and had my father summoned to the gate. He seemed to know, without my telling him, what had happened at home. Several of his men, with that informative solicitude which we often show when information can work tragedy, had shown him yesterday's *News*. He could not read; but he had had them recite every painful word to him. He carried the paper in his hand now.

"So you've killed your mother," he said, bitterly.

That was all. We walked together in silence to the house. My mother seemed to be quiet now; I could hear only her occasional sobbing, and the crying of my sisters. But when my father came to her she began to call upon God with the same wild cry as before.

I went into my room, but I left my door open. A moment later my sisters entered, Edna holding the *News* in her hand.

"Jack," she said, "this is a terrible mistake, isn't it?"

I tried to tell them that it was all true; but I had no voice. Then they flung themselves wildly on their knees before me, caught hold of my hands, and begged me:

"Jack, Jack, tell us it isn't true!"

What could I answer them? They saw from my silence that I had nothing to say, and they burst into hysterical sobbing, their heads on my bed. I ran from the room half insane, and down the stairs, and out to the nearest telephone. I begged our family physician, Dr. Robison, to come at once. He answered that he could not come for two hours.

"But, Doctor," I implored, "my mother has had a stroke; she is in convulsions, and I am afraid she is losing her reason. Please, please come at once."

"All right," he said, "I'll come." He had never failed us.

I went home, and sat in the kitchen waiting for

him. I could hear my father trying to soothe my mother. She seemed to ignore him; she walked up and down her room, and every now and then she would fling herself on her knees and repeat that awful cry, always the same:

"My God! My God! Give me back my son!"

When the Doctor came I explained the matter to him quickly. He was sympathetic. "I'll give her something to put her to sleep," he said, "and tomorrow she'll be all right again."

I followed him upstairs, and went into my room as he entered my mother's. I heard him talking to her, but she answered only with the same unrecognizing words which she had been repeating for two hours. He offered her a sedative, but she turned away and refused to take it. Then I heard him arguing with my father:

"Don't be too hard on the boy. He's passing through a change. He'll get over it."

My father's long-controlled anger suddenly overflowed.

"Look here," he said, "you're called to give medicine. Don't tell me what to do with my children." They were almost the only harsh words I had ever heard him utter in my life; and he had had a world of provocation.

The Doctor gave me a moment as he passed out.

"I'm afraid I can't do anything to-day," he said.

When he had gone, my father came into my room.

"Listen to me," he said. "You're the most ungrateful boy any mother ever had. We've been patient with you long enough. I'll give you three days to get out of this house."

I said nothing. I felt that I deserved it all, and much more. As soon as he turned to go I began to pack my books.

When I awoke the next morning the house was quiet. My mother was in bed, and seemed to be asleep. My father was downstairs making his breakfast. I put all my belongings into one suit-case, except some of my books, which I left in the little desk that I had used ever since my childhood. I wrapped a cloth around my typewriter, and bound it up chaotically with cord. Ben wanted to come with me, but I dissuaded him gratefully.

I stepped into my mother's room, and watched her for a moment as she slept. She looked utterly worn out. I could see, even through her sleep, that hope had passed out of her and left her face lifeless and dull.

"Ben," I whispered, as we looked at her, "tell her I wanted to say good-bye, but I couldn't bear to wake her up. Tell her I'm not as bad as she thinks, and that I will try to lead a good life."

"Where are you going, Jack?" he asked.

"I don't know."

I had not thought about it yet.

174

"How about meeting in your office at three o'clock to-morrow?" I suggested.

"All right, Jack."

I went downstairs with my suit-case in one hand and my typewriter hanging from the other. I must have seemed a highly fantastic figure to impartial eyes. As I neared the foot of the stairs I heard Edna's voice behind me. She and Evelyn were standing in the doorway that led up to their attic room. They were red-eyed and almost voiceless.

"Good-bye, Jack," they whispered.

"Good-bye," I managed to answer.

I opened the front door, and then turned and faced my father. He always rose at five o'clock, long before the rest of us, made his own breakfast, and said his morning prayers kneeling on the hard floor of the kitchen.

"Good-bye, pa," I said, timidly.

He looked at me sternly without replying.

Suddenly a cry came from my mother's room.

"Don't send him away! Don't send him away! He's my boy!"

And then the same passionate prayer as on the day before:

"O God! Give me back my son!"

I walked out, closed the door quietly, and went up Laurel Avenue. It was the longer route to the trolley, but it led through a deserted part of the town. Half way up the hill I realized that I had no strength left. I put down the typewriter just as it was about to slip from my fingers. I threw myself upon the soft grass by the side of the road, and let all the floods that had been held in for days have their way with me.

"My dear mother!" I cried helplessly. "My dear mother!"

PART TWO

THE NEW WORLD

I MAKE A FLYING LEAP

THAT evening I found myself in a room over a saloon in West Nineteenth Street, near Sixth Avenue, New York. I could hear the voices of men who, on a lower floor, were drinking and carousing without fear of the Sabbath laws of God or the policeman. Every few minutes the house shook as an Elevated train rumbled by. The room was so small that a bed, a chair and a wash-stand almost exhausted its space. The landlord, who was also the keeper of the saloon, collected three dollars in advance for a week's rent, turned up the gas for me in fear of my rural ignorance, and left me. I called him back a minute later.

"I'm terribly cold," I said. "Doesn't this room get any heat?"

"What do you want for three dollars?" he growled.

Nevertheless, he brought me an old gas-stove, and connected the hose to a pipe in the floor; and soon I was rubbing my red fingers, sore with a day's porterage, over the jets of fire. The hose leaked, and I had to open the window to clear the air of gas. I tried to bandage the leak with my one handkerchief, but it would not work. I found that my choice lay between

179

freezing with the window open and the stove burning, or freezing with the gas turned off and the window closed. Despite all the instructions which I had received from the *Physical Culture Magazine* I shut the window and opened the door into the hall. I tried to read, but found my books strangely insipid; for an entire page I was engrossed almost to the point of unconsciousness in memories and anticipations. I closed the book and locked the door, undressed, opened the window, and with the stove on full blast I went to bed.

I was slipping into sleep when a gruff voice aroused me.

"Say, you greenie, what d'ye mean by running that stove all night? What a bloody nerve!"

"Put it out," I said, too tired for argument.

"Put it out? I'll take it out." He loosened the connection, and carried the stove indignantly from the room.

I turned around, huddled up for warmth, and tried to sleep. But it was too cold. I closed the window, and threw all my clothing on the bed. For many hours I tossed and shivered, thinking of a thousand things; thinking of the absurdity of coming to live in this unfamiliar city, this noisy street and this gloomy room; counting my resources, and concluding that besides my typewriter and a few books I had ten dollars; and always haunted with visions of my mother lying on the floor and calling upon God. What an insane world it was that could so tear mother and son apart because of simple faith and honest doubt! What a humorless absurdity that a difference in theology should be considered of more importance than the bonds of blood and love!

I was not bitter, nor was I lonely. Even in the heat of the event I understood what base ingratitude my apostasy must seem to parents who had stinted themselves for years that I might have an education and be a priest. After all, I had been exiled gently, without violence or hatred. It was an inevitable incident of the Great Change. Perhaps it was a common incident in every generation, as the young tried their growing minds against the dogmas and authority of the old. I thought of the fermenting days of the Renaissance, the Reformation, and the Enlightenment: in those times too there must have been apostate sons and divided homes, bewildered fathers and broken-hearted mothers. Perhaps every age had known the growth-pains of transition.

And I was not lonely, because I had already had four years of nocturnal solitude, and could not feel at once the moral isolation that was to come out of this new division. Indeed, mixed with the hot sorrow of that day there was a strange feeling of acceptance and reconciliation; in a sense it was good that the cloud had burst, and that the doors had closed behind me. Let all the doors be opened in front now, even if they should lead into lonely roads. I was an outcast, but I was free.

Towards dawn I fell asleep.

I remember little of the next day. Doubtless I spent a part of it in bed; it is remarkable how well we can sleep in the morning. It was Saturday, and I did not have to report at School. I believe it was that afternoon that Harvey Keap came to my dingy room and tried to console me with his latest poetry. For the rest I wandered about through the lower West Side, half dazed with visions and memories, trying to understand the new life into which I had been flung.

Here at last was New York. What a chaos! How could people think clearly in this uproar, or find any serenity in this degrading haste and competition? The trolley's warning bell might have had some music in it if it had sounded only now and then; but its insistent clang shrieked with impatience and irritation. The horses that still drew the city's freight over the cobbled streets were glorious animals, vibrant and firm; but the lumbering trucks which they ignominiously dragged behind them were monstrous things, that drowned the poetry of life in their shapelessness and their noise. Here and there, still in a proud minority, were automobiles, graceless in line by the side of their coming progeny, but giving to the prosaic scene a picturesque element of fleet and almost silent motion. And everywhere there were men.

It was as exciting as an esoteric and forbidden thing. It had the lure of the abnormal and unnatural. I knew that this neurotic life was not the kind

182

of existence that would make for health of body or poise of mind; but I was attracted by the intensity of it, its variety and fulness, its adventurous complexity. The noise irritated me, almost frightened me; but I had no doubt that I would soon be hardened to it; within a week I would not hear it. This awful city had drawn me to itself, as it was drawing a million young men every year; I recognized the fatality of the process, and for my part agreed to it; here in this bedlam I would live my life, here in the heart of things, and at the foaming crest of the wave.

In the evening, hungry for companionship, I walked down to East Twelfth Street, the home of that same Freedom Association for which I had given my historic lecture on the origins of religion. The Association had been formed as a result of the execution of a famous Spanish liberal—a man whose ideal had been to establish schools that would be independent of religious domination, and less authoritarian than schools were wont to be in Spain. No doubt in America he would have been a harmless liberal. But the anarchists of New York were the only group moved to action by the cowardly association of church and state in the assassination of this great educator. As a memorial to him they proposed to organize a school in which not religious freedom only, but freedom of every kind, would be the soul of the curriculum. To teach people to be free, to let them know the happiness of a natural and spontaneous existence: what better program could there be for any school?

As I approached the little flat which had become the hot-bed of radicalism in New York, I saw an excited youth making for me with arms outstretched and face radiant with welcome. It was Dawson—redhaired, brown-eyed, bare-headed, open-hearted Dawson—one of those who through thick and thin remained loyal to their faith in a free world. He embraced me in the most passionate French style.

"What luck!" he cried. "Do you know I've been hunting all over Arlington and Newark for you?"

"What's the trouble?" I asked.

"You're wanted at the Center this evening. There's a meeting of the executive committee. Miss Bridge will certainly be glad to see you; we thought we'd never find you."

I followed him into the little office, and was introduced to Viola Bridge, Director of the Freedom Association. I stood in amazement before this strange and fascinating woman. She was so frail that her energy made me uncomfortable; at any moment it seemed that her physical resources would be exhausted, and she would fall to the floor consumed in the fire of her own spirit. Every word she spoke dripped with feeling. Her large dark eyes looked out on the world with a mixture of passionate resoluteness and brooding love; she would remake this sorry scheme of things whether it consented or rebelled. I found later that she was a poetess, whose lines trem-

184

bled with the ardor of the soul that made them. It was fitting that a poetess should be the head of a group of splendid dreamers; but it was extraordinary that this sensitive plant should be the director of any association whatever. I liked her so much, after a few minutes with her, that I was prejudiced in favor of anything that she might ask.

"We are organizing the Freedom Modern School," she said, as softly as a mother speaking to her child, "to give a libertarian education to ten or fifteen children. It will be a glorious experiment; and if it succeeds, it will affect the practice of every school in America. We want you to take charge of it. We can't pay you well; and if you come to us you will be losing something in security and worldly position. But we thought you were the kind of man who would dare to make the sacrifice."

How could I escape this inveigling compliment? I wanted to say yes; it would be an exciting game, this trial of teaching without compulsion or authority; many times I had felt the absurdity and the inhumanity of the discipline which I had been forced to impose upon my pupils in the public schools. But was I ready to associate myself with the exponents of the most extreme of all movements in the world of politics and industry?

"You see," I said, "I'm not an anarchist."

"Never mind," she smiled, confidently; "you will be. And you believe in libertarian education, don't you?"

"I do." On that point I was prepared to go with the farthest.

"And you are a good teacher. That is all we ask."

I can resist one compliment; but two in a row have always overcome me.

"I should like to do it," I said. "But you ought to give me a few days to think it over. It's a decision that may affect my whole life."

"Yes," she answered; "it may. And it is hard to ask you to make your decision now. But we too must decide quickly. Mr. Black, who is the only other man whom we have in mind for the place, is leaving New York to-morrow for his school in Oregon. He will abandon that and teach ours if we ask him, but we can't delay any longer. If you refuse us, we must take him. If you are willing, we would rather have you."

I was conquered.

"I will come and do my best for you," I said.

She rose and grasped my hand as if she would embrace me.

"I knew you would," she said.

I did not learn till almost a year later what a hard fight Viola Bridge made for me that night in the meeting to which she went on leaving me. Emma Goldman, the most influential member of the executive committee, supported Mr. Black; he had had experience as a libertarian teacher, and was loyal to the anarchist philosophy. I think it was agreed that Mr. Black had everything in his favor except that his hair was gray while mine was still brown with the color of youth. Perhaps some secret and anonymous influence worked for me. At all events, I became, on the following Monday, the principal, sole teacher, and chief learner of the Freedom Modern School. In the eyes of the world I had become an anarchist.

CHAPTER II

MY FRIENDS THE ANARCHISTS

I was prepared to find my new acquaintances a rather wild lot. I looked for long whiskers, disheveled hair, flowing ties, unwashed necks, and unpaid debts. I had been led to believe that most of these men and woman were criminals, enemies of all social order, given to punctuating their arguments with dynamite. I was amazed to find myself, for the most part, among philosophers and saints.

I had a good chance to study the group at a lecture which I gave on "Love and Marriage." I was still young enough to suppose that one could speak an hour on this subject without providing humorous reminiscences for his maturity. Perhaps the expectation that I would make some heretical and regrettable remarks explained the large attendance. The little hall was full; and as I spoke I could see the chaotic variety of individuals which composed the actual anarchist type.

The long whiskers were there, but on one or two faces in a hundred and fifty. The disheveled hair was there, but on heads that I later found to be empty; these careless ones were neither the leaders nor the characteristic personalities of the movement. There were flowing ties a-plenty; I can still see before me the magnificent cravat of Radkon Vicoberci. As to the necks, I was too far away from them to see just how much of mother earth they carried on them. But all about me I saw fine faces. There was Stuart Dare, tall, handsome, gray-haired, quiet; a soul softened and saddened by some youthful Old-World tragedy. There was Dr. Freer, whose beard made him look more like an orthodox anarchist than any other person in the group, but whose spotless cleanliness and twinkling eyes prepossessed me at once in his favor. There was Alexander Berkman, who had, not long since, completed a fourteen-year term in prison for shooting a steel magnate in the Homestead strike of 1892. As I looked at him I felt quite secure; this man would never hurt anyone again. Not that he was too sensitive for it; he looked strong and masculine enough; but he spoke with such calm intelligence that I could not picture him reverting to the futility of violence. Years of suffering had given him a profound sympathy for the unhappy and oppressed. He joined in the discussion that followed the lecture, and with the politest indirection suggested that I was slightly mistaken in certain of my facts and views.

Near him stood his life-long friend, Miss Goldman. She listened impatiently to my prattle; she had heard these things a thousand times before. We disliked each other, I suspect, from the time we swam

into each other's ken. There was something of the
stern authoritarian in her which made a strident discord with her pæans to liberty; where she could not
dominate she could not work. I missed in her the
kindliness which I found in so many others of the
little circle: they wished to help the world to peace
and freedom; but she brought with her always a
fiery sword of act and speech, and threatened with
dire punishment a world that would not take the
form of her desire. Yet she too, like Berkman, had
earned by suffering the right to her opinions. From
her point of view I was a young intellectual whose
seminarian past made him unreliable material in the
war of liberation; at any time, she felt, I would slip
back into my ancient faith, and hug the old ortho-
doxies in which I had been bred.

Most interesting of all was the chairman, Ronald
Dalton. I believe he had been born in England; certainly he had lived there in his youth; I was jealous
when I heard him speak, from personal acquaintance,
of William Morris, and Bernard Shaw, and Sidney
Webb, and H. G. Wells, and those other brilliant
apostles who had made socialism intellectually respectable for the British mind. I was jealous, too, of
his tall figure, his dark brooding eyes, his handsome
and sensitive face. He came of a well-to-do family,
and showed in every gesture the evidences of a semi-
aristocratic origin. He was an anarchist not because
he wished to use violence, but because he had a horror
of violence of any sort; unless he could persuade

through patient reasoning he went away with his sad smile, regretful, but as friendly as before. He was incapacitated by nature from quarrelling with any man; and I doubt if ever in his life he said no to a request that fell within his physical powers. He suffered with those he saw suffer; every bit of evil that came within his experience found him, like Shelley, all nerves, and cut him to the soul. All who knew him loved him. The women in the group gazed up at him with eyes dripping with admiration and devotion; and even the men, some of them hard and cynical, looked upon him as the redeeming angel of the anarchist movement.

What did these people mean by anarchism? To the outside world, and to a certain "lunatic fringe" within the group itself, the word meant the approval of any means, moral or physical, peaceful or violent, that the exploited classes might care to use in their war for freedom. But to the finer spirits in the movement anarchism meant just the opposite of this: it was the absolute rejection of physical force as unnecessary in human affairs. This difference of opinion made the circle a nest of controversy. I can recover in fairly accurate outline one of the many disputes that made the little hall ring in those days of my radical novitiate.

"Why should we limit ourselves to peaceful means?" asked Leon Bremer, whose disheveled hair symbolized the condition of his mind. "Does the exploiter limit himself? Doesn't he hire criminals to hound out his enemies at the polls, or empty the ballot-boxes into the river when the vote goes against him? Doesn't he buy up newspapers to fill the public with lies? Doesn't he pay gunmen 'detectives' to shoot down strikers in peaceful meeting? Doesn't he organize state militias and constabularies whose secret function is to keep down the working-class? Doesn't he build armies and navies to grab whatever parts of the world he can get, by force or by fraud? And meanwhile he preaches Christianity to us: we are to be meek and humble of heart, and turn the other cheek. Well, we won't be fooled; we'll use words, or books, or guns, or dynamite, just as they come handy. Let the cowardly socialists fill the parlors with talky-talk. An anarchist is a man who dares to do things, and if necessary dares to kill."

Such language was a little startling to a beginner like myself; and loving argument almost as much as life I plunged into an animated rebuttal. I hinted to Bremer that his violence of speech covered a secret fear of action; when the time came for quick decisions and resolute enterprise he would still sit at a table in a basement, drinking tea and talking social metaphysics, as we were doing now. What he really hungered for was not freedom, but power.

"Nearly all of us love power," I announced, with that mad obstinacy which has always made me talk conservatism to radicals and radicalism to conservatives. "Freedom is an empty shell until it is filled with power. It dies almost as soon as it is born, because it

192

is an instrument and not an end; those who get it become the exploiters of those who cry for it in their turn. The very desire behind the cry for liberty sets liberty its bounds."

There were excited interruptions, and many a head of hair shook from side to side in scandalized disagreement. It showed a fine tolerance, after all, that these passionate propagandists allowed me to go on at all. I proceeded to tell them, in my learned way, that anarchism might be possible in a simple agricultural society of the kind that Tolstoi desired, but that it would be out of the question in a highly developed industrial order; in such a society thousands of unequal functions were performed by unequal abilities demanding unequal rewards; and every increase in the complexity of industry placed the average person more thoroughly at the mercy of superior ability, cunning, or power. We were born unequal, and we became more unequal as we grew up; every new invention added strength to the strong and weakness to the weak. My discourse ended with the inopportune suggestion that anarchism was a survival of primitive isolation and simplicity, and was perhaps a secret and reactionary yearning for it; it was the beginning rather than the goal of a civilization, and became more impossible as civilization progressed. Disciplinary regulation was the alternative to industrial and political disintegration.

A handsome bearded poet stopped me.

"That is just the point," he said, with admirable

calm. "Civilization and anarchism are incompatible; let us agree. But you conclude that therefore anarchism is impossible. I conclude that therefore civilization is intolerable. We do not desire a continuance of this complex and materialistic industry which, you say, requires compulsory regulation. For my part I am willing to abandon your cities and your factories, your brothels and your slums, and go back to that primitive life in which all men were substantially equal and all were free. Yes, anarchism is an enemy to modern civilization, and to that modern culture which means the leisurely pursuit of subtleties by a few favored individuals at the cost of the slavery of nearly all mankind."

He was wildly applauded; and I could not help admire the simplicity and directness of his thought. I was ready with a crushing rejoinder, when Bremer captured the floor again, his great mop of red hair streaming out from his head like the rays of the setting sun.

"The regulation and order you talk of," he said, pointing his finger at me as if I carried the scarlet letter on my brow, "is the fetish of cowards and slaves. We don't want order, we want liberty. Order is a means, liberty is an end; for liberty is the free expression of ourselves. I don't care for production" (it was obvious); "I care for my soul; I had rather be free than possess millions. What are laws? The rules that criminals make for the quiet acceptance of slavery. Every law is an enemy of the spirit. Only when we have broken all commandments, and violated all prohibitions, shall we become men."

A pale but dark and sombre Jewess took up the argument timidly.

"If we answer murder with murder," she said, so softly that we could barely hear her, "there will be murder without end, until the most cunning and cruel brutes will be the only men left on earth. I became an anarchist because I thought it meant that all force used by one man against another is immoral. The more force a society uses on its members or its rivals, the less civilized it is. Anarchism means to me that we can get more peace without armies than with them, and more honor by trusting one another than by binding ourselves with laws. How could we do without laws or police if we were not resolved never to raise our hands in violence?"

"You can't apply the perfect law in the imperfect state," said Bremer, rising noisily from his chair.

"Then," said the girl quietly, "the perfect state will never come. We become what we do; and if we kill we'll be brutes like the rest. Only when we are brave enough to live without violence even in the midst of violence will we deserve a better life. Some one must begin."

"What's the difference between that and old-fashioned Christianity?" asked Bremer over his shoulder as he moved from the room.

"I don't know," said the girl simply.

For days the words of this little woman rang in my memory like receding bells. I was disconcerted to find so many resemblances between my old faith and this strange and disreputable philosophy. I developed a new tolerance for anarchism, and began to read its literature with sympathy. I was surprised to learn how old the theory was, and how persistently it had survived twenty centuries of political change and speculation. I was attracted above all by its educational ideal. Doubtless the adults of our own generation were too violent and insensitive a lot to get along without policemen and magistrates and jails; but why should we not take the virgin soil of childhood and sow in it the love of liberty? And then would it not be a delight to see children freed from the hundred compulsions of class-room discipline? Too long the underpaid and overworked teacher had solaced himself with the practice of absolute monarchy; democracy had shaken every citadel but that. What if the best school, like the best government, was that which governed least? To be a guide, philosopher and friend, and never a disciplinarian; to be a comrade and fellow-student rather than a teacher; to let children grow up freely without artificial pedantry or unnatural constraints: surely that would be a delight to the soul, and perhaps an illuminating test? We would try education by happiness.

So you picture me—now a slightly saddened and meditative but still vigorous boy of twenty-six—en-

196

tering the portals of Freedom's school on a cold January morning. Twelve children were frolicking about with noise joyfully unconstrained. I fell in with their games, turned the play slyly into an arithmetical rivalry, and suddenly captured them with the exciting story of Columbus' voyage from Palos to America. They gathered about me hungrily; some sat on chairs, some on the table; some stood beside me, competing for the privilege of putting their arms around my neck. At this lucky juncture Viola Bridge appeared, and her poetic soul burst into sunshine as she saw how well we were getting along.

When twelve o'clock came we explored our lunch-baskets, and had a merry meal together. The children were not easily persuaded that in this world of freedom they must clean away their crumbs; but they did their best, and accepted my suggestion that those who had an abundance of food should share with those who had too little; though even a theorist like myself could see that nature had not fortified them with any instinct for such communistic generosity. Then we galloped out to the park at Fifteenth Street and Second Avenue, posed for a perambulating camera, tumbled about on the grass, and had a lesson or two in between. They never had enough of my stories of great men; when one was finished they clamored for another. "Tell us more, Jack, more," they pleaded. Astounded passers-by wondered what manner of man this was who, hatless and coatless, tumbled about with a dozen children a-top of him,

197

and then suddenly subsided into science or history. Occasionally those who came to scoff remained to listen to these tales. Parents too would join us when they could; simple, timid mothers who had had little time for education amid the poverty and oppression of their native lands. What happy hours we had together, we big and little children, on those sunny afternoons!

There were many virtues in our libertarian theory; but there were some difficulties too. One little girl insisted on skipping rope noisily while I expounded the evolution of man; and when we suggested that she go to another room for her exercise she could not see the necessity. I thought to solve the problem by taking the class into the yard; but the pretty miscreant followed us, and jumped about more bacchantically than before. I tried the direst threats: we would none of us speak to her for a long, long time; we would let her poet-father know how inconsiderate she was; we would not let her come to our Freedom School any more. The dance went on. Finally I took her by the arm and escorted her into the street. She resisted, and protested that this was a libertarian school, where the pupils were never to be subjected to compulsion. Out she went nevertheless; and something of our educational theory went with her.

But for the most part our experiment fared reasonably well. The parents came for conferences with me, and I gave them scholarly disquisitions on the needlessness of spanking. They promised they would try to dispense with it, but begged me, meanwhile, to instil into their childrens' savage breasts some respect for a parental authority shorn of its supporting rod. The young students made good progress for a while under my easy-going rule. Some of them had known the rigors of public-school discipline, and romped through the hours inexhaustibly now, fearful that at any moment this incredible freedom would come realistically to an end. They did not call me "teacher," for that word reeked of prim authority and indigestible erudition; they called me "Jack," and looked upon me as a big brother who knew incomparable stories. When we parted at three they clung to my coat-tails till I had to shake them off and take to my heels. Many of them gave me their affection with a trustful abandon which made their parents jealous. All in all that first half-year was a bright rosary of happy days. I shall never forget them, nor those natural little anarchists, my pupils. Time and tide have borne us far apart, each from all the rest; yet in my memory very often we meet again. They are young men and women now, and would not know me if they met me on the street; but I hope there is some little place still left in their memories for their brother "Jack."

CHAPTER III

I AM BLOWN UP

It takes my breath away even now when I think of
that precipitate passage, within a few months, from
the quiet conservatism of a Catholic seminary to the
turbulent radicalism of the most reckless organization in America. I had not accepted anarchism; but
I was passionately interested in its theories and its
hopes, and I admired without restraint the moral
heroism of its leaders. I wondered whether these
strange men and women might not also have their
share in wisdom and their function in society. Our
industrial development was multiplying coercions
and destroying the traditional independence and in-
dividuality of the American character; our political
development was littering its path with a hundred
thousand laws. Democracy, incompetent and corrupt, had become a tremendous machine for the dis-
couragement of personality, the disfranchisement of
education, and the nationalization of provincial prohibitions. Never had there been greater need for a
check on the insolence of elected persons, for a guard
over our ancient liberties. Eternal vigilance was the
price of freedom.

Therefore, when my new friends urged a battle for free speech on the peaceful streets of Tarrytown I joined them with all my heart and soul. On this matter, surely, we would all agree,—that we had every right, legal and moral, to denounce the economic and political evils of our time as publicly as we wished. How could America advance if that last weapon of minorities—unhindered criticism—was taken from them? Here in Tarrytown, we thought, was the head of a great industry; we would make his aristocratic village resound with our description of the ugly exploitation which that industry was guilty of in Colorado and a score of distant states. We would bring to his own guarded ears, to the walls and fences that shut him in from the poverty and suffering of the world, the story of what his menials were doing with the slaves he had never seen.

And so we went to Tarrytown: Berkman and Dalton and Carney and Johnson and Greb and I. Greb was a morose and silent Dutchman whose anarchism went back to the days of Johannes Most. Johnson was a Swede, tall and blond and strong as every Swede seems fated to be; he had all the qualities of his people except their geniality, which had gone from him when his younger brother, whom he loved with all the ardor of a bachelor, had been sent to jail for his part in a violent strike. Carney was a handsome and fiery Irishman; he had had much the same experience with Catholicism as myself; our common disillusionment had made us friends, and we lived together now in a lofty room on Lexington Avenue. I was French, Dalton was English, and Berkman was a Russian Jew. To an Anglo-Saxon eye we must have seemed the physical embodiment of the Black International.

We drove to the center of the town, and Carney, our finest orator, spoke for us from the rear of a touring car which a rich radical had dedicated to the "Cause." A crowd, not of workingmen but of clerks and shopkeepers, gathered about us, some curious, some hostile, most of them dully apathetic. Carney described the strike in the Colorado fields, the expulsion of the workers from their homes, their encampment in tents with their impoverished families, the battle with the company's guards, and the promiscuous slaughter of men, women, and children. Then he drew a picture of the vast estate where lived the man who, as we naïvely thought, owned the industry and the fields in which the tragedy had taken place.

"I see him at his table," said Carney, passionately; "he is surrounded with servants, and his table is heaped with luxuries. Everybody about him is silently subservient; nothing is left undone to meet his wants. He eats the assembled delicacies of a thousand fields from every continent. Suddenly, upon the white table-cloth before him a great blotch forms, deep red; and as he looks at it in fear it spreads and spreads. He puts out his hand to find out what it is; he feels something warm falling upon his fingers. He

draws his hand back in fright and looks at it in ter·
ror; it is covered with blood. He stares at the ceiling
and sees a large patch of it dripping red; as he looks
a heavy drop falls upon the cloth. And then another
and another and another. Putt! Putt! Putt! They
come faster; now it is a steady drip; now it becomes a
stream and a torrent of blood. He draws back from
the table in horror; he tries to hide the sight with
his hands, but his hands are bloody too. He turns
around, but blood is dripping everywhere. 'My God!'
he cries, 'what does it mean? What have I done?' But
the blood continues to fall, silently, mercilessly; it
forms in widening pools at his feet; it spatters his
head and face; it soaks through his clothing to the
skin; it covers him. It is the blood of the men and
women and children shot to death by his hired murderers. Their blood is upon his head."

It was the most eloquent bit of vituperation that I
have ever heard; it made me think of Robert Emmet
and Patrick Henry; it was a pity that it could not
go on to its natural close, if only for the honor of
American oratory. But at this logical point of
punctuation a piece of fruit (there were to be disputes about its species) fled through the air and
struck Carney full in the face. He had not seen it
coming, and his mouth was half open with the next
sentence of his impassioned speech. Almost choking,
he spat out as much of the fruit as had gone within,
and wiped away something of the rest with hand and
handkerchief. While Carney gasped for breath his

friend Johnson leaped to his feet and into the fray.

"The brute who did that is a rotten coward," he cried. "Let him stand out from the crowd, and I'll go down and give him a chance to fight like a man."

No one accepted the challenge; but instead, from one corner of the group, came a volley of edibles which overwhelmed our second leader. Most of us were harmlessly bespattered; but Johnson's lip was cut with the pit of a peach, and blood streamed down his chin. The younger ones among us burned to jump out and fight; but Dalton urged us to be patient.

"If anyone is seriously hurt here," he said, "we shall be blamed, and not those who provoke us. Perhaps there are Americans enough in this crowd to give us a hearing."

But at that moment a voice contradicted him.

"Down with the dirty anarchists!" it cried.

"Ride them out of the town," suggested another.

"Tar and feather them."

"Hang them."

Johnson leaned out from the car and spoke again, biting out each word with bitter emphasis.

"Very well. You don't believe in the right of free speech. You refuse to let us make our protest against industrial feudalism and tyranny. But there are other ways than words to make ourselves heard. You've had your choice."

At that moment a patrol-wagon clanged and clattered alongside us, and disgorged a squad of policemen. They were led by an enormous officer, puffing

with patriotic authority, and longitudinally orna-
mented with brass buttons that looked like super-
numerary glands. He mounted our car and took
Johnson roughly by the arm.

"You're under arrest," he said. And then, survey-
ing us magnificently:

"You're all under arrest," he announced.

I had been excommunicated, but never arrested;
this was a novel experience for me. We were escorted
unceremoniously into the patrol-wagon, and our ride
to the station began to the accompaniment of jeers
from the crowd. Those who sympathized with us
maintained a dignified silence. As we rode along
Carney cleaned his face and clothing, Johnson wiped
the blood from his lip, and I prepared a speech for
the court.

But the sergeant whom we faced at the police-
station had no literary taste, and would listen to no
speeches. He scowled at us over his spectacles, asked
us questions with the rigidity and invariability of
a mechanism, took the bail which our rich friend sent
up for us, and ordered us to appear for trial the
following Monday morning. We marched back to our
car without enthusiasm, and drove towards New
York debating methods of revenge.

That Saturday evening I stayed late at the Center,
and did not reach home till midnight. Carney was already in bed; and thinking he was asleep I undressed
without turning on the light. But when I was lying

still beside him, in the darkness of our little room, he startled me by saying, quietly:

"Jack, I want to tell you something."

I was all attention.

"What is it, Will?"

He hesitated strangely.

"Do you believe in anarchism?"

"Yes and no. But I thought you were going to tell me something."

He was silent. Then——

"I won't see you after to-morrow. I'm leaving town."

This had the air of a prelude.

"What's up, Will?" I asked. "Trust me; I'll stick by you to the end."

He laid an arm across my body affectionately.

"Jack, I'll trust you. We're going to blow up John D.'s palace to-morrow."

My heart stopped. I had heard so much talk of violence that I had never taken it seriously; I had supposed it was a theory, and would never come to deeds.

"Good God!" I whispered, "who put you up to this? I know: it was Johnson. Tell me."

"Johnson, Greb and I have sworn to do it. We don't want to kill anybody; but if we do, it's their fault. If we can't tell the old man what we think of him we'll put him where he won't care."

He laughed the pleasureless laugh of an embittered man.

206

"Which is better," he asked,—"to be a live pauper or a dead millionaire? Perhaps I shall soon be a dead pauper."

He had been out of work for some time, and had long since reached his last dollar.

"You're going too fast," I said. "You don't really want to do this. You'll be caught, and they'll give you a life-time in jail."

"Well, I'll have regular meals," he answered.

"But this man you're going to kill may know less about the Colorado affair than we do. He's an old man; he doesn't play any active part in the industry any more. It is possible he had nothing to do with our affair in Tarrytown. Perhaps he was a thousand miles away."

Carney could not realize the actual truth of this conjecture. He sat up and looked at me angrily. A ray from the moon came through our solitary window and set off his silhouette against the dim light. His red hair disheveled, his body naked to the waist, he might have represented either a devil or a ghost.

"Look here, Jack," he said, "you never did believe in anarchism, did you?"

"If you mean trying to live without bossing people, I'll go as far as you like with you. If you mean killing people, I think it's insanity."

"Don't they kill us?" he growled. "Do you want us to stand for all their damned murder and robbery without lifting a hand?"

"We have to educate them," I said, lamely. "It's

slow work, but it gets results sooner than killing."

"You're rotten with books," he replied. "You think too much. We're tired of thinking and talking and reading and educating. One bomb will educate faster than a hundred schools."

For a while we were silent. He lay down again, and turned his back to me.

"Suppose you kill them all," I argued, "all the exploiters. Don't you know that new exploiters would come up out of the exploited? Isn't that what has happened everywhere in the clothing industry? What's the use of merely changing masters, unless we can change the minds of people so that they won't care to exploit when they get a chance?"

"Rot," he said, wearily. "Even if you were right, I'd go on with this job just the same. I'll have revenge."

I talked on, accumulating arguments; but when I paused for a reply I discovered from his regular breathing that he had fallen asleep. I lay awake beside him all the night through, facing the problems of social strife as I had never realized them before, and wondering how I could save the life of an enemy whom I had never seen, without endangering the freedom of my friends.

At eight o'clock the next morning some one knocked softly at the door. Carney must have been half conscious, for he jumped up at once and admitted Johnson and Greb. Johnson carried a black suit-case, whose very color seemed ominous to me. He

208

laid it on the floor side downwards, and then looked at me dubiously as from the bed I gave him greeting.

"Is Lemaire coming with us?" he asked of Carney.

"No. He thinks we're crazy."

Johnson scowled.

"Did you tell him?" he asked.

"Yes," said Carney.

"You're a fool," said Johnson.

Carney sat on the bed, quite naked, and brushed his hair sleepily from his eyes.

"Maybe I am," he muttered. "Maybe we all are."

"What do you mean?" Johnson demanded.

Carney made no answer, and did not move. Greb took out his watch, and remarked on the need of haste if they were to make the train to Tarrytown. I still lay in bed, wondering what to do.

"Johnson," I pleaded, "don't go."

He looked at me scornfully.

"Pussyfooter," he said. "You stay where you are, and keep your mouth tight. If the police hear of this we'll know who told them; and we'll get you if it takes a life-time. Remember."

"I'll remember. And you haven't anything to fear so far as that goes. But for your own sake, for the sake of the whole movement to which we belong, don't do this. You'll put things back half a generation."

He ignored me, and turned to Carney.

"Are you quitting too?" he asked, towering over him.

Carney looked up at him wearily.

209

"Sit down, Johnson," he said; "let's think a little."

"Think?" Johnson cried,—"what for? The time for thinking is past. I'm through with thinking."

"Yes," said Carney. "But I'm beginning."

"So you're afraid."

"I don't know. I'm not afraid of death, I'm afraid to kill."

"You lie. You're just trying to cover up your cowardice. Why didn't you quit at the beginning? It's too late now; you'll have to go through with it."

He went over to the suit-case, unlocked and opened it, and took out a bundle of rags which he laid upon our little table. From the rags he drew a black box half a foot square. I could see no fuse, but I knew it was a bomb, and I breathed faster. Johnson held the bomb in his hands and laughed the same dry laugh which had struck me in Carney the night before.

"Here," he said, "is the present we have for the old man in Tarrytown. Ladies and gentlemen, let me introduce you to his majesty, Death. With this little black box you solve all your problems. You never have to pay the landlord again, you never have to drag your weary body to the shop again, you find a way of making your wife love you once more. With this you escape the next war, and the hell they call peace. Who will have it?"

Greb lost something of his taciturnity.

"For God's sake, put that down," he begged.

Carney was not afraid.

"Let's see it," he said, quietly.

He went over, and took it carelessly out of John-son's hands.

"If you drop it," said Greb, "we'll be smashed to a thousand pieces."

"Yes," said Carney, meditatively.

He went over to the window, and examined the bomb. I was more alarmed by his unnatural calm than I would have been by his normal vivacity and passion. I watched him intently, and only vaguely saw, across the court, an old woman hanging clothes upon the line. Through the open window the voices of children playing reached us. Strange thoughts came to me. "I shall die in a moment," I said to myself. "I shall never have a home, or a child."

"Get away from the window," said Greb to Car-ney, "and put your clothes on."

Carney surveyed his own nudity, and laughed.

"Isn't it funny?" he commented, leisurely. "We come into the world naked, and we go out of it naked. I was born naked, and now——"

He raised the bomb over his head, and threw it with all his might upon the floor.

They tell me that they came upon me as I lay unconscious, blackened and burned and bruised, upon a shattered bed. The upper floors of the house we had lived in were a chaos of débris; nothing was left of our room except the twisted iron bed, the broken spring, and the torn mattress. Apparently the bed had been raised aloft and had fallen amid the ruins while I lay on it; or perhaps I had fallen back upon it after a flight into the air. It is incredible, and I should be the first to ridicule such a story. But there in that bed I was found, without covering of any kind; the sheets were gone, and I was clothed only with dirt and blood.

In the hospital the police gathered about, and questioned me; but I looked at them stupidly and would not answer. Their promises and threats seemed trivial things to me: what could jail or freedom mean to a man who was nearly dead? I did not care about anything; I was too weak even to fear death. For days I lay listlessly upon that clean bed; a week passed before my strength began to return, and I cared to talk about the affairs of life again.

Friends came, and told me that Carney, Johnson and Greb were dead. Their bodies had been found in the ruins, and surrendered to their relatives. Among the débris, in a tattered coat, the police had discovered a letter from Carney to his mother, in which the outlines of the great plot were revealed. It was that letter which persuaded the police of my harmlessness, and forestalled my graduation from hospital to jail. The bodies of the three men were cremated, and the ashes were placed in a pretty urn designed by an anarchist sculptor. The members of the Freedom Association held ceremonies in honor of these new martyrs, as they conceived them, to the cause of liberty.

I thought it a little foolish, but I could not long

protest; my heart went out to these simple souls who fled from poverty and injustice into ideal and perfect realms, and covered with passionate poetry the harsh realities of life. I came now to feel toward anarchism very much as I felt toward Catholicism: I could give it respect and sympathy even though I withheld belief. But I bore from that moment a new sadness in my heart as I realized that I was fated, bit by bit and day by day, to lose my Utopian aspirations as I had lost, in younger days, my hope of immortality and heaven. This double bereavement—of faith in a redeeming happiness beyond the grave, and then of belief in a paradise for our posterity on the earth—was to be part of my inevitable destiny, as it was part of the destiny of my generation. We were caught in the chaos of transition, and would have to live through it as best we could, until a new order and a new stability of soul would come to give our children's children peace.

CHAPTER IV

I ESCAPE MARRIAGE

I HAD been but a week out of the hospital when a letter came which lifted me to happiness. It was from Henry Alden, and was postmarked "Vienna." Alden was a great traveller, and almost every summer saw him wandering in Europe or Asia. I have lost his letter; but I remember the heart of it well. "I am glad to hear," he wrote, "that you are making good progress at the school. There is only one thing you need now to complete your education; and that is travel. Would you care to join me in a tour of Europe? Of course I will pay all the expenses."

Would I care? I filled with laughter the quiet room to which I had retired after my adventure with dynamite, and rang half a dozen telephones to announce my good fortune to the world. I wrote to Alden telling him that this was a boon I had done nothing to deserve, and that it was ungrateful of me to doubt Providence now. Had I not dreamed for years of the day when, after long stinting and saving, I might sail off to see England and France and Spain and Italy and Germany, and perhaps even Greece; dreamed how I might at last murmur a prayer in the Acropolis like Renan, and worship in the Sistine Chapel like the pagan Goethe, and bask like Nietzsche in the sunshine of St. Mark's? I could scarcely believe that I was about to see those sacred monuments of man's creative passion; not till I stood in the flesh before them would I know that this vision was something more than the mirage of my youthful fantasy.

The days passed anxiously for me after that letter was despatched. I calculated again and again the time it would take to reach Alden, how far it had gone now, and whether he would reply by letter or by cable. Meanwhile, nervously resolute, I carried on my work at the School until my summer vacation began. Eleven days went by, each more feverish than the day before. Then a messenger stood at my door with a cablegram:

"Meet me at the Hotel Europe, St. Petersburg, July 10–12.—Alden."

"Good God!" I cried; "Alden writes as if he were asking me to meet him around the corner. St. Petersburg—it's half way across the world. Can I make it by July 12th?"

Within half an hour I was at a steamship agent's office. The *Mauretania* was sailing on July 1; there was still time to make reservations and get a passport. I rushed back to my room; and though I had five days left me before sailing, I began to pack at once.

On the eve of my departure I went to Arlington. I had not seen my parents for half a year; and they had uttered no word of reconciliation. Brother Ben had kept me informed: my mother, after three weeks of illness, had resumed her routine of household cares, and never mentioned me. Yet I could not go to Europe without bidding her good-bye. I exaggerated the risks of an ocean voyage, not knowing that the dangers were chiefly internal; I thought, dramatically, that this might be the last farewell of all. But would my mother receive me? I held my breath as I rang the bell at the door of my old familiar home.

There was no answer. I rang again, and again there was no answer. I felt myself caught in an anticlimax: I had prepared the most touching speeches, and could not bear the thought that they might never be uttered. I walked alongside the house to the rear, and there, at the farther end of the yard, I saw my mother working among the flowers. She turned white as she recognized me.

"John," she said, almost inaudibly.

She came over to me silently, and embraced me. I had feared that my visit would give her new hopes of my return to the faith, and new pangs of hope deceived; but she saw at once that I had not come for that; and her face quieted into a melancholy resignation.

"I'm going to Europe," I said. "I'll be back in three months. I just wanted to say good-bye."

"Europe?"

She could hardly understand. I explained Alden's generosity; and I could see it pleased her to learn that any one should think enough of her wayward son to extend him such bounty.

"It's dangerous to cross the ocean," she said. "I'll pray God to take care of you and bring you back safe. And you, John, pray God to bring you back to your holy religion."

Poor mother! What did it matter which religion we professed, or which philosophy we believed, any more than which language we spoke or what clothes we wore? The chromosomes had more to do with us than these external and accidental things. What really mattered was that you were the tenderest of mothers, and that I, having none of your faith, could love you and honor you more than this pen can ever say.

A week afterward I was in mid-Atlantic. No later experience on my trip meant as much to me as those five days of uninterrupted sea. I tired at last of looking at it, but not till I had studied a score of its endless forms: the chaste light of the chill morn turning the dark deep into white-capped vales of green; the blazing glory of the noon-day burning a pathway from the horizon to the ship; the changing rainbows of the setting sun reflecting their kaleidoscope in the sea; the new moon silvering the waters with her rays; the waves mounting gigantically to smash in fury against our iron sides, then calming themselves into the smooth billows of some inland lake; and most fascinating of all, the wake of our great vessel, the churned white froth that danced and laughed behind us, in a narrowing path, mile after mile, till we lost its ending in the sky. No wonder the proud poet had bowed in awe before this turbulent immensity, whose helpless passion outdid his own; surely there was nothing in the world so impressive as this infinite and sombre sea.

Tossed up and down in the hollow of the ocean, our giant liner seemed but a bit of unguided wreckage, and we humans who blackened its decks were microscopic animalcules creeping blindly on a floating spar. Sometimes when the prow of our vessel sank down into some abyss between the waves I thought we should never rise again; and when the hills of foaming water gathered and hurled themselves upon us I wondered would they not topple us over into a choking death. One night there was no moon, nor any star; then our great ship, ghastly alight in the engulfing dark, seemed like a phosphorescent insect struggling in the sea. But as we neared the rocks of Britain's ancient shore the mood of my thinking changed, and I marveled not at the vastness of the ocean but at the courage of man, who had ribbed it everywhere with the paths of his floating cities; who had dared to make great arks of heavy iron and fill them with thousands of tons of the products of human hands; who had built upon these frames luxurious homes for many hundred men; who had made engines capable, through the expansion of a little steam, of propelling this enormity of steel and flesh safely and quickly across the widest seas, making the rage of the ocean impotent. It was man that was marvelous, I said, as I stood secure and relieved on the solid soil of England.

I passed through London with but an hour's stop, and found myself at Dover, again upon the waves. It was raining; but the water was calm, and I reached the Continent still unacquainted with the power of the sea upon the digestive tract and the semi-circular canals. I slept fitfully as we crossed the fated soil where once Neanderthal men had waged their savage wars, and where, so soon, German and French millions were to kill one another with all the improvements of civilization. The next afternoon I was in Berlin, experiencing the orderliness and cleanliness of a Prussian city, and the proud clatter of Prussian military feet. I climbed up to bed in a "wagon" at the Friedrichstrasse station, and took care not to awake as we passed through Königsberg; perhaps old Kant was still promenading there, and might insist on beginning the argument all over again. The next morning I was in Petersburg, picking my way through a thousand heavy-laden people, and besieged by *isvost-chiks* who, in the middle of summer, were surrounded with innumerable coats, and topped with enormous hats which must have been stolen from some imperial hussars. I tried three cabbies before I found one who could translate my "Hotel Europe" into the proper combination of Russian sibilants. I held on breathlessly to my seat as we bounced over the barbarian cobblestones of Peter's city, and then suddenly I was deposited at my hotel. I suspected that the driver cheated me in the fare he charged, but I bore it patiently, anxious to begin my wooing of Europe under the auspices of peace. The English conversation that came to my ears as I passed through the lobby made a strange concourse of sweet sounds; I had never known the language was so lovely. And I was delighted to find that the clerk at the desk knew nineteen tongues, including mine. But I was shocked at his reply to my inquiry for Henry Alden.

"There is not any Alden here," he said.

I almost lost consciousness. I had a vague sense of the ridiculous calamity that would encompass me if I failed to find my friend. So much of my money had been consumed *en route* from New York that now, in this distant country, where I was so helpless and useless, I should be reduced to my last rouble unless Alden appeared. I pictured myself walking, like Napoleon's army, across the wastes of Russia through western Europe to France, and then shoveling my way to America as a stoker. I begged the clerk to see if there was any message addressed to me. He assured me there was none.

But then another clerk came up.

"What did you say?" he asked. "I think we have a message for you." He thumbed a hundred envelopes while I suffered. "Ah, yes," he said; and I lived again.

"Dear John," the message read; "we found the Europe crowded, and had to go to the Imperial. Take a cab and come over. We are awaiting you.—Alden."

And then more lifting of luggage, another *drozhky*, more cobbles, and at last my hands were held by the man who had cabled me from four thousand miles away to come and see the world. He was buoyant as a lad of twenty despite his gray hairs and his fifty years; his face was ruddy with health, his eyes were alert and sparkling.

"John," he said, "this is my dear friend Dan Newton. And this is Alexis, who is going to guide us through his country."

I liked Dan at once—strong son of a New York farmer, as cool and quiet as an Englishman, and yet the most genial companion in the world. Alexis— alas, Alexis and I did not get along well, and I must say nothing about him. No doubt it was my fault at least as much as his; as a lover of the philosophers I should have known how to meet all men peacefully. I send him my greetings and my apologies; and I trust that even in the present chaos of his native land he has found some happy port.

This is the story of one mind, and not the description of a continent. I must not stop to tell of Petersburg, nor of Moscow, nor of Nijni Novgorod, nor of Kiev, nor of the many other cities that we saw. After a week in the capital we took a fast express to Moscow; it went over twenty miles an hour, and stopped less than thirty minutes at each of a dozen stations on the way. It carried no dining-car, and waited contentedly three times a day while we ate our meals in

the depot restaurants. There is so much more time in
Russia than in America. Moscow was picturesquely
Asiatic, with its vari-colored buildings and costumes,
its mixture of many peoples from many "governments," and its onion-towered churches with their
ever-ringing bells and their incomparable choirs.
When we left Moscow for Nijni I bought a return
ticket in order to come back overnight to hear the
Sunday singing at St. Basil's.

I had not calculated on the fact that there were
girls in Russia. At Nijni Dan and Alexis and I became conscious of them as we walked along the banks
of the Volga. We begged Alexis to translate our
compliments to the ladies whom we passed, but he refused; Russian morals, he assured us, would not permit such familiarities. Dan and I, having our doubts
on this question of sociology, took the matter into
our own hands, and spoke to the next fair couple in
the international dialect of smiles. The smiles were
understood, and in a moment we were walking together in the park. Alexis did not admire the way in
which Dan engrossed the attentions of one girl, and
I the other's, and would not act as the interpreter of
our love. However, mere words were superfluous. We
spoke with eyes and hands and arms, and soon
mounted to perilous heights of tactile endearment.
Suddenly Alexis broke in upon my happiness.

"Your train for Moscow leaves in an hour. It will
take you all that time to get to the station."

Villain!—how can I ever forgive this untimely

presence of mind? And how shall I forget the ready
way in which my Beatrice, as I moved away still
dazed with the ecstasy of love, allowed Alexis to take
my place around her waist and upon her lips? Was
there any morality in that?—And yet it was wonderful singing that rewarded me when I reached St.
Basil's; never shall I hear such bassos again.

A few days later we were steaming with Russian
leisureliness down the muddy Volga. I saw the boat-
men at their work, but they did not sing their famous
song for me. Then we were at Kiev, and passed
through a gauntlet of beggars into the great Lavra
monastery, where the bony relics of some medieval
saint oozed sacred blood whenever the kopeks deposited in the basket before him were sufficient to inspire his ooze.

For a week we lived with moujiks at a little village
in the province at Chernigov. Simple, kindly, harassed, timid, greedy people; so poor that their absorbing thought was of the gifts that Alden might
leave them; so oppressed that for days they feared
we had come to steal their children; and yet so hospitable that for a week our peasant host put us up
on such extra boards as he could find, and regaled us
with bread and lard. It amazed me to see how these
men and women could become hardy and vigorous
on a diet inferior to that of an American dog, and
how they managed to find some measure of happiness
in the midst of poverty and fear. I thrilled with patriotic comparisons when I learned that every year

their youths were taken away, sometimes by force, for distant and dangerous service in the army.

The young people of the place gathered at the house where we were guests, and danced their wild and heavy steps for us; the men stamped the ground with their boots, and whirled the girls madly through the air. An old poet, as blind as Homer and with as good a memory, sat against a tree, and to the monotonous accompaniment of his balalaika narrated in sad chant the legends of his people. Alden rewarded them lavishly, and they departed singing their plaintive songs.

In the evening my friends strolled off to a wedding party, while I, who preferred sleep to such unreasonable jollity, stayed behind. All of our host's family went except the daughter, a buxom girl who had posed for her picture with my arm around her waist. My bed was a bench in a little cabin some distance from the *isba*. One blanket served to wrap me in from the hard board beneath and the elements around. I tried forty positions, but I could find none which had the *virtus dormitiva*.

About eleven o'clock the door of my cabin opened, and I saw the substantial figure of the daughter of the house enter timidly, guided by the light of her candle. She wore only a night-gown, through which my sleepy eyes made new researches into the ancient male problem of the female form divine. I was surprised into an unwonted silence. I wondered why this visit, at this time, in this dress. She spoke some tender words in Russian, and then, seeing that I was stupid, resorted to a smile. I thought for a moment that she had come to inquire whether I needed any further covering. I did, but I had no words to say so. Suddenly she turned and walked quickly back to the house, leaving my door open. At last it dawned upon me that the poor girl was suffering from innocuous desuetude, and was disgusted with my inability to prescribe for her. The abominable sociology of Alexis had misguided me. Unseen, I went to the door and caught a look at her angry candle-lit face as she entered the house. I returned to my board a little lonelier than before.

A few minutes later Alexis, with whom I had quarreled bitterly that day, came in and lit the lamp. As I tried position forty-one I comforted myself with the thought that I had had a narrow escape from becoming a Russian moujik.

CHAPTER V

I DISCOVER AMERICA

ASIDE from, and in addition to, this incident, those were revealing days for me in Russia. My marveling mind was pried open ruthlessly, and forced to broaden itself, by the sights we saw as we traveled down to the Crimea. Only in the chaotic melting-pot of New York had I come upon so great a variety of peoples, so many sorts and conditions and strata of men. It was good to see unique and picturesque cities like Moscow and Kiev, vigorous new types like the moujik and the Cossack, Byzantine and Asiatic enormities of architecture, and the startling *bizarreries* of Russian faith. But my general impression was of a vast country moving slowly out of poverty, ignorance, and filth. Here the Middle Ages were still darkening the minds of men, still holding them in abject superstition and autocratic rule, still stopping that development of education which would be necessary before Russia could develop her immense resources and become one of the civilized nations of the world. Who would cleanse these stables, and clear the air, and open the roads to growth?

Of course I had no right to see Russia so darkly. I had come as an ordinary tourist, and had seen only the exterior of the land. I had had no access to great scientists like Pavlow or Bechterev, nor to great composers like Rimsky-Korsakov or Stravinsky, nor to great writers like Gorki, Andreëv, or Artzibashev. I know now that out of that backward country, whose inhabitants seemed never to have had a bath, there had come the finest literature of the last half-century; that in fiction and prose drama these barbarians had given to the world the greatest work ever done in those literary forms. I did not have eyes enough to see, behind the apathy of 1912, the furious energy and miraculous devotion of 1917.

At Sebastopol Alden engaged a three-horse *drozhky*, and with this lively *troika* we galloped from one end of the Crimea to the other, past the palaces of the Czar and the playground of Tolstoi to the Newport of the Russians, Ialta. I became accustomed to butterless meals, and *tschav*, and *borscht*, and *pirozhkin*, and the ubiquitous samovar. I learned that every diet is a prejudice, and that the small intestine will make humanity out of anything reasonably resembling food.

At the same time Alden learned the arts of bribery. We steamed back to Odessa, and wished to take the first boat thence to Constantinople. That vessel, however, was leaving the next morning, and Russian law required that the police should have our passports three days before we could be permitted to

depart from the country. It cost Alden a pretty sum
to abrogate that law; but then, no doubt, the law
had been made for such occasions, and such purposes.

I did not see much of the unfortunate people who
have to call themselves Constantinopolitans. All
that I remember of them is the patience of their
shoulders (which served them as horses and trucks),
and the indecent spaciousness of their pants. I
hardly dared look at those fierce Turks, and I wondered whether they had stopped beating their wives
yet. You see that I was an unimaginatively provincial person, incapable of leaving my environment at
home, and secretly wishing that all the world were
like the familiar faces and places of my youth. I
growled at the people of Smyrna, and wished they
would make more use of the water which nature had
so lavishly offered them; and I vowed I would never
eat figs again if they came from this filthy port.
But in Athens everything pleased me except the heat.

Even Pericles would have been glad to have so
fair a capital,—the cleanest and most orderly city
I had seen since passing the customs' gauntlet at
Wirballen. I went in swimming at the Piraeus, because I had heard that Socrates had bathed there
some years before,—though this item of information
was quite out of keeping with all else that I had
learned of the habits of that famous idler. But there
were more rocks than gad-flies in that sea, and I
came away with a bad cut which I still display as

an evidence of my philosophic lineage. I had my picture taken in the prison of Socrates (so our guide called it, but the villain had no reputation for archeological veracity) ; and I reflected how sweet it would be to take the gentle anesthesia of hemlock as a martyr to metaphysics, at the age of seventy-one. And then I stood in the Theatre of Dionysus, marveled at the vast mountain-side of stone and marble seats rising in a semicircle before me, and imagined that I saw Antigone leading blind Œdipus to Colonus, and Hector bidding farewell to Astyanax and Andromache. For a moment that ancient and youthful civilization came back to me with the reality of things seen rather than of things read: I saw Æschylus writing his warlike epitaph, forgetful of his tragedies; and Pericles sitting at the feet of the learned and yet lovely Aspasia; and Socrates inviting his executioners to support him at the public expense; and Aristotle teaching Alexander to die of drink at the age of thirty-three. They had no sanitary plumbing then, and no electric lights, and no motor-cars; but they had *parrhasia*—that brave liberty of mind and speech which is more precious to the world than all its engines and all its laws.

At Athens Alden and Dan, having seen Western Europe many times before, deserted me, and alone I took the train for Patras. Riding through a paradise of vineyards I munched for half an hour luscious and seedless grapes larger and sweeter than any that had ever entered me before. And then the boat to Brindisi, and lo, I was in the fairest land of all.

Others have raved about Italy, and does it follow that I should not? But long since I have upheld it as the greatest of all the nations of Europe. Greece had her incomparable epoch; but it passed like the flush of love. Italy never quite reached the exhilarating heights of the Periclean age; and yet for two thousand years she showered genius upon the world. From Numa and his laws, and Ennius and his verses, and Cæsar and Cicero, and Lucretius and Virgil, and Horace and Ovid, and Trajan and Hadrian, and Antoninus and Aurelius, and Julian and Justinian, and Leo and Gregory, and Dante and Petrarch, and Giotto and Donatello, and Leonardo and Raphael, and Michelangelo and Cellini, and Correggio and Titian, and Machiavelli and Bruno, and Tasso and Ariosto, and Galileo and Palestrina, down to the weary wisdom of Leopardi's verse and the weary music of d'Annunzio's prose,—tell me, all ye Muses of history, was there ever elsewhere such a dynasty? Has any other nation held in its loins the seminal virtue and fruitfulness of this passionate and inexhaustible people? Look into their eyes, and you see the burning sun mirrored in twin lakes; look at their carriage and you see royal Cæsar; feel the hot lava of their volcanic speech and you know the ambitions of the Borgias and the passions of the *Inferno.* Alfieri was right: the man-plant grows

230

stronger in Italy than anywhere else on this planet Earth. Oh, when shall we see Italy again?

I passed over the Apennines and through Sorrento, and put up for a time at Naples. I liked the people more than their cities; I hated the dirt and stench of Naples, but I envied these handsome and terrible men their beautiful and terrible women. One of these—not the least beautiful, and not the least terrible—allured me with her great black eyes and her voluptuously rounded figure as she passed me on the street at night; I followed her for half a mile as if a chain had bound me to her, until at last she disappeared into a pretentious dwelling. I remained for a long time outside, wistfully looking up at the closed door, fretfully wondering why I might not enter and tell her how beautiful she was, and consumed as I had never been before with the hunger of flesh and blood.

When I trace in memory the incidents of those happy days I mourn to think how much escaped me, and how little I carried away with me from Italy. I passed through the ruins of Rome, sad embers of a flame that burns now on other hills (or is it destined to light those hills again?), and through the streets and galleries of Florence, where beauty is lavished upon one as it might be in paradise; and always my insane ambition was to see as much as possible in the shortest time. I left myself no leisure to study these immortal things; I came to them without background or context beyond a name and a date

231

or two; I was all eyes and no brains; and too late
I found that eyes without brains cannot see. I forgot the sights of yesterday as soon as I saw to-
day's. Though I was twenty-six I was not yet prepared for travel; I was too immature to know what
beauties to seek, and too uninformed to understand
those that I found. Life will be merciful to me, perhaps, and will let me see again that bright fairy-
land of genius. Then I shall look at less, and see a
little more.

For Venice I needed less instruction; St. Mark's
would open any eyes, and the music of those omnipresent waters would stir responsive harmonies in
any breast. How picturesque the gondolas were; and
how I liked to sit in them for hours, and talk in my
pitiful Italian with those philosophic gondoliers!
On every side majestic edifices challenging mortality,
graceful bridges throwing friendly arms over mean-
dering canals, sombre cathedrals whose beauty bore
the memory of a thousand patient hands, and whose
cool naves, large enough to hold a city, felt only
the step of aged women and irreverent travelers. In
the Piazza San Marco, where Nietzsche loved to sit
and write, till the sunlight hurt his eyes, I wondered
how the great iconoclast could have been so bitter
against Christianity, here where it had uplifted men
with its legends and inspired them to dream of loveliness. From my little room I could see the flowing
life of the city's peopled streams, and yet hear no
noise but the ripple of the gliding boats and the

voices carried on the water. Byron did well to come here with his Guiccioli, and a thousand geniuses with their Muses and their mistresses. Shall not we too, some sunny day, in the peace of that floating marble, renew our youthful love and write masterpieces for eternity?

I saw Vienna hurriedly, and Frankfort and Mayence; and there I took a steamer down the Rhine. From Cologne I went by train to Brussels, and thence, after a day, to Antwerp. They were all beautiful cities, mellow with recollections, and ruled with such a minimum of incompetence and corruption as would be considered indecently abnormal in America. And then I boarded the boat for England.

I had not known seasickness yet. Now it came to me with such force that the experience should suffice me forever. I believe our little ship pointed her nose at every invisible star on that unlucky night, and distorted herself into every figure known to geometry. It was impossible to stand, or to sit, or to lie in bed; even the sailors moved cautiously along the railings, and stopped at every turn to pay their tribute to the sea. Rolled ruthlessly out of their berths, precipitated ignominiously from their chairs, and cheated at every turn of the solacing liquors with which they would have drowned the memory of Neptune's insolence, the passengers decided that the one safe position was to lie upon the floor, from which there could be no further fall.

I lay prostrate with the rest, indifferent to human affairs. Perhaps it was at that time that I lost so much of what I had absorbed upon my tour. My very vitals seemed to have cut their moorings, and resolved to explore the external world. The thought came to me that our tiny steamer could never weather such a storm; that the next lurch would flood us, and the next one empty us out into the hungry sea. I waited impartially for the event. I had no desire for further existence or experience; the supposedly everlasting instinct of self-preservation was asleep or dead. Nothing in the dark beyond could be any worse than these repeated convulsions that tore the flesh from one's throat, and spewed one's blood upon the floor. The grave would have been a victory now that death had lost its sting.

The little drama continued all the night. As we neared Hull in the morning the water calmed, and those of us who cared to stand found it a possible position. An hour later we sat shivering in an early train for London, drenched and almost blinded with fog, sick and pale and emaciated as if we had passed through a Thirty Years' War. I can always reduce the misfortunes of life to a modest perspective by remembering the tortures of that endless night. The English Channel should be abolished as an enemy of the human race.

How could I love England after that? What traveler could forgive the embarrassment of such an introduction? And yet, as I left my hotel the next

morning to walk to the British Museum, I found
myself muttering: "This, at last, is civilization."
Here were order and quiet and cleanliness, good manners and self-control and a reassuring leisureliness
of motion and speech. These people would not stab
me for differing from them in philosophy; they
would not disfranchise me for loving books, or im-
prison me for passing through political schools and
theories as children pass through colic and the
mumps; they would provide a great park for the
free and open explosion of my oratory, and then
they would go home and sing hymns or drink beer,
confident that the fog would absorb my poison
harmlessly, and the earth would remain solid and
respectable beneath their feet.

I went to Edinburgh and climbed Arthur's seat;
and to Abbotsford and Melrose Abbey and many
places long forgotten by me now. I crossed to Ireland and was almost drowned in the lakes of Killar-
ney. I mounted to the crumbling roof of Blarney
Castle and stood in line waiting to kiss the "Blarney
stone" that was guaranteed to give the "gift of
gab." But as the line was long, and I had the gift
of gab already, I came away with lips untouched,
and left the green fields of Ireland for the crowded
boulevards of Paris.

What a change that was! In Ireland the girls
had had a fresh and natural beauty, and the young
men, though poorly dressed, had shown the flush of
health and an open life upon their cheeks; they were

talkative, those Irishmen, but jolly and friendly, and capable of the finest tenderness. Here in Paris, of course, life was far more brilliant and intellectual, and civilization had reached a subtlety and a sophistication which even the Athens of Alcibiades had never known. But sex seemed to run through all the fibres of this hurried existence; every man seemed to be hunting a woman, and every woman seemed anxious to be taken. And there was talk, infinite simian palaver, circling madly around the lure of love. All the erotic sensitivity of France flowed centripetally into Paris, and all the erotic curiosity of a million tourists gathered in this capital. It was the Cloaca Maxima of the world.

I was as curious as the rest. Before looking at Napoleon's tomb, or promenading through the Louvre, I joined a Cook tour of "Paris by Night," resolved on seeing as much as I could of the gayeties of the town. We went first to "L'Enfer," where we were waited on by a corps of red-velvet devils under the personal supervision of His Satanic Majesty Himself. I found this hell a little tame, having experienced the English Channel. At midnight we were deposited at the "Bal Tabarin," and left to our own resources, moral and financial. I wandered about among the crowded tables, timid and prurient, avidly absorbing this novel atmosphere. My first impression was of feminine shoulders and bosoms emerging in such profuse generosity as I had never seen before. Then it seemed to me that all the drink-

236

ing and smoking in the room were being done by these lively and gorgeous ladies. The men—heavy-cheeked sight-seers from every land but France —looked blandly about them, obviously at a disadvantage with their *hetairai* in the matter of making words. On the floor below, the scenery was wilder: the girls of the ballet, inconspicuously dressed, sat upon knees that had grown fat in Liverpool or Chicago, and murmured the nothings for which men risk their lives. At midnight these step-daughters of joy danced for the edification of the crowd. At one o'clock they paraded through the hall led by an Eve in the garb of Eden, leafless. At four o'clock I was back in my hotel, an older and a wiser man, breathless with accelerated education.

When I sailed for New York in September I had already begun to feel something of that nostalgia which acts within us like the homing instinct of the bird, and draws us back mysteriously to our wonted haunts however far the migratory impulse may have led us into alien lands. The weather was bad, and I missed more meals than I ate. Our ship was slow; we took seven days for the passage, and my hunger for America grew with every hour. As I sighted the Statue of Liberty (which had not yet followed the Liberty Bell of Philadelphia into disablement and decay) I felt the same emotion of happiness and gratitude that warms the heart of every returning traveler. We had been very critical of our country

while we fought, within its gates, the cruel battles
of economic life; we had credited ourselves with all
our successes, and had assigned to institutions the
blame for every failure. We had compared our country not with the other nations of this earth, but with
some perfect state which we had pictured in our
dreams. We had longed for the beauty, the culture,
and the moral freedom of the old world, and had
spoken with a certain scorn of that deceptive female on Bedloe's Island. But the hardiest radicals
among us forgot all this as we passed that massive
monument, noble if only for its aspiration. One good
lady, who belonged to the most advanced heretics of
New York, and had come from a year with her
parents in Russia, wept with joy as our ship cut its
way into the familiar harbor, and Manhattan's gran-
ite mountains rose into our view.

"Oh, I could kiss the ground," she said.

Even the sunshine seemed richer than any that I
had felt since Italy's. Two weeks before, Paris had
shivered with cold, and all England had been armed
with top-coats and umbrellas; half our voyage had
been through a chilling rain. But here how bright
and warm it was! It seemed to me, in the prodigal
enthusiasm of that moment, that America had become the favored child of the sun. I was glad, after
all, that I belonged to this vigorous people, and
that this turbulent and towering city was my home.

I do not know what subtle changes had gone on
in me during those hurried months of my European

tour. In some way a larger perspective had come to me. I saw my country in the light of her youth, and vaguely understood the necessity of her faults, the unavoidable passage of this feverishly growing land through mental immaturity and a chaotic adolescence to the leisurely fulfilment of her unmeasured possibilities. Our commercialism and our vulgarity were historically inevitable things; the ruthless exploiter of soil and brawn was the fated protagonist of the initial scene. All these other countries that I had traversed had passed, or would pass, through like transitional puerilities; once Europe too had been a wilderness, and its people had been artless and soulless brutes. Something of the fire of my young rebelliousness had been cooled by these hundred days; I felt the immensity of time, and sensed the unhurriable pace of evolution. All things would come to us, but they would come slowly, and in their own way. There would be generations of suffering yet, and blind injustice, and coarse corruption; but we would grow out of it; our very disgust with ourselves, our thousand experiments and enthusiasms, were the trial-and-error of our progress, the signs and pains of our growth. Therefore it was good that we should rebel, that our protests should stir uplifting ferment in the soul of our country; it needed every stimulus in its development. Soon we would catch up to Europe; some day we would go beyond it, and top its greatest glories. I could love America a little more, now that I had seen the world.

CHAPTER VI

ARIEL

A MONTH later, love came to me again.

Nature is as persistent as the sex in which we personify her. Many times she had tried to lure me into the tricks of procreation; and here I was, at twenty-seven, still unyoked to the chariot of the race. But her hand lay heavy upon me; I fretted under the unnatural restraints of my solitary life; I looked longingly after every fair face that passed; and I brooded in solitude over the mysteries of love.

Ariel was the oldest of my pupils in the School; and yet young enough to make my passion for her the scandal of a season.

"You know, Jack," she said to me in later days, "I knew you long before you knew me. I was in your audience that night when you spoke on your impressions of Europe. You were just back. I didn't like you; you talked with a queer French accent, and we couldn't hear you well in the rear of the hall. I said to Miriam: 'If that's the teacher, I want to go to another school.' "

But she came to mine just the same, so that I think she deceived me about that original dislike; we can

240

always trust the tongue to conceal the heart. It would be so much more satisfactory to believe that Ariel fell in love with me at first sight! As for me, I do not know if we should call that first-awakened curiosity by the full-bodied name of love; but from the first moment there was something in Ariel that captured my eyes and possessed my memory. I was attracted by her high spirits; she romped and babbled and laughed and sang with the innocence of a girl who had never known theology. In the park she jumped the highest, and ran the fastest, and tired the last or not at all. Vividly I remember still how we would stand alert in our handicap positions on the gravel-paths of Central Park, I on the starting-line and Ariel only a bit ahead of me, and a gay-colored rosary of children strung along the line; and how that wild fairy of a girl would leap like a spirit over the earth and race to victory. That is why we called her Ariel: she was as strong and brave as a boy, and as swift and mischievous as an elf.

In class she found it difficult to be quiet; she was not made for the artifice of study, and her vibrant body was like a string stretched taut and waiting for release. Yet she took the lessons patiently, listened in wide-eyed rapture to the stories I told, and helped me to keep the younger ones in leash. After class she was the last to go. Many times I looked through the window to see her darting across the street to her home, her brown arms swinging, her perfect body singing aloud with health. I called her my "Whitman girl," for surely she personified the *Song of the Body Electric*, and the spirit of the open road, as no other girl that I have ever known.

When Ariel danced into my orbit she was such a contrast to me as might have augured immediate incompatibility. I was all learning, and she was all life; I knew ten thousand books, and she knew only what nature and hardship had taught her,—though these lessons were sounder, perhaps, than any that had been dreamed of in my philosophy. When I heard her story I marveled at the resilience of the human body and soul. She had been born in a Russian ghetto fourteen years before; and many the story she could tell of Mershe Lebe and the other scholars in her family. Her mother had been the belle of that Proskurov village;—I could believe it, seeing her beauty now, and that inexhaustible health and energy which made her the sister of her children. What tragedies they had had! What wars, and famines, and pogroms! What bloody memories of Cossack and Pole invading homes to steal and rape and slay! I could hardly credit those tales,—men would not act so—until I learned how they behaved in the wars and revolutions of our own day. No wonder there was bitterness in the souls of those who had survived these terrors, a lingering fear of neighbors from whose apparently civilized ranks murderers might at any moment step out to tear their children limb from limb before the mothers' eyes.

"We had heard of America," said Ariel, "as a

refuge for the oppressed and the home of liberty. So father and mother resolved to come here. They might never have left home if they had foreseen the suffering they would go through on the way. Father came first, and worked and saved; then mother came with six of us—Morris, Sarah, Harry, Flora, Mary, and me. In London Mary nearly died, and Morris had to play the part of father, running about for doctors and medicines and food. Mother spent then nearly all the money she had saved. We were sick every day of the trip across; they gave us filthy food, and wherever we went the odors of the kitchen suffocated us. When we reached Ellis Island we were all thin, and penniless."

Yes, it was the story of thousands and thousands of eager souls who had bravely cut their old-world roots and taken the adventure of America. Many of them, I knew, had still to find their footing here, and were unhappy; some of them were to be sent back in that wave of cowardice which came upon us after the war; but the great healthy majority of them had risen with miraculous courage out of this prelude of despair; everywhere in America now they were tilling fertile fields, building homes, and sending their merry children to school. And here was Ariel, after all those sufferings, as healthy as mountain air, as happy as love returned, and as bright as the sunlit sea.

One evening I sat alone, in the dark, at the same table at which, that afternoon, I had told the children the story of Spinoza. (I had an absurd passion for telling them the lives of the philosophers.) In an hour or so I was to lecture on "free love." It was unwise of me to take such a theme, and to flay the unfaithfulness and insincerity which hid under that fair phrase, before an audience of men and women who for the most part believed that legal marriage was slavery, and lived in unions sanctioned only by mutual consent. But in those days I cared as little for convention and tradition as any youth; and it was not for respectability's sake that I protested against these fly-like matings on the wing. I was hungry for love, and would have preferred to have it free of all bonds and costs. What I saw as I looked about me, however, was that the men were profiting, and the women losing, by this pleasantly primitive marriage. I was resolved to ride forth, like another Galahad, and defend the still dependent sex against this subterfuge of the irresponsible male.

Then into the dark circle of my brooding came a quick step, a dim figure, and Ariel sat across the table and smiled into my face. As I looked into her eyes I felt myself in the presence of life itself. Here was the primal mystery—that subtle and yet inexplicable power of expansion and growth which had spread in a million forms over the earth. These brown eyes danced and burned as if behind them all the forces of creation surged; this softly-rounded face quivered with sensitivity, this tense body, even when still, trembled with action and desire. Now I

knew that the body and the soul were one. Instinctively I understood that I had come upon a force as
strong and persistent as my own, and that it was
enveloping and absorbing me. Ariel could not know
how the race was speaking through her, through her
slender little hands, the smooth skin of her cheeks,
the fragrance of her hair, the rich color of her lips,
and the alluring lines that drew my furtive eyes
from her soft throat to her breast.

"Miriam sent me," she said gently, "to ask if I
may listen to your lecture to-night."

I knew the lure of prohibitions, and how useless
they would be now. Here, I told myself, was the first
girl I would save.

"Yes, Ariel; though I'm afraid you won't understand."

"I may understand a little," she said, humbly. "I
so want to learn, and grow up, and be a woman."

Poor Ariel! What queer fever of growth was it
that made this happy girl long to pass from her carefree youth to the sufferings of womanhood? What
powerful tide of development was pushing her on
to the brink of death that she might snatch a little
life from nothingness?

Now she stood beside me, trembling, and looking
timidly into my eyes.

"Do you believe in free love?" she asked. Then,
seeing my surprise, she drew away, and stood across
the table from me, sorry that she had been so frank.

"I'm going to talk about it in my lecture," I said.

"Some time you'll tell me what you think of what I shall say. But don't think too much about it; you've plenty of time. Why should you want to grow up so soon?"

She looked at me trustfully, and smiled. I rose hastily, and retreated from the field of battle to the safer monologue of the lecture-room. What can one weak individual do when the species announces to him that his time has come?

I never looked upon Ariel as merely a pupil after that. I became concerned in no impersonal or scientific way with her looks, her clothing, her language, her body; unconsciously I reached out in my turn and tried to absorb her being into mine,—not knowing then that this was a definition of love. I found myself one day, in the midst of my pedagogy, discussing with her which ribbon would better match the color of her hair. She responded to my interest, and began to care more meticulously for the hundred items that make up the beauty of a woman. She grew quieter and gentler; she anticipated my needs, and helped me at every moment with the children. Sometimes, when we gathered together for the daily story, she would sit next to me, and put a hand upon my shoulder or my arm. I became conscious of that hand as never before. It was really a pretty hand,—perfectly formed, small and delicate, and just chubby enough to be comfortable. I began to look at it stealthily and possessively.

246

And then one day the tide came to a flood, and all the moorings were torn away. It was after three o'clock, and the children had gone. Ariel had stayed to help me put things in order. By some fated accident our bodies touched, and my whole being was swept electrically with a current of desire. I, who had spent so many hours with the philosophers; I, who had read Schopenhauer's bitter description of women, and his disillusioning analysis of love; I, who had smiled appreciatively at every hit which the rejected Nietzsche had scored upon the subtler sex —I should have controlled myself; I should have paused and weighed circumstances; I should have considered that this was my pupil, that I was her teacher, that here was the last place in the world for love. But I caught her wildly in my arms, and kissed her hair, and her eyes, and her mouth.

She made no resistance, and no response; a strange sadness stilled her joy. It was as if she felt, in that delirious moment, what penalties she would have to pay for that embrace; how every friend and relative in the world would denounce her as a traitor to her race. And yet she was glad to give me this happiness which I was drinking from her lips. It was so innocent; how could it ever be wrong to make another happy? As for me, I knew now an intoxication such as had never come to me in the past. Fate had placed miraculously in my arms just such a girl as I had fashioned in my fantasy; I held her close to make certain it was not a dream. And I hungered and thirsted for her as if in all the world this was the woman whom nature had made for me.

"Will you forgive me, Ariel?" I whispered.

"Yes," she answered. "But I love you too."

We kissed no more that afternoon; perhaps some sense of guilt had crept within the hot consciousness of our love. As from a height I saw the widening consequences of this act; the break-up of the school; the clash of hostile races, families and creeds; the surrender of my freedom and the end of my solitude; the assumption of new tasks and new responsibilities in the world. But through it all I felt the joy of a new comradeship, an almost mystic sense of fulfilment and completion. I was content and happy to be caught up in the great web of the continuity of life. As I rode home alone I lived the scene over and over again, and saw something of its content and significance, but never with a moment of regret. I had been a fragment long enough. I would not be afraid of life. I wanted to live forward; I was glad that again all the doors were closed behind me, and that new doors and new avenues had opened in front. I have never been happier than on that afternoon. After all, what does it matter what price we pay for love?

CHAPTER VII

I EXPLORE THE HUDSON

WHAT was I to do now? I was caught in such a maze of unforeseen and chaotic circumstance that for a while I felt like letting the whole mesh and welter of things fall upon me unresisted. I would follow the path of love without looking to the right or the left, and I would let the world talk and snarl and bite. Her parents were Jewish, mine were Catholic; very well, I would do nothing about it. She was my pupil, I was her teacher, and I had done a shameful and immoral thing, subject to a thousand uncomfortable imputations; well, I would do nothing about that either. We would go off and bill and coo, and thrill and woo, and all the dogs in Christendom might howl their moralic protest unhonored and unheard. Love seemed to me so much more important than those other things, than all those other people.

That Saturday Ariel and I went to a park, and wandered all day along its brooks and across its fields. We did not talk of marriage, for that had a prosaic sound; I spoke only of the new happiness within me, and of my gratitude to her who had brought it; and Ariel told me with her girlish simplicity that she was happy too, and would go to the end of the world with me. That afternoon, however, we got no farther than Bronx Park. We sat down near a hospitable tree, whose spreading boughs sheltered us from hostile eyes, and we stayed there for hours, shoulder to shoulder, head to head, and (though not quite for hours) lips to lips. Ever since that sunny day I have honored the ritual of love.

When a week had passed I resumed the relationships and amenities of society, and acknowledged that under the supremacy of Eros there might be room for the consideration of parental and fraternal sensibilities. I decided that I would go no further without revealing everything to Ariel's mother and father, and that I would at once offer my resignation to the heads of the Freedom Association. I wrote to Ronald Dalton, and told him that having fallen in love with one of my pupils I was presumably unfit to be any longer the teacher of the school, and would relinquish my position as soon as they could find some respectable person to take my place. It was characteristic of my intoxication that I despatched this letter without considering for a moment that it would in all likelihood result in my being thrown penniless into the streets at the very time when I was preparing to become a full-fledged man. Luckily the executive committee of the Association asked me to stay till the end of the school year; and I had a chance to catch my economic breath.

The other aspect of the problem was not so smoothly settled. One of Ariel's pretty sisters invaded the school and denounced me for misleading a girl only half my age. I protested mildly, but I remember having a moment's lucid interval in which it occurred to me that perhaps Flora was right. Then the tide of love swept back upon me again, and I let the charge go unanswered and forgotten. During the next few days Ariel's family made every effort to keep her from school; when she finally broke away from them she came in horror and tears to announce to me that one of her brothers was going out to buy a revolver, and would shoot me presently. But I was so absorbed in the new consciousness of love that I could not find time to think of that revolver. I walked bravely past Ariel's home, while she implored me to hurry on. The next day I went to see her mother.

She had just come home after a heavy day's work, and was so tired that she could not find energy to resist me. Ariel put a soft arm around my neck as I expounded the honorableness of my intentions.

"Ah, yes," said the mother wearily, as if knowing that love would have its way no matter what she might do, or what dearly purchased wisdom she might endeavor to pass on, "you speak fair words, but I know what men are. You wish to take her for your pleasure, and then you will leave her."

Ariel protested that I was too fine a fellow to do that; but her mother suggested that she was not yet an authority on the psychology of the esurient male. We made some progress, however, merely by talking; there has always been a certain innocence about me (which has stood me in good stead when I meditated villainies); and as Ariel's mother studied me, and listened between the lines of my amiable harangues, she grew more reconciled.

"Do you know," she asked, sadly, "how dear a mother's children are to her?" She took Ariel around the shoulder and kissed her hair. "My daughter, my Khaya, do *you* know what you mean to me, and how I suffered for you?"

I was won to her completely.

"I think I love you too," I said.

She looked at me wistfully, silent; but I felt that from that moment she had put her trust in me, and that the barriers between us had begun to fall away.

What was the rest of my life during those happy days? If I remember well, I was spurred on to additional industry. I taught better, I studied more, I lectured with greater spirit, than before. Often I traveled several hundred miles for my fare and a few dollars' fee, solacing myself with the joy of overwhelming new audiences and hearing new applause. In those days I dealt in superlatives, scorning modifiers; and the energy of my speech helped the dogmatism of my thought to please the little groups of heretics who welcomed me. I had a smattering of all the sciences, and an engaging way of bringing them together to prove any theory that came upon my tongue; my hearers were comforted to know that all the wise men of the earth agreed with them. I was young enough to hope that after yielding my place at the Freedom School I might earn sufficient pennies as a perambulating sophist to warrant the high adventure of marriage. Yet all my little fees, aside from my wage as teacher, amounted to three hundred dollars a year. Such is the optimism of love.

In those days I was well rewarded by a little transient decency into which I had fallen six months before. Returning from Europe I had found some seventy-five dollars remaining of the six hundred which Henry Alden had given me in Athens to finance the remainder of my tour. My fingers had itched to keep that surviving sum, and my ready reason had found a hundred syllogisms for it. Reluctantly, I had sent the money back. Now, when Alden heard the story of my new love and my resignation from the school, he asked me, in the simplest way:

"What do you propose to do?"

"I don't know yet," I answered, still unconscious of the imminence of this problem.

"What would you like to do?" he asked.

"If I were free," I said, "I'd go to Columbia University and study there for three or four years."

"Well," he said, quietly, as if offering me a cigar, "go to Columbia, and study to your heart's content. I'll pay your tuition, and add enough to your own earnings to keep you alive."

Why should I not be an optimist? Time and again, when things have apparently taken an evil turn for me, Fortune has emptied her horn of plenty into my lap. Here I had been penniless and (economically) forlorn; and in a moment my fate was changed to a second youth of quiet study. For a while I hardly knew what to do with my rosy opportunity. I thought of studying medicine, and curing the world of all disease. But then, with that distaste for practical things which has always kept me out of the more lucrative walks of life, I forswore medicine and vowed myself to philosophy. Some one had told me that the highest of all degrees was the Ph.D.; well, I would become a Ph.D. Of what use that ornament would be when I secured it, I had no conception, and no thought. Alden smiled patiently at my decision, tried in his gentle fashion to steer me back to prescriptions and pills, and then, seeing me obstinate, let me have my way. It was arranged that I should begin graduate work at Columbia as soon as my engagement with the school came to an end. I looked forward eagerly to the new life.

My friends were not pleased at the prospect of my marrying; they knew that love is a cannibal of friendships. Some of them pictured me falling from my meteoric radicalism into the bathos of domestic respectability. Some wanted to know what degrees

Ariel had taken, how many languages she knew, and whether she was acquainted with Spencer and Marx. Others asked how much money she would bring me, what was her father's social position, and whether I was financially equipped for this voyage into that dark and perilous country from whose bourne so many travelers return. I could not answer them to their satisfaction; but I smiled in a way that perhaps made them understand how trivial these considerations seemed to me.

Nevertheless, as March came and went, and April and May, I myself began to ask questions of this love that raged within me. Had I a right to marry? Was I the kind of man who could earn for a woman the comfortable home which every mother ought to have? I counted my savings, and discovered that they came to three hundred dollars. I had no prospect of adding to that amount; and a breath of illness or misfortune might sweep it away. It would be several years before I could win my degree at Columbia; for while studying there I should have to prepare and peddle the popular addresses which were to be my main economic resource. Ought I to ask this guileless girl to cast in her lot with such a reckless Jack of all sciences and master of none? Or should I ask her to wait three years till I had gained a little practical wisdom?

During those days of doubt I saw Ariel almost constantly; and her presence always tipped the beam of my thoughts in the direction of precipitate advance. It was simple enough, in the quiet of my room, to plan three years of patience and abnegation; but the sight of her welcoming eyes and the touch of her warm hand were irrefutable arguments for instant marriage. Suddenly I determined to isolate myself for a week, at whatever cost in loneliness and yearning; I would go off like Wells's Samurai, and in the valley of two waves I would cast up the accounts of Yea and Nay, and come back resolute.

We sat on a great rock overlooking the lake at the northern end of Central Park.

"Ariel," I said, "I want to leave you for a week."

"You want to leave me?" she protested, her big èyes opening wide. "Why? What have I done?"

"You are too beautiful," I said. "I want to get away into the woods by myself, and think."

She looked at me sadly.

"Yes, I know," she whispered. "You want to think if you really love me." Then, after a long pause: "Go, Jack. I'll wait for you."

Three days later I was in Albany. I had pedaled my way up from New York on an old bicycle which had survived from my irresponsible years. After a night in the land of the politicians I bequeathed my bicycle to the friend who had sheltered me, and canvassed the boat-houses along the river in quest of a second-hand canoe. It was my luck to find a young man who was ready to solve my problem at once.

"I'll sell you my canoe at a bargain," he said. "I'm getting married next week, and I need all the cash I can get."

It was a fine boat, a little too large for my purpose, but so well made that I should probably be able to sell it in New York for as much as I was asked for it now. I surrendered eighteen precious dollars, with a guilty feeling that I was spending money that belonged to Ariel as well as to me. Then I went up to the town, bought a folding cot and a carton of food, brought them down into the boat, and pushed off into the river. The Albany fiancé, still on the dock, wondered what I was up to.

"Where are you bound for?" he asked.

"New York," I answered.

"All alone?"

"Yes."

"Can you swim?"

"Enough to get back to the canoe."

He shrugged his shoulders.

"It's no fun alone. You ought to have a good swimmer with you."

"I'll take a chance on it," I said.

"Well, here's luck to you."

I returned his good wishes, feeling that he needed them as well as I.

Soon Albany was behind me, and for a while I drifted quietly with the ebbing tide. Never had I known such peace. I was not worried about what might befall me; for I was too young to fear death.

And I was not troubled with thinking; instead of debating the problem of marriage I found myself looking down the stream contentedly, seeing at its end the face of Ariel ready to welcome me.

The summer sun shone down upon me, and I accepted gladly its heat and its light. I kept in midstream to catch the force of the tide; there, too, the noises of the brickyards and the boat-houses on the shore came muffled to me, and left me the stillness that I sought. The passing water lapped my boat with a pleasant music. Sometimes a barge would go by, leaving a wake that lifted me gently on a lullaby of waves. At other times the great boats of the Day Line would meet or overtake me, and my canoe would rise to perilous angles on the crest of mighty billows, and then slip down into a valley of swirling water that covered me with spray. Occasionally the wind would stir the river into an almost oceanic fury, and I would be so buffeted on every side that no skill of management could keep the point of my boat to the wave. But for the most part the weather was fair and the wind was calm. I could paddle then almost without thought, letting my fancy weave a hundred visions of what the future ought to be. Perhaps if I faced every danger bravely I might go to my love as a tested man, warranted in asking her to ship with me on a longer cruise. And so I kept my courage through all anxious moments, looking steadily ahead, and seeing always, across the chasms and the foam, far away under the bridges and through the ships, the girl who was waiting for me.

At night I drew my boat up on the bank, opened out my cot, and slept the sleep of fatigue. The problems I had set out to solve seemed to have dissolved in the light of the sun and the heat of the day's work. I had been washed clean of the concerns of the world; the immensity of the forest and the eternal flow of the river made my affairs so small that I was ashamed to think of them. The quiet stability of natural things, the imperturbable persistence of the sea pushing itself into the uplands with the silent and irresistible tides, laid their spirit upon me, and soothed me with their peace. Day after day I drifted with the ebbing water, or paddled patiently against the flow. In the midstream solitude of my little boat I became for a time a part of nature; the trees and the waves murmured and babbled to keep me company, and the sun and the clouds befriended me.

On the fifth morning I rose at four and set out from the banks of Ossining with the hope of reaching Ariel that afternoon. I had written to her that if the wind proved kind she might expect me in the evening. But the wind was more unkind than man's ingratitude. The worst of the storms I had encountered caught me soon after I had started out. It began with a rain that rapidly swelled into a torrent, as if all the elements had turned their friendship into war. Soon I was drenched and cold. My little bark, shipping water at every moment, had to be bailed out breathlessly in the intervals between the great waves that attacked me from every side in cruelly endless succession. But for the tide I should have made no progress whatever. The wind turned my prow around so persistently that at last I compromised, and paddled backward, watching the waves anxiously over my shoulders, and letting them splash me to the neck as the weighted stern of my boat sank below their crests. In five hours I made five miles.

I struggled on till three o'clock, and then I surrendered. Boatman after boatman called to me, and commanded me to take refuge on the shore. When I felt myself quite exhausted I followed their advice, and pulled up my canoe on the docks of the Yonkers Yacht Club. I changed from my bathing suit to the equally drenched clothing that had lain in the bottom of the boat; and made the rest of the voyage to New York by train. I walked my way wearily to Ariel, and laid my head in her lap; and while she fondled my hair I fell asleep. I felt that I should be content to stay with her now all the days of my life.

CHAPTER VIII

I GO THE WAY OF ALL FLESH

ON the following Monday I began my studies at Columbia. Here at last was the atmosphere I had thirsted for: the "clear, cold air of science," and the quiet surroundings of modest scholarship; the sense of human progress as resting not on politics or strife, but on silent and inconspicuous research, on the organization of inquiry and the dissemination of knowledge into every corner of the land. I drank in with delight the unassuming psychological erudition of Professor Woodworth and the brilliant biology of Professor Calkins; I watched Professor Morgan pursuing chromosomes and genes through countless generations of *Drosophila,* and for two years I followed the thorough-going courses with which that perfect teacher, Professor McGregor, initiated thousands of students into the lore of the biological laboratory. I squirmed uneasily as I took live worms and dropped them into alcohol, and shuddered as I pinned their still quivering bodies to a board and cut away their delicate skins. I pored for years into microscopes, and studied the animalcules from which, I was assured, I had been evolved. I dissected a dog-fish, a bird, a frog, and a hundred

other unfortunates that had to die to make Ph.D.'s.
I came away from those laboratories a little tired
of malodorous carcasses, filth-filled digestive tracts,
and shameless reproductive systems; but grateful
nevertheless for such solid instruction as I had never
had before.

And then I passed from Schermerhorn to Philosophy Hall, and found Professor Woodbridge in his
prime. Of all the lecturers I heard in those four
years, he was surely the ablest and most alert. I knew
after one session with him that I was to enjoy the
intimate self-expression of a mature and genial
mind; that here was a man who had circumnavigated
the intellectual globe, and could see our little problems now in that total perspective which is philosophy.

Finally I came to Professor Dewey. I smiled as
I saw him cross the campus on a winter's day,—
hatless and overcoatless, collar turned up and hands
in his pockets, hair unsubdued and neck-tie awry;
none of us would have supposed, from his bearing or
his appearance, that he was the leading figure in
American philosophy. Nevertheless his lectures were
almost the worst in his university. His voice was a
monotone and his pace an even drawl,—except when
he sought Flaubertianly for the fittest word, and
stared out upon the lawn till it came. Some of us
went to sleep; others of us copied his lecture in long-
hand word for word in order to remain awake. But
he was slow because he did his own thinking, and

262

ploughed virgin soil. Most lectures are compilations;
and if they flow easily on it is because they follow
a beaten path. But where Dewey thought there
were no paths; he had to make them as he went; and
like a frontiersman he had no time for ornamental
delicacies. When, in the leisure of the evening, we
read over what we had taken down during the day,
we discovered gold in every second line. We found
that without excitement, and without exaggeration,
this man was laying a firm basis, in biological psychology, for the progress of his country and his
race. Sometimes he spoke so radically that only the
obscurity of his speech and the modesty of his manner saved him from the sensationalism of reporters
or the hunters of heresy. And then at times, with a
quiet sentence of irrefutable analysis, he annihilated
a theory or a movement, and brought the eager ideals
of youth within the circle of reality.

I am afraid that those four years at Columbia
undid me as a radical, and completed that subsi-
dence into liberalism which had begun with my experience as a conspirator, and had been carried on
by my European trip and perhaps by the retarded
tempo of my blood. I had come to Columbia from
the center of American anarchism, as I had come to
anarchism from a seminary; and this new change,
though less sharp and sudden than the first, was as
fundamental and revealing. I passed from the clash
of controversy to the calm of study and research,
from the discussion of discordant hopes to the analy-

sis of impartial facts. It was not that these teachers were conservative. Most of them were genuine liberals; some of them contributed to the support of the Socialist press; others had followed the career of Emma Goldman with some measure of admiration; not one of them but sympathized, and in no hypocritical way, with the aspirations of the common man.

Yet as I studied with them my Utopias moved farther back in the perspective of the future. I had thought of the world in ethical terms, and had talked of rights and wrongs; now I learned that behind rights and wrongs were desires and powers. I heard something of the impulse of mastery, and discovered that it existed as strongly in the leaders of the proletariat as in the Manufacturers' Association of America. I learned something of the acquisitive propensities of man, and saw their roots in that terrific struggle for existence, generation after generation, which had required such an instinct, which had for the most part destroyed those who lacked it, and had intensified it ruthlessly by the selection of those in whom it flourished. As long as struggle continued, and material goods remained the prime necessities of survival in the individual and in the group, that instinct to possess would continue to operate in the human soul; and Utopias that reckoned without it were compensatory castles in the air. I did not throw all my castles down, but I remade them more modestly, and nearer to the earth. I found myself fighting to keep my social faith from disintegration as I had once fought to preserve my religious belief from the assaults of this same dissolving science.

"Perhaps," I said to myself in those meditative days, "it is science, and not socialism, that will revolutionize the world. Medical science may lessen epidemics, may weaken the virulence of disease, and may teach us how to keep ourselves clean and strong. Economic science may lessen industrial tyranny by showing that when the flood of immigrant labor subsides, and contraception reduces the abundance of proletarian brawn, it will be wasteful to ruin the human resources of industry with long hours and unclean homes. Mechanical science may lessen slavery by making electric power less expensive than the muscle of the unskilled worker, and man will become only the intellectual factor in production. Historical science may rid us of superstitions, and leave us freer to understand and control the world. Psychological science may cleanse our minds of ignorance and fear, and teach us to understand and control ourselves. Perhaps these very scientists, isolated in their laboratories and silent amid the noise and argument of the rest of us, are the great changers, the great destroyers, and the great builders."

And then I asked myself, Wellsianly:

"Suppose that these scientists everywhere should realize that, united, their knowledge would be more indispensable, in war and industry, than the gold of the capitalist, the courage of the promoter, or the brawn of the proletaire? Why should they not take control of the world and make a newer Atlantis? Perhaps that would be the greatest of all revolutions!"

At that moment one of the most famous physicists of America crossed the campus. He was tall but very thin, and looked too frail for this rough world. He peered timidly through his thick glasses, and walked with his eyes upon the ground. He was evidently a sharp and subtle mind, but not a masterful man; I felt that he would run from power rather than towards it, that he would make almost any sacrifice for peace. It dawned upon me that the scientist is not a warrior and not a ruler; that the same nobility and cleanliness and modesty of soul which keep him bent obscurely over his tubes and microscopes might make him a malleable medium in the hands of men equipped at birth with the instincts of domination. Nature does not like to give two gifts to one man.

In October of that year Ariel and I were married.

After all my denunciations of free mating I found it irksome nevertheless to submit to the routine of securing a license for our love. I vowed that we would go through the formalities of the marriage ceremony with a scornful dispatch, making our required obeisance to society and the state, but flying back to our treasured privacy as soon as the formula would permit.

And so one sunny afternoon I met Ariel as she

came from the secretarial school where she was studying; and though she had her roller-skates in one hand and her books in the other, and I had a briefcase bulging with every science and a dozen philosophies, and both of us were hatless, we sallied forth to the City Hall. There we met Frank Haughwout, a Columbia associate, and his lawyer friend Harry Winter; a little later Ariel's mother came, hesitant and diffident; and together we approached the desk of the man who might legitimate our love.

"How old did you say?" he asked Ariel.

"Fifteen," she answered, fearfully. She stands before me in my memory as she stood there that day, her hair flowing down over her shoulders in schoolgirl fashion, her eyes flashing with excitement, her cheeks red with health and all a-blush with modesty, her muscular body thrilling with our great adventure.

"You're under age," said the clerk sharply. "You can't marry here without the consent of both your parents. Are they with you?"

We had known something of this, but we had had a queer hope that the clerk might have forgotten the law. Ariel's father had refused his consent; under no circumstances would he help us; indeed, had he known what we were doing he would have appeared and protested with all his soul against his daughter's apparent treachery to her people.

"The mother is here," I said, as politely as I could; "will you let her speak?"

"Perfectly useless," said the clerk; "get the father too."

We were brushed aside. Ariel had tears in her eyes, and I hot words on my tongue. But Winter quieted us.

"We'll go and see chief clerk Tully," he said.

We took an elevator to the fourth floor, and there, fortunately, was the man we sought,—bald-headed, round-faced, short, fat enough to be good-natured, and intelligent beyond the custom of public officials.

"Mr. Tully," said our lawyer, introducing me, "this new victim is a graduate student in the department of philosophy at Columbia."

I wondered at this selection of details; but Winter knew his man; philosophy was a private hobby of this master of matrimony. Tully invited me to explain my trouble; but suddenly he led me into irrelevant discourse on the current issues in science and philosophy; he found delight in leaving the dull routine of his desk for a sally into the airy world of speculation. Then he returned to earth.

"I'm forgetting what you came for," he said with a smile. "Of course you know it's against our rules to let you marry a minor without the consent of both parents."

I said nothing. I had learned that this is usually the best thing to say.

"Do you really want to marry this young lady?" he asked.

"With all my heart," I answered.

268

"Well," he said, "I'll take a chance on you."

He wrote a brief note, and gave it to me. We thanked him, and filed back to the clerk below. This gentleman growled at the violation of rules and precedents, but finally handed us our precious license.

"Well, if you're bound to do it, go ahead," he said, grimly.

I was quite bound. I had done all the thinking I intended to do; there has to be some cloture on thought in these matters if the race is to go on. We passed from the license-bureau down into a basement where several aldermen were marrying couples as fast as the formula could be recited. Once more we stood in line. I shuddered a little as I saw the anxious faces ahead of me—this must be a terrible thing that we were doing. And then, couple by couple, we were passed into marriage, almost as if we were buying tickets for a ball game. When our turn came I lost my head, and had to have the questions repeated and shouted at me before I could understand them. Suddenly an unforeseen question startled me:

"Where's the ring?"

"What ring?" I asked, stupefied.

"Your marriage ring, of course," shouted the awful alderman. "Do you think I can marry you without a ring?"

I had forgotten all about that damnable formality. I hated rings unreasonably as a relic of savagery, and I had never thought of them as a necessary implement of marriage. It was my modest mother-in-law who saved the day.

"Perhaps you will lend me your ring for a minute?" she whispered to the girl who had preceded Ariel to the sacrifice.

"Eh?" the girl asked. "Why should I lend you my ring, when I just got it?"

"Here's a dollar," said Ariel's mother, quietly.

"Oh," said the young lady, and handed over the ring.

The alderman frowned as I tried to fit upon Ariel's finger this borrowed bond of matrimony. But he was unwilling to be cheated of a fee which he had almost earned; and he grumbled his way through the remainder of the ceremony. "Say, 'With this ring I thee wed,' " he commanded.

I obeyed blindly.

". . . love, honor, and obey,"—I heard Ariel murmur the words, though she denies it now.

Then he handed me the certificate. We surrendered the ring, paid our fee, and rushed out into the open air, relieved and happy.

"Hurrah!" I shouted; "it's over at last." (Commencements look so much like completions.)

Ariel smiled through her tears, happy too, I hope, but fearful of the new responsibilities we were facing. Then it dawned upon me that I had not yet kissed her since our marriage. I caught her in my arms, and before the amazed hundreds that swirled around us I kissed her passionately.

"Now," I said, remembering Whitman, "shall we two stick to each other as long as we live?"

She looked up at me trustfully and resolutely.

"To the very end," she whispered.

CHAPTER IX

WANDER-YEARS

WE sought rooms near the University, but the rents there were too high, and we found ourselves forced up the hill to 136th Street. Thither we moved our combined belongings,—a bed, a typewriter, a desk, and my books. We had hired a small truck, and it was stipulated that I should have to help the driver carry our furniture three flights down from the old rooms and four flights up to our new ones. When the day's work was over I fell down upon the floor, and could hardly be persuaded to rise for the little meal which Ariel had conjured up for me out of the chaos of the kitchen. How quietly resourceful she was, how quickly and contentedly she took over the task of caring for my big appetite and our little home! Never was food sweeter to me than in those days, when we were too poor to enter a restaurant, and everything that I ate came to me from her hands, seasoned with comradeship and love.

During the day we studied at Columbia together. People stared at us, surprised to find us always arm in arm or side by side. They were not quite certain whether I was husband or brother or father, though

they might have known by our tenderness that we
were newly wed. Yet with all our cooing we mingled
an abundance of argument; for Ariel was young
and hopeful, while I, nearing thirty, felt already
old and wise, and leaned to a grave moderation. Our
philosophy is a function of our age of life. We pass
through Utopias and idealism to knowledge and
limitation as we pass through a hundred illnesses
to a certain moderate health.

At Columbia once, wandering among the book-
shelves, I came abruptly face to face, round a turn
in the stacks, with a bent and white-haired man of
perhaps some eighty years. For a moment we looked
at each other with a vague hostility. "Ah," he
seemed to say, "I too was once like you, eager for
change, voracious of knowledge, hopeful of great
achievements, and with a fretful passion for taking
the world apart and putting it together again. Now
I spend my hours reading the frayed yellow pages
of the magazines that were popular in my youth."
I felt, as I saw him moving timidly along, that given
a little time and I too would look back longingly to
the days of my hope and my strength, and would
crawl reluctantly and fearfully towards the dark.
—Another time I paused at the sight of an old
man, with side-boards and Prince Albert coat, lean-
ing on a cane and watching with awe the Missis-
sippi of automobiles that passed the Public Library.
His face showed the subtle tragedy of a man rudely
left behind by a changing world. Finally he turned

to an antique carriage which a precariously exalted
driver had been keeping for him at the curb.

"Take me home," he said, wearily; "this confusion tires me."

Perhaps it was for the sake of such men, in mercy
to them, that the mills of the gods had to grind ex-
ceeding slow.

Those days at Columbia were among the happiest
of our lives. It was there that we discovered together
the true City of God; not the gloomy abode of saints
which the stern Augustine dreamed of, but that fair
and pleasant Country of the Mind where all the
great dead are still alive, and wisdom makes with
beauty an eternal music. We saw Plato there, still
handsome in his eighty years, telling his students
of the perfect state; and grave Euripides writing his
mournful tragedies in his cottage near the sea at
Salamis; we stood beside Praxiteles as he carved the
tender likeness of Aphrodite for the Cnidians; we
followed Dante as he wandered through Hell and
Purgatory seeking Beatrice; we drank and laughed
with Rabelais in the Abbey of Thélème, and heard
the merry quips of Shakespeare and rare Ben at the
Mermaid Inn; we suffered in prison with Verlaine,
and lay on the grass, on a transparent summer morning, while the poet sang to us of the life-long love
of comrades. We were filled with a strange and quiet
happiness when we thought that the geniuses of
every land and every age stood always ready to walk

with us and be our friends. No matter what misfortunes and disappointments might befall us, we
should always have a refuge here; these endless
treasures were ever at our call, and would be poured
out for us with a lover's lavishness. For years we lost
ourselves in this fairy-land, hearing immortal voices,
passing freely among all peoples and all periods, and
taming our savage hearts with the music of philosophy. "It was bliss in those days to be alive; but
to be young was very heaven." Not for many
years were we to know such happiness again.

Nevertheless, when vacation came we decided that
we had had too much of books and too little of life;
now we would do something hardy and physical for
the sake of our bodies electric. So we set off one
morning to walk to Philadelphia; what could those
ninety miles mean to our sturdy youth? We stopped
the first night at Bound Brook, where my sister
Delia awaited us with her unstinted hospitality. We
slept fitfully, every muscle taut and sore. The next
day Ariel found it almost impossible to force her
swollen feet into her mud-encrusted shoes. All morning we walked along the tracks of the Reading Railroad; and many a time we felt like waiting at some
station and boarding one of those fleet expresses that
would take us in an hour to our destination. We
made the mistake of sitting down occasionally to
rest; when we tried to get to our feet again we found
that we were sorer and stiffer than before.

All day long we plodded, pushed on by a quite

irrational pride, and trying to make ourselves believe that this was delightful exercise. At night we spread our blankets in the field near the tracks, and tried to sleep. But interminable freight-trains came along, with snorting and belching engines; sparks flew up into the air, and fell as hot cinders upon our heads. Though we moved our dwelling-place away from the railroad, we could not escape the noise.

The day had been tropically warm, but the night was sharply cold; our single blanket was not enough, though we embraced each other the whole night through. The earth, which we had loved so much in our theories, proved inhospitably damp and hard; the dew rose up mysteriously around us, covering our hair with moisture and chilling our bones. Even the stars stared at us frigidly, as if unreconciled to our sharing with them the open spaces of the world; they glared down upon us like a million spies, Puritanically hostile to our entangling love. And then we saw them withdraw, chastely and coldly, fearful of the sun. We were glad that the night was over; we rose at four and marched shivering towards the bridge that spanned the Delaware. Behind us the horizon grew white and clear, then yellow and gold; and we turned to watch the dawn. Suddenly the sun caught the edge of the earth with shining fingers, and lifted himself triumphantly, inch by inch, into the sky. We bowed to it as father of all the gods, lord of creation from whom all blessings flowed. We wiped the dew from our locks, shook the chill out of our bones, breathed deeply the virgin air of the morning, and marched breast forward, loving life again.

Towards noon, when we were raving with hunger and seemed fated never to find a store, we passed a caboose from which the odor of food came with an intoxicating lure. On the platform a burly-headed railroad man, be-spectacled and overalled, was peeling potatoes as if this were the most masculine and satisfying occupation in the world.

"Oh, for a potato cooked in a fire among the stones!" sighed Ariel.

It was said just loud enough to be heard, and it brought us good fortune.

"Where 'ye bound for, brother?" asked the man on the caboose.

"Philadelphia," I answered.

"Ain't our railroad cars good enough for ye?"

We explained, rather lamely, that walking was more fun than riding. He laughed heartily.

"Maybe, for the first ten minutes." Then—"Had any dinner yet?"

We thrilled at the question.

"No," said Ariel, sweetly.

"Want to eat a bit with us?"

We consented.

"Can we help you get things ready?" Ariel inquired.

"Everything's ready now, lady, 'cept these here

potatoes. I'm going to fry them right on the stove."

I envied the directness with which he passed from thought and word to action. He blew a whistle, and soon a crew of jolly and vigorous workers clambered up the steps into the caboose.

"Here's something for dessert," said one of them, handing the *chef* a pailful of blackberries.

"Hello, folks," came another greeting; "tramp-in'?"

And so they welcomed us; in a moment we were at our ease, the twelve of us sitting on benches at a rough table, and eating hungrily till we were gloriously full. I wonder was that not the most savory dinner that ever found its way into our history. Meanwhile not one curse, not one questionable remark, from these honest sons of toil.

"How much finer they are," Ariel whispered, "than the fat-jowled business-men who sit in their chairs, smoke their cigars, and ask Congress for cheap immigrant labor." Her eyes flashed with indignation as she thought of those terrible business-men, and then melted to tenderness as she looked at these simple proletaires who, as Ariel hoped, would some day rule the world.

When we left the caboose we tried to pay for our meal with the finest phrases our vocabulary knew. The *chef* brushed our weak words aside.

"We'll be here three days," he said. "If ye pass us again we'll have a bite left for ye."

We were walking down the track, turning our

heads to say a last good-bye, when we heard a shout:
"Jump! Jump!"

I looked ahead, and saw a train rounding a curve
and rushing towards us at the rate of seventy miles
an hour. It was less than a hundred yards away. I
am filled with pride when I remember that, even as
in the story-books, my first thought was for Ariel.
I dragged her clumsily across the rail, and we
crouched in fright as the great mass of steel pounded
by us. In one brief second it had passed, and was
narrowing to a line far up the road. Ariel fell limp
upon my shoulder and began to cry, while perspira-
tion drained some of the poison with which fear had
filled my blood. Now that the danger was over I
trembled and grew pale, and found it difficult to
stand.

We did not walk along the railway after that.
Timidly we crossed the bridge over the Delaware.
We fell upon a bed of hay that strewed a new-mown
field, and warmed with the mid-day sun we slept a
troubled sleep.

CHAPTER X

SENTIMENTAL

OUR life was most peaceful in just those years when
20,000,000 boys were going to their death in Europe. We went on studying biology and psychology,
philosophy and history, literature and art, as se-
renely as if the world were not being wrenched by
one of the periodical quarrels of our inhuman species
for the emoluments of trade and the resources of
the soil. It never entered my provincial head that
America would join in this competitive murder, this
co-operative suicide. The President was making the
prettiest pacifistic speeches in the history of his office; I admired their content almost as much as their
form. And I was repelled in the extreme by the ex-
hibition of sword-eating which his strenuous rival
was providing to various newspapers and magazines
in the effort to recapture some of that public attention which had become his vital medium. Only when
the campaign of 1916 began, and the sword-eating
became so voracious and exciting as to threaten the
peace of the country, did I sense the proximity of
war.

I belonged at that time to the Socialist party, and

occasionally I attended the meetings of the Local at
125th Street. Though I had become sceptical of the
whole theory of governmental operation of industry,
and had acquired a certain respect for initiative and
enterprise, I admired the devotion with which the
Socialists gave themselves to their "Cause," and the
courage with which, in the face of every form of
contumely, they fought the undertow of martial
imagination that moved beneath the pacific idealism
of the American people. But when the issue seemed
so clearly drawn between "He Kept Us out of War"
and "Fear God and Take Your Own Part," I decided
that the socialist commonwealth would have to be
postponed for a few years while we kept the country
out of war by re-electing Mr. Wilson. I was read out
of the Socialist Party for this new heresy; but as I
had been excommunicated before I did not take the
matter too much to heart. I was a little more sensitive to a Socialist editorial which denounced me as a
traitor and a fool. The first name slipped by un-
felt; but the second has rankled in my memory ever
since, as names have a habit of doing when there is
much truth in them.

"You are too occupied with immediate issues,"
said a loyal and intelligent socialist to me in those
exciting days. "In every election the major parties
concoct an issue and have the press of the nation talk
about it so much that the people begin to think the
issue must be very important; men believe they must
vote either with the chief protagonist or with the

281

chief antagonist of the idea; otherwise they will
'waste their votes,' and the country will go to pieces.
The result is that nearly all the votes are wasted.
This year, they say, the issue is peace or war. But it's
only a trick again. No matter which party wins, the
question of peace or war will be decided not by the
election but by the desires of the economic masters
of the country. Watch and see."

At times I felt that he might be right; on all my
theories of government, the political power would
yield to economic compulsion; and dollars, not votes,
would decide whether we should have war or peace.
But one Saturday afternoon I went out, with thousands of others, to hear the President speak from
his porch at Long Branch; and when one of his
aides pinned on the lapel of my coat a pretty ribbon naming me as a member of the arrangements
committee, and entitling me to a seat on the speakers' stand, I became an enthusiastic Wilsonite. I was
disappointed with Mr. Wilson that day; he looked
uncomfortable as he talked to us, and his manner
was so constrained that for a moment I suspected his
sincerity. But I came back with the crowd; and by
the time we reached home I thought with the crowd.
On the following Monday I joined the "Wilson Volunteers" on a speaking-tour of New York state, and
explained to street-corner audiences how the President had kept and would keep us out of war.

Was there ever a more exciting campaign? On
election night Ariel and I hovered constantly about

the headquarters of the "Wilson Volunteers," and as the returns were read we swung back and forth between delirious joy and black despair. When it appeared that Mr. Hughes had won we retired to the waiting room of the Grand Central Station, where Ariel's brother Harry fed us on successive editions of the morning papers, and listened to my Jeremiads. Harry did his best to console us with his infinite humor; but Ariel sat glum and silent, while I tried to cover up my tears with rueful smiles. It seemed to me so great a smash-up of fair hopes, and so shameful a betrayal, by the American people, of a man who had stood by them, apparently, against a horde of Prussian swashbucklers and an ocean of British propaganda, that I dropped into utter despondency, and could hardly be prevailed upon to get up and go home. At that time we were living with "Big Bill" Perlman, a jolly host, ex-engineer and nascent dramatist, who had shared with me the toil and enthusiasm of the campaign. Wearily and sadly we went to bed, just as the night was passing into morning. We were hardly asleep when the telephone rang; my friend Jonathan Day was calling me:

"I thought you might sleep better," he said, "if you knew that the tide is swinging towards Wilson. He has North Dakota; if he gets California he wins."

I woke my host and together we did as triumphant a dance as our dignity and his weight would permit. The next day, and the next again, we stood on crowded curbs reading the votes of distant states, shouting and sobbing over figures as surely mathematics had never made men shout or sob before. And when at last Mr. Wilson's victory was conceded, and Mr. Hughes had unkissed his wife, we retired to our homes proud and happy, forgiving our enemies, and confident of peace. Everywhere in America men and women went more joyfully and securely about their work because they had resisted the million-mouthed demon of militarist propaganda, and had saved a great nation from violating its finest traditions and plunging into the maelstrom of foreign war.

In March 1917 came the news of the Russian Revolution. We were delighted to hear that the most ignorant and cruel despotism in Europe had come to an end almost without sacrifice of blood. We were thrilled by the romantic figure of Kerensky, conquering cities with oratory while tubercle bacilli gnawed at his lungs. We looked more sympathetically upon the cause of the Allies, and hoped that their victory would bring a new growth of liberty throughout the world. Then suddenly the Russian front caved in, and Russia was out of the war. A million German troops poured from east to west, and it seemed for a while that Paris would fall, and the German eagle would once more dictate to Europe from the palaces of Versailles.

I like to believe that it was this Russian débâcle

that sent Woodrow Wilson, the pacifist, to war. I did my best to understand the motives of a course that seemed to me drenched in treachery. The President's ancestry and culture and traditions were British; he confessed frankly enough, when the battle was over, that no matter how little formal cause had been given, he would have asked for war whenever it seemed that the Allies, without us, would be destroyed. He was accustomed to an English universe; he could not bear the thought of Teutons bestriding a Prussianized world. That he sent our young men to death to secure the loans of our bankers to European governments, or to ensure American domination of South American finance and trade, was a hyper-Marxian conception which I was too tender-minded to entertain. I liked Woodrow Wilson's prose too well to believe him capable of such brutality. And even to this day, somehow, I have an affection for the man.

I thought he was grievously mistaken in going to war, though God knows I thought so with some measure of humility. I had learned my lesson by that time, and could conceive the possibility of my being wrong. I was filled with awe as I contemplated the complexities of statesmanship; how could I, in the midst of a hundred other concerns, and still adolescent mentally, understand the secret factors that determined international events? And I too preferred—perhaps through time's irrational habituation, and the accidents of place—a British to a Ger-

man world; like all my tribe I thought the educated
Englishman the finest gentleman on earth. But I
could not believe that England, which was sending
so many troops to capture Asiatic soil, would be defeated unless we sent our happy youth to her aid;
it seemed to me that the effect was as if we had dis-
patched our troops to the East to win for this crafty
Lion the oil and wheat of Mesopotamia. Nor could I
forget that England had loved Kitchener on account
of his ferocity, that she had her own sorry list of
swashbucklers, fire-eaters, and tyrants, and her
crimes of black oppression in distant lands,—crimes
muffled, for our ears, by the intervening seas. Was
the difference between these German cousins so great
as to warrant the forcible alienation of the American
people from their age-long loyalty to peace, and the
surrender of our moral meaning in a world that
might have begun to unlearn war if we had shown
that a great nation could live without it?

They told me that peace would be cowardice; but
was not our war itself a conscripted cowardice? Was
there any glory in a victory enforced by fear of the
artillery behind us? Yes, the volunteers had courage:
I saluted them; they were brave. But we others, who
found mothers to support, or married in haste, in
order to evade the draft; and those lofty ones who
sat comfortably in their office chairs and spoke or
wrote of glory—was that bravery?

I thought the better courage would have been
the courage to be ourselves. I thought, as the Presi-

dent had thought, that courage would have been to say: "America does not carry war across the seas. America will cherish unsullied the British tradition of freedom, and it will not let itself become a Prussian camp. America will never set forth to conquer other nations, never force her ways upon them at the point of arms." What an experiment in peace and liberty our history might have been! How much fairer than our years of conscription and imprisonment, of deportation and suppression, of governmental corruption and reviving bigotry, in a land that once was proud of Washington and Franklin and Jefferson and Paine! What if for our brief glory we forfeited the soul and significance of America? What if America could be for us now not the reality of peace and freedom, but only a memory and a hope?

One morning in April I found the spacious approaches of the Library at Columbia University crowded with thousands of babbling people.

"What's up?" I asked a student.

"Don't you know? We're cutting the eleven o'clock classes to protest against the acceptance of Professor Beard's resignation."

Professor Beard had resigned because, though he favored our entrance into the war, he felt that an injustice had been done to Professor Cattell. Cattell had been one of Wundt's students far back in the seventies, when that encyclopedic German had

established at Leipzig the first psychological laboratory in the world. With Stanley Hall, another of
Wundt's pupils, Cattell had founded experimental
psychology in America. Almost out of nothing he
had created the department of psychology at Columbia; he had assisted valiantly at the painful delivery of the new science by that ancient mother of
the sciences, philosophy. He had grown old in the
work; and it was expected that soon he would be
retired with honors and a pension. The old professor
had a son, on whom he had lavished twenty years of
love and care. He could not bear to see this boy taken
from him now and sent off to die forsaken on a
foreign battlefield. He wrote to the Congressman of
his district, asking him to vote against the bill establishing conscription. He wrote that letter, as he
had written thousands of others, on the stationery
of his department, bearing the letter-head of his
University. The University authorities dismissed
him.

Some leaders of the protesting students were
gathered in a circle on the lowest flight of steps. Another group of students, dressed in khaki, formed
above them, and suddenly descending upon the rebels, dispersed them, knocking many of them down
upon the pavement. In the solitude of my home I
had concluded that it would be useless to resist the
war; the economic masters were in the saddle; and
until the madness was over I would keep my peace
and love philosophy and Ariel. But here at the first

provocation my good resolutions melted into thin air. I spoke to one of the protestants.

"Don't give in," I said. "Let's re-form on the upper steps; they'll find it harder to push us up than down."

"All right," he said, "you lead the way and we'll follow you."

Three months before I had been made an instructor in philosophy in the Extension Department of the University. The youth who so readily accepted my lead was more conscious of my position than I; I marched ahead quixotically oblivious of my prospects as an official philosopher.

"Speak to them," urged one of the rebels. "Tell them why we protest against the loss of Professor Beard."

I stepped out upon the great stone wall that rose at the side of the Library steps, and began to speak, never suspecting that the President of the University sat in the Secretary's room behind me, grimly watching the scene through a window. Gradually, while I spoke, our warrior enemies fell into line again, and prepared to rush upon us once more. One good shove, and we partisans of peace, followed perhaps by some vigorous lovers of war, would tumble in unpremeditated comradeship to broken necks thirty feet below. Discretion came to the aid of my valor. I stopped my oratory, and addressed the leader of the siege loudly enough to be heard by the crowd.

"Are you an American?" I asked.

"You bet!" he replied.

"Well, then, you believe in fair play. You may be right or you may be wrong. I shall take five minutes to tell this audience why we protest against letting Professor Beard go from this University; then we will listen quietly while anyone whom you may choose tells us why you protest against our protest. Is that fair?"

The crowd was with us.

"That's fair," many voices cried.

And so I made my speech, keeping one eye on the besieging force, and taking good care not to override my allotted time. I have never been so brief again. When I had finished, the enemy spoke; but as no one proposed to push them off into thin air, the crowd lost interest in the proceedings and went off to lunch. We were left with a victory of words.

A month later, when the arrangements for the Fall term courses were being made, it was found that so many young men had volunteered, and so many others would be conscripted, that some sections of "Philosophy 1" would have to be dropped. I was informed, with every courtesy, that in such cases the teachers most recently admitted to the staff were the first whose classes would have to be disbanded. I did not teach at Columbia any more.

I love it none the less. I thrill even now at the sight of its great domed library, and that quiet, vaulted reading room where for many golden years,

with Ariel beside me, I explored the treasures of our
race. Sometimes I pass the door where Professor
Woodworth still smokes his pipe, and I remember
with gratitude the days when he taught us how psychology could be a science, vowed to exactitude and
objectivity, and destined to the noblest victories of
all. I look into the class-rooms and wonder will there
be any days in the future brighter than those student years. I climb again the cruel stairs of Schermerhorn Hall, though not three steps at a time as
in my youth; those stairs which Professor Morgan
called an instrument of natural selection, letting
only the most resolute come up to the great science
of biology that rules the topmost floor. Even the
laboratory, with its kegs of dog-fish and its smell of
alcohol, is dear to me, and the pans in which we
scissored those helpless and innocent worms. Here in
these rooms, and in Avery and Havemeyer and Kent
and Philosophy Hall, I know that honest knowledge
still finds encouragement and a home. The war was
an illucid interval; we shall forget it at last and
refind our better selves. That illiberal interlude, in
which we hated one another because our eyes saw
differently the values of life, was not characteristic
of us, nor of the spirit of our Alma Mater. The years
will pass over our little wounds and heal them, and
we shall understand how accidental they were, given
and received in a moment of unbalancing excitement,
when wisdom had been blinded with strife. Perhaps
some day, when Ariel and I are old, we shall go and

sit once more among the students in the library, and feel the current of man's lore passing down to unstained generations, giving them the light and the power to make America again a land brave enough to be free.

That part of my life stands in my memory as the conscription years. I see, as vividly as the fields before me now, my brother-in-law Harry taken from his home, led away with other youths, behind bugles and drums that could not drown our grief, to the station where they were to take a train for camp. The recruiting sergeant was as lenient as his work allowed; and at the station he permitted us a last good-bye. Harry smiled and joked bravely; but his mother suddenly caught him in her arms, burst into cries of frustrated love, and would not let him go till the sergeants tore her hands away. Can men understand the tragedy of a mother who rears a son for twenty years, and then sees him forced to go and kill, to shoot and stab, and wallow in his own blood, and die, for a cause utterly without meaning to him or to her? Can we grasp in our thin imagery the million-hearted agony of the mothers, helpless and numberless, who saw their sons dragged from their arms in those proud flag-waving years? I can never hear the bugles blow now, or the drums beat, without seeing that last farewell, and hearing the cries of the mothers whose bodies had been racked with pain to give these sons to death. Harry came back; but how many there were who never returned, or returned maimed in body and mind, or coarsened forever by the filth and brutality of war?

I see twenty million corpses strewing a thousand battlefields. I know with what despair they went to war, and how loath they were to kill. I hear them praying to their gods, as they advance with drawn bayonets and broken hearts, that they may be spared from murder and from death. And then I see them crazed with the passion of strife and slaughter; snarling and crying out with hatred and fear; sending a bullet into this lad's head, pushing the sharp bayonet into that lad's breast; rushing on over the crumpled body of the fallen foe; stepping perhaps upon the quivering and bloodied face that some mother once admired; then stumbling for a little moment, and looking up too late; feeling the cold blade entering the body, twisting and tearing the vitals; falling under the onrush of battle, under a thousand heels impinging cruelly, again and again, on every muscle and bone, on nose and eyes and mouth; remembering in one brief flash a thousand happy days of far-off youth; then hearing great hammer strokes upon the brain; moaning and asking heaven why these things should be; struggling, struggling, to keep one little bit of life from the universal conqueror; tiring, yielding, sighing out the last hope with the last breath; and sinking down heavily, under a thousand stifling weights, into the darkness and futility of death. That is how they died, those twenty million men.

And then peace came, more suddenly than the war. Shall I ever forget that first Armistice Day, when all America came out of her madness and sorrow to blow the trumpets and sing the songs of peace? Did we not parade all night, unwearied, covering ourselves joyfully with streaming bonds of brotherhood renewed, and greeting with tears the long-awaited dawn? Your soul was revealed on that day, my country; never had you celebrated war as then you celebrated peace. And it was not your victory that you sang; no lust of bloody triumph coarsened your voice, or darkened your shining eyes; you beat and pounded for peace, you knew her holiness once more; you were glad that now you could raise your hand in fellowship to the world, and not to kill. That night you knew happiness again.

But in a door-way on Lexington Avenue I saw a woman weeping.

"Why are you crying?" I asked. "Don't you know that the war is over, and that we are all friends again?"

"Yes," she said, and her voice broke out into a bitter wail. "But it's too late, too late."

"Have you lost one of your boys in the war?"

"My only boy," she whispered. "They told me

yesterday. O my boy, my George, you'll never come back to me, you'll never come back to me."

As I bent over to comfort her I saw a hundred thousand mothers, everywhere in America, standing or sitting in doorways or at windows, looking dull-eyed and empty-hearted on our joy, and waiting for the sons whom their arms would never hold again.

CHAPTER XI

I PLAY POLITICS

ONE would imagine that by this time I had become sufficiently disillusioned to retire into a studious corner, and protect myself, as far as might be, from the harsh contacts and bubble-bursting pricks of life. One would suppose, at the very least, that I had come to understand the futility of an intellectual plunging into the labyrinths and shady catacombs of politics. But my scepticism and rationalism have always been matters of the head, that never crossed the medulla into the deeper roots of my behavior and my being. At bottom I am as romantic and sentimental as a high-school girl or an old maid. I think I shall never grow up.

So it was that in 1919, still burning with hatred of war, I accepted the invitation of some friends to join them in the high and mighty game of making a new political party. It seemed a comparatively simple matter: Providence had arranged everything for us; we had only to reach out our hands and take the fruits of office. Was not America secretly resentful of having been dragooned into the war? Were not the Republican powers attacking Woodrow Wilson with a campaign of vilification unprec-

edented since the days of Abraham Lincoln? The
Democratic Party might be destroyed, in this election, beyond any possibility of resurrection. As to
the Republicans, had they not joined in the war-
making as merrily as any Democrat? And were
they not on the verge of nominating a Prussian
general as their candidate for the presidency? Here
was our opportunity, if ever opportunity would
come, to gather together the scattered and shattered
forces of the old Americanism and the new pro-
gressivism; to bind them into a party, and offer to
the people the chance they had been longing for—
to vote for peace and freedom. "America waits," we
said. We never dreamed how long America would
wait.

It was J. A. H. Hopkins who brought us together. I always liked everything about him except
the initials. To begin with, he was the handsomest
man in America. I was convinced that if he would
only let us nominate him for the presidency half the
population would vote for him on his face value.
And he not only looked like a gentleman, he behaved
like one. All who met him wanted to do anything he
asked. Even his relatives liked him. He had left a
remunerative business in order to give all his time,
and nearly all his savings, to the work of establishing a third party. He burned with a tenacious idealism that never lost hope or acknowledged defeat; we
might come to our meetings with him despondent to
the point of cynicism, but in a moment he was carry-

ing us along enthusiastically towards Utopia. No
man could be a pessimist about America after knowing "Hop."

We met in a little office in East Fortieth Street,
and laid our plans like breathless conspirators. At
that first meeting, if I may trust my memory, there
were, besides Hopkins and myself, Allen McCurdy,
McAlister Coleman and Arthur Hays. It was arranged that we should write a "Call to Americans,"
inviting liberals throughout the country to send us in
their dollars and their names. We received more
names than dollars, but we were encouraged to go
on. Our executive committee grew to ponderous pro-
portions, and our meetings took on the dignity of
a movement to save America. I thrilled once more
with the enthusiasm of younger days. Something of
the warm faith which had burned within me for religion flamed up again as I thought of the new era
that our great crusade might usher in. It was the
final fire of my old idealism; if this too should flicker
out and die, nothing would be left to me but a cynical and crabbed age. It was the last fling of my
youth.

We might have learned from our own behavior,
and from our own turbulent debates, how impotently
divided American progressives were. The younger
ones among us argued for co-operation with the Socialists and the new "Farmer-Labor Party"; the
older heads, like George Record and Amos Pinchot,
believed that it would be wiser to work alone, and

take no chances of being manœuvred into an extravagant and futile radicalism. Our youthful eloquence won; and in July 1920 we sallied forth to Chicago with a program for the amalgamation of the two conventions that were to meet there, Labor and Liberal, and with our hearts full of the great deeds we were to do for our country.

When our convention gathered at the Morrison Hotel I was pleased to see that there were four hundred liberals in America. But a goodly number of "cranks" were among us too: people who felt pinched in one special spot, and wished to cure all our social ills with one idea—free silver, single tax, governmental monopoly of banking, equal distribution of wealth, or what not; until I began to realize that I was something of a "crank" myself. Nevertheless we had sober-headed and big-souled men with us also; and if we had supported them well we might have come home with some success to our credit and some gladness in our hearts. A message was received from Senator LaFollette that he would gladly be our candidate if we could unite both conventions on a moderate platform; and a telegram from the most influential newspaper-owner in the United States pledging his support on conditions which we had already written into our program. We were as happy as college boys at a football game; and we had no doubt that we were making history.

Meanwhile, in Carmen's Hall, the Farmer-Labor Party was holding its own convention. Pinchot

called it "Carmen's Barn," and it was immense
enough to deserve the name. A great overspreading
roof, and four bare walls; a stage crowded with labor leaders, mostly from Chicago, and an auditorium
pullulating with a thousand delegates and visitors.
These men were not so well-dressed as ours, and they
could not talk coherently for more than a minute at
a time; but they knew—or they had been told—
what they must do; and they did it with a brutal
directness and an uncritical unanimity which gave
their leaders an enviable power.

These leaders came to the Morrison, and for two
days they sat in sleepless conference with our own
tacticians. They had their platform as we had ours;
could the two be made one? At every point they
fought for the socialist and radical position; at every
point except that of a free and unmilitarized
America we pleaded for moderation. We reminded
them of the individualist traditions and tendencies
of the inland American, of the acquisitive instinct
that lurks in even the idealist's heart, of the unwill-
ingness of workers to be called "labor," of the
American fear of anything that might be labeled
"socialistic," of the almost innate conservatism of
the propertied farmer, of the need for a platform
simple and brief and modest enough to unite every
group in the land that hated war and poverty, and
still loved liberty. We wanted a program on which
the great Senator from Wisconsin would consent to
run; with such a program and such a candidate, and

with a united front, we could go to battle with the
hope of laying a sound basis for victory in 1924. The
labor leaders replied that they cared more for principles than for any candidate, more for truth than
for expediency; they would make no compromise to
catch a few more votes; they were resolved to demand justice from A to Z, and let America grow up
to understand them if it took a century. Whether
their truths would still be true after the changes of
a hundred years seemed to them academically irrelevant.

I speak as if I had shared in that struggle to
educate in a day men who were trying to see a continent in terms of their shops and locals, their individual hopes and sufferings. But I was not so
privileged; the Convention, with the folly which
characterizes crowds, had not chosen me to serve on
the Conference Committee. I subsided to a Committee
on Resolutions and Platform, and labored there for
days to find a clever formula. When we thought we
had succeeded, old George Record, gray, disheveled
survivor of a thousand political battles, entered to
announce that our meditations were worthless, and
that the two conventions had suddenly united over
our heads.

Then there was wailing and gnashing of teeth,
cursing and bitter tears. One of our leaders, un-
nerved by fifty hours of continuous struggle over
points of theory that were to him matters of political life and death, threw himself upon a bed, and

cried with a child's abandon. Record, meeting us younger ones, glared at us silently and grimly, as if to say: "You insisted on co-operation with the Labor Party; now you have it; go and co-operate."

"How did it happen?" I asked McAlister Coleman, who, like a good newspaperman, always knew what was going on.

"Our delegates were sick of hearing speeches," he said, "and took things into their own hands. A Labor Party man had a motion introduced to amalgamate the conventions at once, and leave all other questions to be decided after that. Our leaders were so buried in conference that the whole show was over before they heard about it. Now the game is up."

Why the game was up became evident when, that afternoon, our convention went over to the "Barn," and merged in fine fraternity with the other. For that other had seven hundred delegates, and we had four hundred; we had to divide and vote according to states, and in almost every state we found ourselves in a futile minority.

"It was an awful mistake," said one of our delegates when I asked him why he had voted for immediate amalgamation. "They talked to us about brotherhood and union, and we yielded to the pretty words. They never told us that once we came here we would be swamped. Now they can put through any motion they like. We might as well go home."

Suddenly the crowd burst into applause. Some one had placed a picture of Senator LaFollette on the platform. The labor leaders frowned, and tried to continue with the discussion then holding the floor. But the convention had a soft spot in its heart for the man who had dared to love peace when all others had lauded war; and they greeted the picture with wild approval. Then the delegates from Wisconsin lifted their state banner on high and marched out into the aisle, singing, over and over again, "We want LaFollette, we want LaFollette!"

"Order!" cried the chairman. "You're out of order. Sit down!"

But they would not sit down; and the noise of his gavel could not drown their songs. We delegates from New York raised our banner and followed them, and others followed us, until there were sixteen states in line. Round and round we marched, shouting and singing like typical Americans drunk with the enthusiasm of politics. We tried to get other states to fall in with us; but their labor delegations were too strong; they clung resolutely to their banners, and waited for the orders of their chiefs. Half an hour later we were all seated again, and the Committee on Resolutions and Platform reported to the convention. Our motion that we should first vote on candidates was defeated. I learned that parades have as much importance in conventions as elections have in determining the policy of governments.

The majority report proposed a socialist platform calling for the nationalization of the larger industries. The minority report, read by George Record, was the platform which Senator LaFollette himself had signed. It was more moderate than the other, of course; but it represented a point of view far beyond that which the mind of America had reached. We knew that our whole fate rested on the acceptance of that minority report.

We stinted no energy in our forlorn effort to stem the tide. Pinchot pled with the convention, in his quiet aristocratic way, not to adopt a class platform. Was there not such a platform already in the field, offered to America with all the eloquence of an imprisoned leader? People did not identify themselves, in America, with the class to which they belonged, but with that to which they aspired, and whose dress and thought they loved to imitate. Record pleaded with these new statesmen to accept counsel of men who had had many years of experience in public affairs, and knew the temper of the country. Americans had a natural distrust of platforms that proposed to rewrite at one stroke the entire political and economic constitution of the land; like Sancho they preferred an island in the Mediterranean to a continent in Utopia. Hopkins pleaded with them for a cleansing away of their hot emotions and their personal resentments. I pleaded with them, with passionate and ridiculous futility. But they would not hear us. The labor leaders had passed the word that their candidate was not LaFollette, and their followers followed them. In the center of the hall sat the Illinois delegation, numbering three hundred men—

one-fourth of all the delegates; they were unanimous against us, and drowned out our oratory mercilessly with their noise. It was not a convention, it was a mob. The chairman acted honestly; he did his best to secure us a hearing, but they would not give it to us. Our substitute resolution embodying the minority platform was voted down.

After that it did not matter what happened. Our defeated leaders sat back exhausted, and said no more. Amos Pinchot, having fought to the last inch, lay limp across two chairs, sleeping so soundly that not all the pandemonium of the balloting convention could awaken him. I found my way back to the Morrison, and went to bed.

In the morning I learned the dénouement. Senator LaFollette had refused to allow his name to be included among the nominations. Then the labor leaders, mostly Irish Catholics, had named a young Irish Catholic lawyer from New York, a man of attractive personality and a matchless orator. His rivals for the nomination sent word around the hall that he was a Catholic. At once the convention ceased to be a political gathering and became a religious meeting, hotly divided according to their ancient faiths. Early in the balloting it became clear that no Catholic could receive the nomination. The young lawyer withdrew his name, and the convention faced the pathetic anti-climax of looking about for a man who would condescend to accept its honors. For hours they talked and waited and voted; and then at last, towards dawn, in order to go home and sleep, they nominated a man whom nobody had ever heard of before, and whom no one will ever hear of again.

That is how I played politics in Chicago.

On the train back to New York I was accosted by a well-dressed, comfortable-looking man, ruddy-faced and gray-haired, with a twinkle in his eye.

"You'll pardon my asking, but aren't you the young man who spoke at the Labor Party Convention yesterday?"

I was more offended at being called a young man than I would be now; people do not call me that any longer.

"Yes," I said, briefly, not anxious to review that ignominy.

"Well, you were right, of course," he said, making himself at home in the opposite seat. "But how in the world did you ever get mixed up with that wild gang?"

"I thought I could be a lion-tamer," I answered, sadly.

He laughed the hearty laugh of a successful man.

"I was passing the place by chance yesterday; I went in because the noise aroused my curiosity. Those labor delegates reminded me of the time when I belonged to the Knights of Labor, 'way back in the nineties."

I began to be interested. This prosperous business man had been a laborer? I should never have suspected it.

"So there were labor unions then too," I remarked. "Were they as radical as Chicago's?"

"Oh, yes," he said. "There's always been about the same proportion of radicals in this country, and perhaps in most countries, since I was born. When radical parties grow, like the Socialists in Germany, or the Laborites in England, it's not because the people are becoming more radical, but because the radical party is becoming comparatively conservative."

"So you think we make no progress?"

"I wouldn't say that. We make all sorts of progress—except in government. And after all, government is unimportant; it's the economic life that counts; that's where mastery lies, and that's where oppression really hurts. Real men go into business, and leave politics to those who don't know better. Hence the progress in politics."

I said nothing; but he was content to carry on the conversation.

"I was a Socialist once myself," he said. "I sympathize with these young radicals, but I know what will happen to them. I'm an awful example. Either they'll succeed materially, or they won't. If they don't they'll continue to complain about 'the environment,' or 'the sins of society,'—they'll plead 'not guilty,' as we used to do in Blatchford's days. But if

307

they learn the ropes and get on you won't see their names in the Socialist membership books any more. Ten years later they'll be voting for the most conservative candidate in the field, on the ground that they would lose money by any disturbance or uncertainty in business conditions. This leakage of ability from the radical movement goes on all the time; the cream rises to the top and gets skimmed away. About the only clever fellows who remain are those who hold positions of honor or leadership. That's why you have so many radical parties; there are more offices to go around."

"I think there are some who are loyal under all conditions," I said.

He smiled.

"They are holy exceptions who can be counted on two hands."

I was silent, too tired and apathetic to make argument. But he went on.

"You see, every radical is a rebel, and every socialist is an individualist. Now you can't organize individualists. They split into a thousand sects, just as individualist Protestantism does. Everyone wants to have his way. There's no possible discipline among them. When one of them is outvoted he goes off in a huff and starts a new party. At last there are so many sects that nobody takes them seriously, and the big fellows who run the country can safely leave them to fight one another to death."

He puffed his cigar, and I looked out of the window moodily. He resumed.

"It might be different if radicals didn't marry. A radical married is already half a conservative. The family is naturally a conservative institution. When you're afraid, you're conservative; and parents are always worried about the future of their children. Nobody is so selfish, as far as the rest of the world is concerned, as the mother who loves her offspring. When the parents begin to save, their radicalism evaporates. Even if they have only a few hundred dollars put aside for a rainy day they are suspicious of any movement that wants to turn things inside out. They don't want any bank failures, much less a government overturn that might make their little savings as worthless as Russian rubles."

"It all sounds very hopeless," I remarked. "And yet you said you believed in progress."

"Why not? You're thinking of something to be gotten by passing laws. It doesn't come that way. Voting is just a modern sport, and means about as much in its results to the country as a world-series ball-game. Wealth will go on ruling, whether we vote or not."

"I don't agree with you," I said.

"Well," he asked, with the good nature of a man smoking a satisfactory cigar, "what do you think?"

I did not want to think, but I tried in my weak way to answer him.

"I think knowledge will rule. To-day it is commercial knowledge that rules—the ability to sell things to people who do not need them. The rich are no longer those who make things, but those who buy and sell things. That won't go on forever."

He smiled patiently.

"Yes?" he suggested.

"A higher knowledge will come. Scientific knowledge. It has come in war; there already the business man's type of knowledge is worthless; it only makes for chaos and corruption, as in our shipping and aviation scandals. Some day science will be applied as far in industry as it is in war; and a knowledge of mathematics, physics, chemistry, engineering, statistics, biology, psychology, and similar fields will be in greater demand, with almost every firm, than the knowledge of where to buy cheap and how to sell dear. Capital without science will be useless, labor without science will be useless. Labor as we know it, manual labor, will disappear. Electricity—clean hydro-electric or aero-electric power—will do the menial work of the world. There'll be no 'working class' at all. There'll be no slums, no poverty, no dirt in the world any more."

"You inspire me," he said, with genial irony. "I suspect it won't come in my time; but in any case it would be better than a bloody revolution."

"There have been only two revolutions," I said, "—the agricultural and the industrial. The third will be the scientific revolution. It will be the greatest and most peaceful of all. Slavery will pass away, and knowledge will rule."

He smiled again, almost tenderly.

"I congratulate you," he said; "you are still young."

CHAPTER XII

NADIR

THAT conversation, dear Reader, was merely an invention of my imagination; I have not the heart to deceive you. And that vague and tenuous business man was only another side of myself, one of the many selves that made me the stage of a bitter debate as I returned from Chicago and politics to life and home. I hesitate to confess the depths of despair, cynicism, and apathy to which I fell in those days. At times I classed all men under various species of villainy; all officeholders were corrupt, all trade-union leaders were politicians, all business men were misers, all conservatives were cowards, and all radicals were fools.

I began to see history as a kaleidoscope of stagnation. The more life had changed, the more it had remained the same. There had been hundreds of political revolutions, and not one of them but had begotten a new ruling class as corrupt and ruthless as the old. Every invention had been captured by the strong, and had increased the gap between them and the weak. The development of machinery had made millionaires of the few, and mere animate tools of the many. The development of transportation had begotten a class of middlemen who absorbed, to the point of diminishing returns, the results of the farmer's husbandry and the proletarian's industry; men rose to position and opulence not by producing consumable goods but by interposing themselves inescapably between producer and consumer; the arteries of the world's economic life were being squeezed tighter and drier every year. The development of communication—of printing and telegraph and telephone and wireless—had merely increased the facilities for spreading misinformation, prejudice, and propaganda; in time of stress these agencies were no longer media for news, but instruments of "morale"; and at all times they served as a vast mechanism of suggestion so irresistible through unanimity and volume that not one person in a thousand could do anything else but think and feel with the crowd. The development of science had made explosives, long-distance artillery, and air-plane bombers, which put subject nations and subject majorities absolutely at the mercy of vigorous governments and imperialist powers. The discovery of the means of contraception had resulted in the sterility of the intelligent and the multiple fertility of the unfortunate; it had nullified the work of education by destroying the social transmission of moral and intellectual culture; and it was gradually repeopling Europe and America with a population reconciled to slavery and wedded to bigotry and superstition.

In this frame of mind I saw nothing in democracy but mockery; a quadrennial or biennial drama which the rulers staged for the ruled as a substitute for the circuses that had soothed the proletariat of Rome. In America the economic bases of democracy —free land, free competition, and open opportunity —had almost passed away; the tools of production had become so complex and costly that only great corporations could purchase them; the differentiation of trades, the growth of land values, and the accumulation of hereditary privileges had multiplied a hundredfold the natural inequality of men; and the specious equality of the vote was the last rag with which America could cover her industrial feudalism and present a virtuously democratic front to the world. And that surviving pretense of letting the people rule had melted away in the heat of the very war that was to confer democracy upon all the nations of the earth.

From complaining that democracy had disappeared, I passed to the inconsistent view that it was a worthless and impossible scheme in any case. I reflected on the growing complexity of political affairs; the transition from the easy-going ceremonial existence of medieval courts, ruling, with the aid of the priesthood, a homogeneous population of peasants, to the harassed life of a modern government, caught in a maze of foreign relations, and called upon at every turn to adjudicate among the conflicting forces of an individualist industrial society. How could that poor abstraction, the average citizen, pretend to have the knowledge requisite for forming, on these entangled issues, any judgment that would be worth expressing? It was only by courteous hypocrisy that the men who decided these issues went through the occasional formality of consulting the nation. And the unreality of the franchise was no greater in the politics of the country than in the affairs of labor unions, or of radical parties; everywhere a few men who had knowledge and ability led by the nose a majority who had none. I concluded that elections were an irksome and expensive futility, and that we ought to ask our masters to rule us without adding to our burdens of indirect taxation the immense cost of these periodical orgies of national delusion.

I tried to comfort myself with the trite consideration that an uninformed electorate might nevertheless choose representatives who, gathered in conference, would meet with fair adequacy the problem of reconciling the brute realities of economic strife with the desires of their constituents. For a time, in Washington, I studied our National Palaver from the Senate galleries; and I discovered very soon that these splendid orators had never been selected for their economic knowledge, or their administrative competence. It was a scandal known to all the world that these congresses and parliaments had been snubbed most cavalierly during and since the War; that the executive power had encroached upon the legislature till the latter had become merely a talk-shop and a register of imperial or presidential decrees. I found that the concentration of economic power had begotten, as its natural heir, a concentration of political power; that state rights were dead; that the business of the world now got itself done through cabinets and councils and expert economic boards; that those very representatives whom we so labored to elect, whom we had prided ourselves on as the obedient voices of our sovereign will,—these representatives, too, counted for nothing, except as voices, capable of endless eloquence, but to no end.

In those dark days I shed most of the social and political ideals that had exhilarated me in my twenties. I, who had dreamed of the time when the workers would rule the world, now found it unpleasant to ride alongside them in the subway. I lost whatever enthusiasm I might ever have had for a dictatorship of the proletariat, or even for "the rule of the people." Socialism, like Christianity, would always be a voice in the wilderness crying out for justice and brotherly love, while the world would go on with the struggle for existence and the survival of the "fittest"—that is to say, the most acquisitive, the most pugnacious, and the most masterful. There would always be strong and weak, clever and simple, ruthless and timid men; and the ruthlessly clever strong would always rule the timid and simple weak. Material comforts would increase; but political

changes would be at best a transition between two
forms of oligarchical power. It might be an oligarchy
of land-owners, as in the Middle Ages; or an oligarchy of industrial and financial magnates, as in
the current world; or an oligarchy of trade-union
leaders, such as could conceivably come in the England of 1950. But an aristocracy of some kind was
inevitable. Why should I disturb myself as to just
which minority would rule or exploit the world when
I should be long since dead? I no longer cared.

No; all these ideals of mine, all the ideals of mankind, were the cowardly self-deceptions with which
we covered up the sharp actualities of life. Socialism was envy; anarchism was a secret lust for power;
democracy was an anesthetic applied to the people
while their pockets were being picked and their blood
was sucked away. Love was the desire for possession,
courtship was combat, mating was mastery, marriage
was monotony, parentage was the subjugation of
the individual by the race. The family was an incor-
porated selfishness, maternal love was a proprietary
instinct, kindness was a timid bribe to peace. Christianity was a lovely phrase designed to conceal the
war of each against all; religion was merely the fear
of death, and the egotistic hunger for perpetuity.

Behind all these fig-leaves lay the naked truth of
the struggle for existence, for food and mates and
land and power. That struggle had always gone on:
the sharp relics of the caves showed how it had filled
the lives of Neanderthal and Cro-Magnon men; the

Homeric ballads wove into one song the lust for
women and for conquest; beneath the exalted culture of Athens lay a chaotic individualism and a
barbarous slavery; history was the Newgate Cal-
endar of nations, a record of war and slaughter,
of robbery and deceit, of crime and exploitation, of
ignorance and bigotry and suicidal vice. And there
was no sign that the future would be different from
the past. Population would continue to press upon
the means of subsistence, filling up the inviting
spaces of the world like water running into pools,
and fighting with stealthy mercilessness for the in-
sufficient resources and luxuries of the earth. There
would be greater and more marvelous machines than
before; but they would enslave and brutalize the
masses, and in every generation they would destroy
millions in the holocausts of war. If, in all this hell
of violence and greed, an individual or a people
should try to realize the ideals of brotherhood and
peace, they would be crushed down into vassalage by
men and races unscrupulously strong. The very re-
quirements of the struggle for existence would force
men to be grasping warriors. Undoubtedly the time
would come when some hardier and more cunning
animal would conquer and enslave or destroy mankind; or perhaps some persistent insect, or the multiplying bacteria, would at last capture the citadel
they had so long besieged, and bring man to an end
with pestilence. And then these species too would
live and struggle, and meet superior foes, and these

again; until the heat or energy of earth and sun would fail, and life in every form would perish from a planet inhospitably cold and dead. Evolution was not progress, it was war; and its end was not Utopia, but death.

I wonder how many men and women were passing through a similar disillusionment in those days; for how many of them the world of hope and faith faded away, revealing for the first time the stark reality and cruelty of life? I believe that there were thousands and thousands of people who could have matched all my despair with theirs, thousands who like me had gone through the double bereavement and the double apostasy of leaving the faith of their fathers and the hopeful visions of their youth. I met them everywhere as I passed through America; I would have met them in Europe had I gone there again. The War had broken the hearts or the hopes of millions who had once felt the fire of social passion burning in their blood. The Russian Revolution had roused in some souls the most fantastic expectations; and when it became clear that the Revolution could not realize their dreams, those who had been most enthusiastic became most cynical. An undertow of pessimism seemed to be dragging the finest, and once the most fervent, souls into a maelstrom of cynicism and despair. Everything had been tried, the most superhuman efforts had been made; but every effort had failed. There was hardly anything left to do, except perhaps, if one could, to eat and drink and be merry while it was day. For the night would come, after which there would be nothing.

I think it was about this time that I became conscious of the sombre reality and quiet certainty of death. I was thirty-five now; and probably the sense that youth and energy were slipping from me had much to do with the loss of my earlier ideals and hopes. I no longer felt the exhilarating surplus of vital income over vital expenditure; every day I used up more power than I could regain. In youth I had been always on the move, excitable, energetic, hasty; now the pace of life slackened in me, and I observed how at every turn I sought to save my strength.

I began to understand the look of fear in the eyes of the old; their lack of interest in the struggles of the world; their long silences and broodings: they had seen the advancing shadow of the Enemy. I began to hear of the death of vigorous men whom I had known in my youth; even of playmates who must have been yet in the prime of life. What futile transitory things we were! Men and women were falling dead around me almost as if we were in advancing battle-line and a thousand shells were decimating us. It dawned upon me at last that I too would die, I who so loved the sun and the green fields and the touch of love and the laughter of

320

children—I would have to leave them, and go down like all the rest into everlasting darkness. Once I stood in the doorway of the New Old South Church in Boston, and read the memorial to its ancient founders. They were two hundred and fifty years dead; and yet they too had been young and strong, full of enthusiasm and ambition, unthinking of the end. How pitiless time is! How every life must pass away, though all the world else continues, careless of our going! Time is our greatest benefactor and our greatest foe—it gives us wisdom and it gives us death. Not death itself is terrible, but leaving undone the things we might do, and leaving behind us forever the souls we have learned to love.

I tried to believe, but I could not believe, that there would be another life for me after this weakening frame should break. What a consolation religion must be, I thought, to all those who see death! I might have faced the matter more cheerfully had I not known in childhood that relieving hope. It had gone from me, and nothing had taken its place; I was left empty and desolate. I belonged to the age of the Great Sadness. They had told me a pretty story when I was young, and now I would always mourn because that story was not true. All man's hopes were false; all things would die; and every heart must break.

CHAPTER XIII

I BECOME A DADDY

AND then Ethel came.

That, though it is here so near the end, was the center and turning-point of my life. For many years Ariel and I had pondered the pros and cons of parentage. We lived in the age and place of the emancipated woman; and the reasonable revolt which had broken out against the mechanical fertility of the old-fashioned wife had passed over into an extreme reaction in which childlessness was the sign of a liberated mind. We had participated in the birth-control movement, and had known its leaders well. We had heard a thousand times of the dangers and tribulations that came with children; we had never been told of the joys they might bring. We took it for granted that discretion was the better part of love.

While we had been growing up, the Industrial Revolution had played many a prank with the happiness of women. It had brought about such changes in their status, their habits, and their minds as rivaled in rapidity the industrial transition itself. It had lured them from the varied drudgery of the home into the dull routine of the factory, merely solacing their slavery with wages. No doubt the first feminine pay-envelope was almost as exhilarating as the first sin. It seemed to bring emancipation at last from the brutal tyranny of the male. That it was another writ of bondage could not appear on that first bright day of freedom. And so one by one the women of our great cities had been drawn into offices and factories by the terrific suction of that economic law which impels all but the finest employers to seek the cheapest labor to produce the cheapest goods.

Ariel had barely known this serfdom of the shop; but even that brief glimpse had frightened her. We thought that she had escaped the evils of the new order; but very soon we found that no woman could save herself from them entirely. For the same industrial expansion which had forced women into the factories had stolen from the home the hundred occupations which had filled the life of women in the past. One after another the old domestic industries had disappeared: the machines of the shop could sew and wash and iron and clean and cook more cheaply than the unaided mother in the home. Nothing was left of the home but a house, and then an apartment or cell in a gigantic hive; and above the proletariat nothing was left of woman but her beauty and her sex. She had no children and she had no work. She had lost her function, and therefore her significance and her happiness; her "emancipation" had made her, unwittingly and unwillingly, a hundred times more parasitic than before. It was brave of her to go into the factory; she sought there the work and meaning that had gone from her; she did not care to remain a functionless ornament, a thing of beauty that would not be a joy forever.

I had been reared by a generation which held it disgraceful that a man should let his wife work outside the home—though it had said nothing of slavery within. That feeling too is caught in the flux of transition, and will shortly pass away. But so it was with me; and in consequence Ariel found herself aimlessly idle, consumed with a sense that her life was incomplete, and her happiness unsubstantial and insecure. This feeling of emptiness and dissatisfaction entered even into me, absorbed though I was in a hundred tasks. I began to be jealous of certain friends of mine whose faces beamed as they looked upon their children. I did not dare speak to Ariel of so old-fashioned and sentimental a yearning; I knew that in this matter she would bear the brunt of the risk and the suffering, and that hers was the right to choose. But one night as we sat in the dark, her arm around my neck and mine about her waist, we told each other of our discontent, and I hinted vaguely at what I thought might be the solution. For a time Ariel said nothing. And then, as my lips wandered over her hair, she whispered her consent.

It was an index of the times that before making this final step into the fulness of life we went to a famous physician and asked him to examine into our fitness for parentage. Were we quite worthy to participate in the reproduction of the race? We took the question very much to heart, and trembled a little as we were put through the tests. The good Doctor decided that the race might take a chance on us, and we walked out with our heads up and our souls elated with this new adventure. I was already proud in presumptuous anticipation of the most common of human achievements, and the most minor of male rôles.

There was a subtle pride too in Ariel's carriage when, a few months later, she knew that she would be a mother. She felt none of the shame that some superlatively modern women have, who hide within four doors, and starve their double selves of air and movement to cover up the crime of pregnancy. Ariel marched forth bravely, and took the sun from morn till night, resolved that her child should have the best start that healthy motherhood could give it. And as I watched her the eternally youthful blood of the race began to course mysteriously through my veins again; I forgot that I was passing the peak of the hill of life, and that love is a prelude to death and replacement; instead, a strange new happiness began to crowd out my political disillusionment and my philosophical despair.

How carefully we counted the days, and prepared

ourselves for the great fulfilment! What discussions we carried on about every article of diet and every habit of life! We sought out the physician of best repute in our locality, and Ariel went to him regularly. It never entered our innocent heads that his examinations were superficial and careless, and that with all our preparations we were sailing into disaster.

We calculated that on Monday, May 12th, the little wonder would mature. About eleven o'clock on Saturday evening Ariel complained of a severe headache; and at once we suspected that the great ordeal had begun. I called up our doctor and begged him to come over. He laughed at me.

"Only a headache? Anybody can get a headache. There's plenty of time yet. You wouldn't want me to come and sit around just for a headache, would you? Give your wife some aspirin tablets."

The truth was that the villain was going to bed, and did not want to be disturbed, even for the sake of the species. I let him be, and gave Ariel what headache tablets we had in the house. We were alone; and there was no friend in the other apartments whom we could ask to run errands for us at that time of the night. The headache continued, and became worse.

"Oh, Jack, there's a great hammer pounding in on my brain," Ariel moaned. "Can't you get that doctor to come? I'm so afraid."

Suddenly her eyes closed, her face whitened, her

body stiffened out on the couch where she had been reclining, and her hands began to paw the air as if fighting off some enemy. I was horrified.

"Ariel, Ariel, what's the matter?" I cried, catching her in my arms. But she did not hear me, and her hands passed aimlessly over my face. Her knees rose convulsively and her head fell back. Then slowly her body relaxed, her limbs straightened, and her hands ceased their wild movement; she seemed to be sleeping.

I rushed again to the telephone, and asked for my doctor's number. I heard his bell ring, but there was no response.

"Ring till he answers," I begged the operator. And at last he spoke.

"Oh," he said, sleepily, "is that you?"

I told him of the convulsion Ariel had had.

"That's bad," he said. "I'll come over at once. Meanwhile call up Fordham Hospital and ask them to come and get your wife. It will be too much for me."

It was an hour before he came. In the meantime I sat beside my sleeping Ariel, anxious as I have never been before or since; praying incoherently that her suffering would be brief, that there would be no more convulsions, and that the doctor would come. Suddenly Ariel opened her eyes, and looked at me wildly.

"Oh, God!" she cried, "I can't bear it. Didn't you get the doctor?"

"Yes, sweetheart," I answered, ashamed; "he's coming. Where does it hurt?"

"In my head," she said, weakly. And then again her eyes closed, her knees jumped up, her mouth bubbled with froth, and her hands moved wildly through the air. I did not know what to do; I put my arms around her and tried to hold her still, though I knew that that would do no good. In those moments I forgot my religious doubts, and called upon God over and over again to come to our aid, and not to let my Ariel die. And then once more she fell back exhausted, and slept.

The doctor came, evidently tired and resentful. He tried the pulse, listened to the heart, took the temperature, and did other learned and traditional things. Ariel did not awake.

"Has she had any abdominal pains yet?" he asked.

"No," I replied; "at least she claims the pain is in her head."

"Well, she ought to know. If there are no abdominal pains it will be a long time before she is ready. Have you called up the hospital?"

"Yes. They said they'd be here soon."

"They will; they're reliable."

And then, despite my protests, he left us.

It was about two o'clock in the morning when he went. At five o'clock the ambulance came. During those three hours Ariel had convulsions every quarter of an hour, with increasing violence. When the young hospital doctor appeared I saw at once from his face that the situation was grave.

"It's an eclampsia case," he said. "It will be troublesome, but she ought to pull through."

"Do most such cases come out all right?" I asked, anxiously.

"About fifty per cent of them," he replied.

So Ariel had one chance out of two for her life.

I helped them place her on a stretcher, and led the way carefully as the doctor and his aides carried her down the stairs. When they had laid her in the ambulance I asked might I ride with them to the hospital.

"No," the doctor said, decisively; "we're absolutely forbidden to let any one ride with us."

"I'll just ride on the tail-board," I pleaded.

"We can't do it. Take the trolley at the foot of the hill, and you'll get there as soon as we will."

I looked at Ariel as if I would never see her again, and then rushed down the hill. There were no trolleys visible anywhere, nor any taxicabs. I was a mile and a half from the hospital. I began to walk, looking back for a trolley or a cab; but when none appeared I broke into a run. I burst into the hospital with a minimum of formality.

"Where have they taken my wife?" I asked of the first nurse I saw,—as if all the world knew Ariel.

"I don't know," she answered, patiently. "But they just brought in a 'clampsia case; is that it?

I think they've gone to Ward Three; on the second floor, at that end."

I rushed up the stairs, and to Ward Three. I found Ariel in the midst of a violent convulsion; two doctors held her lest she should fall to the floor, or hurt herself against the iron bed. One of them greeted me.

"I'm Nelson, one of your old students at The Workers' Church. So is Dr. Cox. You may trust us to do the very best we can for your wife. We've already sent for Dr. Telfaer, who is our consulting specialist in these cases."

"But will she come through?" I asked, in a breaking voice.

"I think so," he said.

They were ominous words for me; and though Ariel had again fallen back into an exhausted sleep, I trembled to think that at any moment she might have another convulsion.

"Will you step into the waiting-room for a few minutes?" Dr. Cox suggested.

I obeyed, anxious to keep their good will; but I feared they were about to do some terrible thing to Ariel. Ten minutes later they called me back.

"We took some blood from her," said Dr. Cox. "She had a very high blood-pressure. Now the convulsions won't be so violent."

I nearly embraced him for this crumb of comfort. Just then poor Ariel drew herself up into a heap, and moaned, and pawed the air blindly again.

The doctors held her hands gently, and one of them slipped a bit of wood between her teeth lest she should bite her tongue.

"Who was your physician?" asked Dr. Nelson.

I named the scoundrel.

"He neglected her criminally. Any honest examination would have shown excess albumin, and it could have been remedied. He ought to be run out of the profession."

Ariel was quiet now, and seemed to me to be sleeping more peacefully and breathing more easily than before. I had time to notice the patient on the cot beside her. She was tossing about restlessly, though her eyes were closed; and she moaned without ceasing.

"Is she in childbirth pains?" I asked Dr. Cox.

"Yes. She's another eclampsia case. We shall have to operate on her to-day."

"What sort of operation?"

"Cæsarian."

I could say no more. I knew that they might have to do that to Ariel,—cut her dear body open, and take out our child, leaving perhaps both of them dead. A dull and suffocating heat spread through me and consumed my strength. I sat down on the nurse's chair near Ariel's bed, and looked blindly at the floor. Why had I been so anxious for a child? How could any child be worth this suffering? What sense was there in making a helpless infant at the cost of so young a life as Ariel's? What a miserable absurdity it was, this business of reproducing the race,—to rear a girl through years and years of patient care, to make her happy and healthy, and then to sacrifice her, as if to another Moloch, on the altar of the species! And what was the species itself but millions of mothers suffering so, and millions of men standing by them, as I stood now by Ariel, guilty and helpless?

When Dr. Telfaer came I was again asked to step aside; but from my chair in the waiting-room I could hear them debating the advisability of an operation. Dr. Telfaer opposed it.

"Wait a little," he said. "Wait till noon."

It was seven o'clock now, and Ariel's family, called by me over the telephone, came to see her. First Harry, always cheerful, and refusing to believe that there was any real danger; what a comfort he was to me during those days! And then Morris and Flora and Mary and Michael, full of tender anxiety, but all confident that Ariel's health and strength would see her through. And finally the mother, gentle and timid, and already in tears as she entered the room. We went to where Ariel was sleeping, her face red and swollen.

"Don't wake her, mother," I whispered.

She longed to hear her daughter's voice, but she said nothing. She wanted to embrace her, but she held herself back. Instead, she went behind the head of the bed, bent down, and kissed again and again

Ariel's dishevelled hair, that streamed over the pillow. Then we drew her away.

"My Khaya, my Khaya," she cried, quietly.

I knew that she was thinking as I had thought: that she had borne this daughter with pain, and brought her up for many years through a thousand hardships, and lavished infinite love upon her,—for this, that she should die, perhaps, in the effort to bring into the world another child fated to similar suffering and similar futility. I could hardly look into her eyes; I felt responsible for this evil, and my shame made me almost wordless.

"Mother," I said, "if Ariel does not live I won't either."

She shook her head sadly.

"No, John," she whispered, "you mustn't say that. It isn't your fault."

I owe them all a great debt for their gentleness to me that morning. The cruel chasm of race had once divided us, and yet they held me now as a brother. Harry above all was kind, and stayed with me throughout that anxious Sunday, and through my two sleepless nights, never leaving me till the end.

At one o'clock the physicians were again in conference. Dr. Cox came into the waiting-room and said:

"No operation yet. We'll wait a few hours longer. She may be strong enough to have a natural delivery."

All this time Ariel slept; and so deeply that every now and then I went in, on tiptoe, to assure myself that she was not dead. Three o'clock came, and yet she slept. Five o'clock came, the hour at which I was to address an audience at the Workers' Church; indifferently I saw the time come and pass; what were lectures to me now? Night came, and Ariel slept it through.

Late that Sunday evening the nurses wheeled a bed, on which a pale, emaciated mother lay, into the room opposite that in which Harry and I were sitting.

"Who is it?" I asked Dr. Nelson.

"The other eclampsia case," he answered reluctantly. "We operated on her this afternoon."

"Will she live?" I asked.

"We hope for the best," he answered. I knew that that was a medical formula for hope run dry.

I sat at the window, looking out into the dark, while Harry slept with his head on the table. I vowed never again to indulge in the pride of paternity. I remembered Ariel's hesitation, and my yearning; what an ignorant criminal I had been to forget, in all my arguments, that no human life is made without risking human life! What should I do if Ariel died?

"If Ariel dies," I thought, "I'll go far out into the woods and lie down on my face in the grass; and I'll never get up again."

I heard a commotion near the door, and went out.

334

Several nurses were gathered about the woman who had had the Cæsarian operation; and in the corridor the doctors were talking quietly.

"She's dying," said one of them, calmly.

"Yes," said another.

As I stepped out of the waiting room I could hear the woman's breathing,—quick, struggling gasps. Her eyes were closed, but her lips opened and trembled convulsively. Even as I looked at her through the door of her room her breathing became heavier, and a queer noise came from her throat.

"It's the death-rattle," said Dr. Cox. "Could you," he asked me, "call up her husband and ask him to come at once? Here's his card."

I took the card and went down stairs to the telephone. I heard the husband's voice, and stumbled for words.

"Come at once," I repeated.

"Is she dying? Tell me the truth," he pleaded.

"I don't know," I lied. "Come."

When I returned upstairs the woman was dead. The nurses had covered her face, and now they left and closed the door upon her.

I went back to the waiting room, and tried to sleep. A few minutes later the husband came, a handsome and passionate young man who knelt beside his dead wife and moaned all through the night. They showed him his motherless child, but he turned away from it blindly.

I could not sleep. In the stillness and the darkness

I heard the death-rattle of the young mother, just one year married; and saw my Ariel, too, lying like her, dead. Monday's sun was rising when I fell asleep, my head on the table at Harry's side.

Two hours later a sharp cry pierced my dulled senses.

"Jack! Jack! I want Jack!"

I stumbled out of the room and found my way to Ariel. She was reclining on her elbow, one hand pressing on her side, a look of pain and fear on her face. A nurse stood near her, but seemed to attach no importance to her cries and her suffering.

"Her pains are beginning," she said, simply.

"Beginning?" I muttered. So all these thirty hours since that first hammer-blow on the brain,—they were painless by comparison with what was coming? I took Ariel's hand, and spoke to her, but she did not know me.

"Jack! Jack!" she cried again, looking vaguely past me. "Where are you? Come to me! Oh, I'm going to die!"

Suddenly she raised her shoulders from the bed, opened her mouth wide for the breath that would hardly come, and moaned:

"O God! O God! O God!"

I put my arm around her neck and kissed her; but she did not notice me. Her face was white with torture, and her eyes, though open, seemed to see nothing but some ghastly vision of suffering and death, from which she wished to flee but could not. The nurse looked at her watch, and wrote something on a pad. Dr. Cox entered, and greeted us.

"How is she getting along?" he asked.

"She's been having pains at twenty-minute intervals," answered the nurse.

At that moment another woman in the ward began to cry out.

"I suppose I'd better go to her for a while," said the nurse, wearily. "Could you," she asked me, "time your wife's pains for half an hour or so?"

Her assumption that the pains would go on for more than half an hour filled me with rage against this irrational universe. My hand trembled as I took the pad.

"Dr. Cox," I said, "you should let every husband see his wife go through this. He would be a little kinder to her for a while."

"We can't afford to let them see it," he replied. "They might never have children again."

"Well," I said, bitterly, "is it worth the suffering?"

"It will be all over in an hour," he said, "and then you'll be more cheerful. You think it's nature's fault, but it's really our own. We turn our women into dolls, choose them for their slim waists, send them into factories, feed them on delicacies, and in general make pretty wrecks of them. Peasant women don't suffer so. In this case it's the result of one doctor's negligence.—Can you take care of the time-chart? Call

337

me when the pains come at five-minute intervals."

I agreed, and he left us. While we talked Ariel slept, breathing always with difficulty. The Doctor had hardly gone when she lifted herself again on her side, her face drawn taut with pain.

"O mother!" she gasped, "O mother! O God!"

I stood there helpless. If I touched her she released herself from me; if I spoke her name, or mine, she did not seem to hear me. She was alone in her suffering. I noted the minute at which the pain had come, while the inevitable tears fell hot upon my hand.

Now the spasms became more frequent, and more severe. I seemed dulled by my consciousness of impotence; and as if in a trance I wrote on the pad, and looked at my watch. As I wrote, two other women, caught in the throes of procreation, sent their shrill shrieks through the room. I felt Dr. Cox's touch on my arm; he took the pad and the pencil from me, and without a word led me to my seat in the waiting room. I had wanted to see it all, to see every bit of this tragedy with which life's comedy begins; now I made no resistance and offered no word as I was led away. But I kept whispering to myself, incoherently:

"I must always be kind to women. I must always be kind to women."

An hour later the child had been born, and Ariel, though still breathing heavily, was silent and still. I bent over her.

"Ariel," I said, "this is Jack. Do you know me? I shall always be good to you."

I think she did not hear me. She turned round with a sigh, moaned for a while, and then fell asleep. I sat by her a long time, grateful that she could sleep at last, and that she had come up from the battle-field where life is won. She was dearer to me now than ever before; dear with a love too deep for any words, and lifted far beyond the passing hunger of the flesh. I knew that she had paid a terrible price for the child she had given me. Dr. Cox entered, and asked would I come and see my little daughter; she was washed and dressed now, and fit for company. But I was absolutely apathetic.

"I don't care to see her yet," I said dully.

He smiled, and left me alone.

A moment later a specialist came and examined Ariel's eyes. They were insensitive to even a bright light placed close before them.

"Will her sight come back?" I asked, almost too weakly to be heard.

"I think so," the doctor replied.

I had to be content with that.

Throughout the day Ariel slept. In the afternoon Dr. Cox took me into a large, darkened room, that had almost the temperature of a hot-house. Here in their baskets were the new-born babes. Some were covered with blotches, others were drooling at the mouth; some had great red marks on their temples, where the forceps had taken hold to pull them, willy-nilly, into the world. Some were awake and crying; others moved restlessly in their sleep. We stopped before a baby that seemed to me cleaner and plumper than the rest.

"This is your little girl," said Dr. Cox. "What are you going to call her?"

I was not ready with the answer.

"We thought it would be a boy," I said.

"Never mind," he smiled. "A girl is much more affectionate. Some day you'll love her more than you could ever have loved a boy."

That evening I went out to lecture, drunk with sleeplessness and harassed with the vision of a permanently blinded Ariel. When the talk was over, friends inquired why I had dragged physicians, hospitals, medicines, forceps, and Cæsarian operations into a lecture on philosophy. I begged for mercy; and in my explanations I discerned already a trace of insane pride in having reproduced my species, however weakly.

That night I slept at home with Harry. Early the next morning I hurried to the hospital and Ariel's side. She was awake, after a sleep of twenty hours.

"Jack!" she cried; "I knew you'd come early."

"Darling," I said, covering her with kisses; "can you see me?"

"See you? Of course. Why do you ask that?"

"Yesterday, sweetheart, you were blind."

"Blind?"

"Yes; don't you remember?"

"No," she said, wondering.

"Don't you remember the doctor examining your eyes?"

"No. Did he?"

"Do you remember how they took you to the hospital?"

"No."

"Don't you remember the convulsions, or the pains?"

"I remember the headache. But did I have convulsions?"

I passed to other topics. It was well that she could not remember.

"Have they shown you our baby, Ariel?" I asked.

"Yes. When they told me it was a girl I cried. But when they showed her to me I fell in love with her. She's such a pretty baby, Jack."

I was comforted to see that Ariel was returning to life and normal reactions.

"Nurse," she said, "isn't it time to give her a little food?"

"Not yet," said the nurse.

"Ah, won't you bring her anyway, and let her daddy see her?"

"It's against the rules," the nurse answered.

But she went out, and soon came back with a bundle, and presented it to Ariel. Why is it that at once I loved that little bundle profoundly, and raised the coverings with the tenderest care? Instinctively I felt that this queer wriggling baby was to be infinitely precious to me. I knew that a million such tots came into the world every day, and were dear beyond utterance to one mother and one father, and seemed to them incomparably beautiful. But I was comfortably like others; I was sure that I had never seen so fair an infant face before.

"She will be pretty," I said, fondly.

"Let me have her," said Ariel, smiling through her tears.

And as the baby clutched at her breast, and finding its food, nestled contentedly against her warm body, she looked down at it tenderly.

"I'm so happy it's over, Jack," she said.

"Will you ever forgive me, sweetheart?" I asked.

She held her arm out to me and drew my cheek down against hers.

"I'm glad she came," she whispered. "Isn't she sweet?"

I sat beside her many hours, listening to her lovingly. I could have knelt and kissed the earth.

CHAPTER XIV

ENTSAGEN

It is right that my story should end here; for since Ethel came my world has revolved about her rather than about me, and I have had the happiness of the nation that knows no history. I should never have expected to be so easily content, and to resign so readily my ambition to remake the world. It astonishes me when I reflect how one breath of creation turned the current of my life and wafted my little bark to port. I can hardly express the change in words; and though I shall try, I know that I shall not be able to tell how happy I am, and why. It is all so unreasonable, and all so natural.

Do you remember, Ariel, how solicitous we were of our precious tot when finally they let you go from the hospital, and we were in our home again? How carefully we laid her in the big crib that our friends had sent us, how we placed the crib alongside our bed at night, and moved always inaudibly lest the babe should lose one wink of sleep? How content you were to be aroused from your slumber by its little voice, and to give your breast to her searching mouth! Why were we so happy? Was it because we had at last surrendered to nature, and she had filled our souls with the music of parental love?

For a time it was difficult for me to realize that there were other children in the world. When I brought Ethel down to her carriage at the door, and saw other infants there, I wondered how their mothers could be so enthusiastic over those puny wriggling legs, those dull eyes in those bulging heads. I struggled to utter the hypocritical compliments that were expected of me; but when the compliments were returned in the spirit in which they had been given, I accepted them as sincere and unavoidable admissions that Ethel's beauty was quite without parallel in the history of mankind. Proudly I took Ariel's place, on many an afternoon, and perambulated through streets and parks with the little princess in the carriage before me. And when it was Ariel's turn, and she had come back from her walk, she would give the door-bell a mystic ring which meant that I must come down and carry our plump and rosy heiress up the stairs to our rooms. I used to kiss my burden at every one of those hundred steps.

Ariel and I were united now as we had never been before. We felt, without putting it into words, that we had passed from mating into marriage. We labored for our little fraction of the future as if she were half the human race. We had always argued against the inheritance of property, as adding an artificial injustice to the superabundant inequalities which nature had established among men; but now, without ever stopping to refute our forgotten arguments, we began to stint and save, just as our parents had done before us, to give our child a better body and a better mind than ours, and to leave to her, when we died, some security against the accidents of life. We behaved as if we had never heard of Marx, and were normal members of the human species. It dawned upon us that the family was more important than the state, that man had become man through parental love, and that nature was right in turning our eyes from the problems of the universe to the needs of our little home. We had found our place, and were content; in the fulfilment of function we had discovered happiness.

"But don't you think it's selfish of us to be happy this way?" Ariel said, as we bent together over Ethel's crib and watched her in her sleep. "Think of the millions of people who are unhappy."

"Perhaps," I suggested, hopefully, "they too will learn the secret. Perhaps they too will find Ariels and Ethels."

"But there's so much disease, and ignorance, and bad temper in the world, so much greed and lust and violence. Shan't we ever get rid of them?"

"Once," I said, "we were all brutes. Do you think, Ariel, that there were souls like Jesus, or St. Francis, or Spinoza, or Raphael, among the cave men? Or minds like Plato's or Leonardo's, or Goethe's? Our violence may be a relic of the hunting stage; we are leaving it behind us as we grow."

She smiled.

"I'm so glad you're learning to hope again," she said.

Yes, I was relearning hope. I had demanded too much of my country and my race. Unconsciously I had been comparing the average of my time and place with the selected best of all past peoples and all the generations. I had complained because our philosophers were not like Aristotle, nor our painters like Rembrandt, nor our poets like Shakespeare, nor our composers like Bach. It had slipped my little mind that these lights had not all shone in the same sky.

And I had forgotten that America was young; that its virgin soil had naturally called the most individualistic and adventurous of Europe's sons, not those timid souls in whom art and letters find their continuity. These subtler minds would come to us later, when we had put our house in order. Wealth such as men had never known was multiplying in these States, and was scattering schools and universities and libraries and museums through the land. Would it all be useless? Would bigotry and intolerance darken again the opening mind of America? No; knowledge would grow from more to more, and would conquer inch by inch the strongholds of ignorance. In another century there would be more enlightenment in America than ever in the history of mankind. America had been a nation for but a century and a half; what would she not do in her maturity? What wealth would she not produce, and what genius?—I began to look again with a forgiving eye upon the sins of my country, its provincial narrowness of mind, its worship of material possessions and display, its crimes against the growth and freedom of the soul. These things would pass away.

Why hope should have this second blooming in my heart I cannot say, except that it came spontaneously with my unreasonable happiness. When I looked at Ethel sleeping, her calm and ruddy face illumined by the moon that seemed to bend from the clouds to caress her, I felt that in such cradles everywhere, rather than in complicated political or economic schemes, lay the future of America. Surely it would be a finer generation than ours, dowered with instrumentalities of growth and culture such as our youth had never known. Those men and women who were to come out of our chaos and uncertainty would be raised on the shoulders of our suffering, and would see with clearer eyes than ours the nobility of freedom and the beauty of peace. Through my own little girl I saw her million growing comrades, children of this new century, unsullied by our wars, uplifted by our care, facing the future with fresh hope, and opening new paths to that ever-promised land which we too had seen, but which we had lost forever because we had stained our hands with blood.

TRANSITION

It is strange, and perhaps ridiculous, that these simple events subtly affected my philosophy. Even before Ethel's coming I had begun to rebel against that mechanical conception of mind and history which is the illegitimate offspring of our industrial age; I had suspected that the old agricultural view of the world in terms of seed and growth did far more justice to the complexity and irrepressible expansiveness of things. But when Ethel came, and I saw how some mysterious inner impulse, far outreaching the categories of physics, lifted her up, inch by inch and effort by effort, on the ladder of life, I felt more keenly than before the need of a philosophy that would do justice to the infinite vitality of nature. In the inexhaustible activity of the atom, in the endless resourcefulness of plants, in the teeming fertility of animals, in the hunger and movement of infants, in the laughter and play of children, in the love and devotion of youth, in the restless ambition of fathers and the life-long sacrifice of mothers, in the undiscourageable researches of scientists and the sufferings of genius, in the crucifixion of prophets and the martyrdom of saints,—in all things I saw the passion of life for growth and greatness, the drama of everlasting creation. I came to think of myself not as a dance and chaos of molecules, but as a brief and minute portion of that majestic process, burning with the impulse to create, to capture truth and fashion beauty, and to leave behind me something better than myself. I became almost reconciled to mortality, knowing that my spirit would survive me enshrined in a fairer mould than mine, and that my little worth would somehow be preserved in the heritage of men. In a measure the Great Sadness was lifted from me; and where I had seen omnipresent death I saw now everywhere about me the pageant and triumph of life.

Every morning Ethel wakes me with the touch of her little hand upon my face; every day I work to the tune of her laughter and her song.

It was Ethel who found a way back for me into my father's heart. She knew no theology, and smiled as radiantly upon him as if the barriers of race and faith meant even less to her clear soul than to the wisest sage. He had come with my mother to see us in our Fordham home; it was a gracious symbol of forgiveness in them to make so long a trip despite their three-score years and ten. When, in July, my father's seventieth year was coming to an end, Ariel and Ethel and I returned that visit gladly, and shared in the birthday celebration with half a hundred reunited members of the family. I had missed these festivals through the days of our separation; and when the night came on which I knew that my brothers and sisters and their children had gathered to do honor to their parents, I spent unhappy hours in lonely meditation. But now we sat again at the same table, under the old-fashioned chandelier, in the old home of my youth; again my father, gray but strong, presided gladly over the two generations of his children; and my mother, white-haired but beautiful, waited on us fondly, overwhelming us with luxuries. And when she laid before my father an enormous apple pie, proud product of her perfect art, she put her sturdy arms around his neck and said to us, with splendid passion:

"I thank God for giving me this dear old man to take care of me these seventy years."

Then I heard my brothers urging me to make a speech, to express something of what we felt towards the tenderest of mothers and the kindliest of fathers. Was I not a professional speech-maker? Of what use was all my training if I could not phrase their devotion now? I refused; I knew that I could not go through with it. But they gathered around me merrily, forced me to my feet, and vowed they would never let me free until I spoke for them. I tried.

"I'm so glad," I began, "that we're all together once more."

Then the old sentimental tears came and blinded me, and a rising tide of feeling swept my thoughts away. I sat down in helpless confusion; but my father, equal to the occasion, raised us all to our feet with a toast that gave simple expression to the hope in all our hearts:

"May we never be separated again."

And now we are in "Utopia." It is no imagined paradise of coming centuries, but a pleasant place

ENTSAGEN

among the hills of this imperfect and contemporary earth. As I sit and write I am surrounded by a hundred thousand pine-trees, eternally fragrant and green. Here and there, almost lost among the spreading branches, are the bungalows of the girls. Pretty girls, almost every one of them; I did not know the world had so many. On the level below I see the boys playing tennis; their wet brown shoulders gleam in the sun; their voices make in the distance the music of persistent life. Farther off I see the lake, nestling quietly in the lap of the hills; and I know that Ethel is frolicking there.

Here she is now coming back, dripping, skipping and laughing, her hair leaping with every toss of her head. She has been in the water for three hours, and yet is not exhausted; she must run to Ariel and then challenge her to a race up the lawn to me. Fondly Ariel lets her win, and she falls into my arms all wet and happy.

"O dad," she cries, "I learned a new stroke to-day. You ought to see me swim now."

What energy! What life! I see that my youth is not gone, it has only been reborn. Surely all things will be possible to man if time is generous.

Ethel is playing with Ariel out on the grass before me, singing. I cannot write any more; I must watch them. She sees me looking up, and takes advantage.

"Daddy, aren't you through with that old book yet?"

"Nearly through, Ethel."

"Come and play with us."

I exact a bribe.

"Do you love me?"

"More than the world." She holds out her chubby arms as if to span the universe. "Even when you scold me I love you."

I close my book, and bid you good fortune, dear Reader. I must go down there and play with Ethel and Ariel.

THE END

.

Printed in the United States
By Bookmasters